Burdens

Sometimes, alone I contemplate my
cross,
And cry with bitterness, against a
fate
That let me look on paradise a while
Before it tightly closed and barred
the gate.

But there are times, when others come
to me
With broken, bleeding hearts,
weighed down with care,
Not knowing that the burden of my
grief
Is almost heavier than I can bear,

Then, when in prayer, I've brought
someone to God,
And left their need before His
wondrous throne,
I lift my cross once more, to strangely
find
That in some manner, it has lighter
grown.

—*Helen Mitchel*

Joe Kotcka

132A

T. E. LAWRENCE
OR
THE SEARCH FOR THE ABSOLUTE

T. E. LAWRENCE. C. 1931.

T. E. LAWRENCE

OR

THE SEARCH FOR THE ABSOLUTE

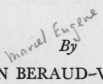

By

JEAN BERAUD-VILLARS

TRANSLATED FROM THE FRENCH BY

PETER DAWNAY

DUELL, SLOAN & PEARCE, INC

NEW YORK

First published in this edition 1959
Originally published in French as
Le Colonel Lawrence ou la Recherche de l'Absolu

© 1955 by Albin Michel

Made and printed in Great Britain by
William Clowes and Sons, Limited, London and Beccles

To my son Marcel
Killed on the 31st of December, 1954
in French Guinea
aged 23

PUBLISHER'S NOTE

This is the complete translation of a work written between 1950 and 1954 and published in France at the beginning of 1955.

In order to preserve its character nothing in the text has either been added or suppressed, despite what has happened in the Levant in the last few years and the books recently written on Lawrence and on the history of the Near East.

Contents

PART III

MAPS

Preface

In the gallery of great men T. E. Lawrence—Colonel Lawrence—is one of the rare men, perhaps the only man, to have been at once a war leader and an artist.

There have been great soldier writers from Xenophon to Napoleon, including Caesar, Joinville, Bernal Diaz and Montluc, but none of them was what one would call an artist, with all that that involves of mysticism, inspiration, instability, strength, weakness and the incapability of self-adaption to the rules of a conventional society: in sum, a monstrosity. The artist and the fighting man are paradoxical entities. Lawrence was as brilliantly endowed with the qualities of the one as of the other: doubtless, from this stems the odd twist in his inner life, and that in his fate which was no less strange. To be an artist is to be egocentric, to be a soldier is to sacrifice and forget self. Two philosophies so contradictory within the same man can but produce anomalies and heartbreaks.

There is no need whatever to romanticise Lawrence's life, as it is already closer to fiction than to reality. For a Frenchman it inevitably evokes the characters of Stendhal, hard-bitten, complex and highly introspective.

Like his predecessors in Stendhal's fiction his mind is full of literary reminiscences. He builds his life by strength of will on an abstract plan, his wish is to carry on the old struggle of the intellect, of character and egotism against conformity. His pride is immense and his ambitions boundless. The shipwreck of his destiny does not cause him to examine his conscience and leaves him in no doubt about himself; it only plunges him into a bitter contempt for men and for life.

He is inhuman by excess of severity, he pursues an absolute that escapes him, and his life reveals at once the triumph and the failure of pure intelligence and of will-power stretched to breaking point. The thought of Bonaparte obsesses him.

The realities of this strange individual are more capti-

vating than the legend, but we must hasten to grasp them
since those who can give us first-hand information on his life
are diminishing in number. The 1914 war is no longer a
contemporary event. It has drifted into that ocean of legends,
lies and indifference that is called History.

*   *   *

It would have been dangerous to have allowed this book to
have developed into an Anglo-French polemic. In an effort to
be impartial, I have striven, in this attempt at Lawrence's
life, to base myself mostly on documents drawn from British
sources as much in my praise as in my criticism of this
fascinating personality.

Englishmen who knew him have been very helpful with
information and advice. I wish to express my gratitude to
them while stressing that I have reserved to myself complete
liberty of appreciation and interpretation and that they have
no responsibility for my conclusions either on the events or
on the men.

PART I

Family

THOMAS EDWARD LAWRENCE was born on the 16th of August, 1888, at Tremadoc in Wales, at the end of the Victorian era, into an essentially Victorian family. Like so many men who were to contribute to the overthrow and almost total destruction of the traditional England of the nineteenth century, he was deeply imbued with her principles and prejudices, and with her undeniable greatness. His most anarchic thoughts, his most revolutionary theories, his jokes and his blasphemies alike were to be coloured by certain ideas typical of an Englishman of the year 1900, who for reasons of his own had conceived a personal hatred against his own background. He was like all who voluntarily lose their social position, incapable of forgetting entirely the class of his origin.

The Victorian epoch ended with the 1914 war, and its opinions, its way of life and its customs, if not its ambitions, were finally buried by the second world conflict. If it were not for the fact that in spite of income tax, Americanisms and the scars of the blitz, traces of it are still to be found in a few houses in the suburbs of London and the counties, in certain colonial cities and in a small number of dusty family pensions in Cannes, Florence and Capri, we should have great difficulty in imagining what it was like.

It is easy enough to laugh at the family table at which the master of the house would not sit down to dinner without having first changed into a dinner jacket that was sometimes threadbare, opposite a wife whose evening dress was less an attempt at sophistication than a badge of class; we may be astonished at the thought of schools where admirals, captains of industry and builders of empires were trained by alternating the liberty of a Boy Scout with the use of the rod, or uphold the hypocrisy of a society that was in fact somewhat pharisaical. The inescapable reality remains that the English of this period built an immense colonial empire in which order if

not justice reigned, that they constructed throughout the
world a considerable number of railways, bridges, aqueducts,
dams, power stations and hotels equipped with bathrooms,
and that the schoolboys who were so well whipped, the
products of austere and starchy families, became incor-
ruptible administrators and excellent sailors, and that they
erected mills of fifty thousand looms without the assistance
of a five-year plan.

*   *   *

It was to this vigorous, tough, enterprising class, that was
none the less puritan and traditionalist in outlook, that the
family of T. E. Lawrence belonged, but its position in it was
not normal, and it lived on the fringe of a highly stratified
world. The father, Thomas Chapman, was an authentic
baronet of an Irish line, not a native Irishman, but the
descendant of the English who at the time of Elizabeth had
settled in the island, a conquered country, and had submitted
it to a severe colonisation. The Chapmans were said to have
through certain foreign connections a touch of Spanish and
Dutch blood in their veins, and to be related to Walter
Raleigh, the courtier, soldier, pirate, littérateur and con-
spirator.

Thomas Chapman had made an unfortunate match in
Meath, his home county, having married a woman who was
so cantankerous that she was humorously known in Irish
society by the nickname of Vinegar Queen. The couple had
several daughters and the baronet consoled himself for the
shortcomings of the Vinegar Queen by courting his children's
governess, Sara Maden. One day he eloped with her, left
Ireland, and having changed his name to that of Lawrence,
lived an uprooted life with no great means (his income was
no more than a few hundred pounds a year). He had almost
broken with the caste from which he came, although he kept
some contacts with it, since from time to time he returned to
Ireland where he had retained some interests and even, at
least officially, the functions of a local magistrate to which his
title gave him the right.

This union, which had every appearance of legality, produced sons. Thomas Lawrence was a tall, retiring and

courteous man. Perhaps because of the prejudices of his class and despite the slenderness of his income, he never adopted a profession. He indulged in sports with the seriousness typical of the Anglo-Saxon, he shot, fished, went yachting and rode a bicycle. He was an expert in photography, a novelty which was then practised with all the paraphernalia of laboratories and dark-rooms. It was said that he never opened a book, but that he was one of the best snipe shots in England. One pities him a little for having given birth to such intellectual sons whose conversation must often have bored him.

As for Mrs. Lawrence, she was the daughter of a Scottish engineer from Sunderland; she had been brought up in the highlands and in the sad Isle of Skye. Courageous, idealistic, moulded by the morals of the Bible and very deeply attached to the Calvinist faith, she applied herself with dignity and diligence to the care of her impecunious household, and to the education of her sons.

She had the dry and passionate spiritualism which has made the Scots and the Hebrews so curiously akin as far as religion is concerned. Harsh even in the profound affection which she felt for her silent husband and for her nest of young eagles, she was seldom fond of making friends, and jealously defended her family from any outside interference. Her puritanism deprived her of the pleasures of life, which to the depth of her soul and with the tormented austerity that is the Nordic equivalent of the Mediterranean ascetic's fear of the devil and horror of the flesh, she regarded as sacrilege.

There is something rather pathetic in imagining this prudish woman, who was as little suited as possible to an irregular liaison, haunted by the thought of her sin, and striving to bring up her children on two contradictory principles. She meant to inculcate her sons with high ideals, austere virtues, unselfishness, upright behaviour and a stoical attitude to the setbacks of life, and at the same time with a contempt for the prejudices from which she had suffered throughout her life. These are ideas that human weakness makes it difficult to reconcile and this inconsistency was to leave a malaise and a lack of stability in the young T.E.'s mind.

People who knew him say that the shock for this precocious,

2

very proud and sensitive child of suddenly discovering that his loved and respected mother and father were living in sin had an effect that lasted all his life. He was deeply wounded by the discovery that his parents, pious and austere to the point of ostentation, did not practise what they preached, that many of their postures were hypocritical, in fact that the desires of the flesh played a major part in the lives of people whom up till then he had idolised. From the day of these revelations he was to conceive a horror of physical love and an obsession with social pretences.

In his voluminous correspondence numerous remarks escaped his pen which support the validity of this thesis, and show that Lawrence hid a secret wound on this score. He asked his biographer Liddell Hart not to give details of his background in his book; his lack of connections with his paternal family visibly embittered him; and for his own name, the very name of Lawrence by which he was to become famous, he had a distinct aversion; it was a borrowed name, as he was to repeat on several occasions, since it belonged neither to his father nor his mother, and after 1922 he gave it up for good and called himself Ross, and then Shaw.

Thus from the beginning we find certain explosive elements in T.E.'s background which perhaps explain some of his peculiarities: the break with the aristocratic family, and the original sin. We find also a mixture of blood: a Scots mother and an Irish father.

We are here of course on difficult ground, because it is not easy to tell in what degree Lawrence was Irish. The Irish Protestant families that have settled in Ireland for three or four centuries generally claim to have kept their blood pure of any mixture with the natives but it is a fact that their long sojourn in the island has left a strong mark both on their mentality and physical appearance. It would be difficult to imagine that they had not, in so long a space of time, contracted unions either official or secret, of a mixed nature, unions which, added to the influence of nurses, servants, their daily companionships and entire surroundings, have transformed them from colonialists and almost completely celticised them, despite the contrasts of caste and religion. Among the descendants of the landowners are found the qualities and the defects of the native Irishry: the same sense of humour, originality and hatred of convention, the same fertile wit, the same taste for artistic licence and bohemia, for indiscipline and heresy, the same courage and love of a brawl.

Thus many of these Protestants, English in origin but transformed by Ireland, have together with the Welsh brought to English life that Celtic wit which the English both hate and admire in certain of their artists, their barristers, their actors, and their most outstanding politicians, such as Swift, Lloyd George and Bernard Shaw, who are the salt of England.

* * *

Without occupation or family ties Thomas Chapman-Lawrence settled nowhere and lived successively in Scotland, the Isle of Man, Dinard in Brittany, Jersey, the Isle of Wight and the New Forest; it was the life of a semi-wanderer.

Four sons were born to him (the fifth did not appear till 1900) and since he had to think of their education, he set himself up in Oxford where all the necessary amenities were to be found. The young Lawrences were sent to the Oxford High School, where the teaching was adequate and the fees reasonable, and to which, besides, some of them and T.E. in particular easily obtained scholarships. They were all day-boys, and the neighbours watched with sympathy each day as these well behaved and well brought-up children, dressed in identical blue jerseys, passed by on their bicycles. Probably for financial reasons or because their parents in reaction to the usual custom of their class wished to keep their children near them, they never knew like most of the sons of the English ruling classes the typical British boarding school, sung by Kipling and other conformist writers, but which many sincere Englishmen confess to remembering as terrible barracks for children. The school-boy life of T. E. Lawrence, day-boy and living with his own family, bears a much closer resemblance to that of a French boy, than to that of the majority of his fellow countrymen.

* * *

While he was still a child, everyone who came in contact with him was surprised and slightly disconcerted by the striking personality of this proud, headstrong, obstinate and reserved boy, with his alert questing mind. His curiosity extended in all directions. He had a passion for antiques, knew all the mediaeval monuments in the vicinity of Oxford and collected pottery and old brasses. At fourteen he had a knowledge of archaeology and had picked up in the excavations made in the town various interesting objects which he took to the big museum of Oxford, the Ashmolean, thus coming into contact with the directors of this institution, Dr. Hogarth and Leonard Woolley, who were to shape the beginnings of his life. He was extremely clever with his hands, he developed photographs, patiently put together the remains of ancient pottery, and above all loved anything mechanical. The need for intelligent and delicate work with his hands, this gift for tinkering, followed him all his life. But above all he was an indefatigable reader. While very young, he was already devouring an enormous number of books, and later he astonished all who met him by his precise and encyclopedic knowledge.

But if many intellectuals passionately cultivate their minds, more rare are those who submit their will-power to a comparable training. Intransigeant in ideals, and manly in pride, the child learnt with obstinacy to master himself. He claimed, he said, to be escaping from the tyranny of the physical world. It is seldom that we find the struggle between the mind and the body, the old Manichean strife between black and white, already taking place in the soul of an adolescent. People who are not yet fully developed are generally more lenient to themselves.

When he was sixteen he broke his leg and astonished his family by the way in which he stood the pain. He seemed to show a vicious indifference to his body and its suffering, which was strange in one so young. There was perhaps a little ostentation in this courage: from now on he loved to play a part, but if vanity carried him to stoicism, it was a vanity that was constructive.

This accident moreover was to weigh on him for the rest of his life. It seems in fact—at least in his mother's opinion— that after this fracture the young man, who until then had developed normally, ceased to grow.[1] He was vigorous and well muscled but he never grew to a height of more than five foot four inches, his body was long and his legs short. He suffered cruelly from being so much smaller than most of his fellow countrymen and this fact partly explains his timidity, his inferiority complexes, and his desire to accomplish physical exploits which would put him on an even footing with men of a more imposing appearance. He never discussed this misfortune, and any joking on the subject drove him into a silent fury. It was in a moment of abandon and because of his strange need to humiliate himself that one day he referred to himself as a 'pocket Hercules': but in general he was mute on the subject of his diminutive height from which he suffered so much.

On this slightly ridiculous body was set a magnificent head: a high brow surmounted by a shock of indisciplined hair, a full nose that was slightly large but noble in shape, a prominent typically Anglo-Saxon jaw and splendid eyes. The mouth was sinuous, and in repose it had a disquieting curve, suggesting cruelty, irony or deceit, but usually it was twisted into a tense smile. This smile which was often accompanied by a rather embarrassed giggle struck everybody who came in contact with Lawrence. Did it reveal timidity or a sardonic sense of humour? It gave his handsome face a slightly taut and on-edge appearance.

But studious and passionately fond of the past as he was, he also loved physical pursuits and even excelled at them. To the great astonishment of his British companions team games such as football or cricket never interested him at all, but everything which required individual effort, and which was difficult, unusual or dangerous, such as rock-climbing, boating on swiftly flowing rivers and swimming in turbulent waters, he adored.

Despite some rather adventurous exploits, however, and in spite of what was said later, T.E. accepted the family discipline without revolt. He showed himself affectionate and respectful towards his excellent parents, who besides allowed their sons a fair amount of liberty. It is not true to say, as we

---

[1] Though, in fact, T.E.'s elder brother was of exactly the same height and figure as our hero.

find in several romantic accounts of his youth, that at twelve he lived in a detached lodge at the bottom of the garden entirely as he pleased, and that he returned home at night at whatever hour suited him. Mrs. Lawrence has formally refuted these stories and adds that her son 'Ned' was a child like the others, that he played with his brothers, took the youngest out in his pram while he was still a baby, went away with his family during the holidays, went to Sunday school and was a member of the Boy Scouts: nor would she have allowed a son of hers to go to bed at an unreasonable hour.[1]

[1] He said later that when he was seventeen he ran away from home and joined the regular British Army, in which he stayed several months. Questioned on this point by David Garnett, Mrs. Lawrence gave the lie to this story. It was probably one of his poetic fables, for he loved, at the end of his life, to foster his own legend.

University

In 1907, T.E., having finished with Oxford High School, thought about going up to the University. So as not to impose too great a burden on the family finances, he decided to obtain a scholarship to one of the colleges. He tried first for St. John's, failed the examination, but was more fortunate at Jesus, and went up in the autumn of 1907.

For a young Englishman the university represents emancipation, the throwing off of the white toga of youth and attainment of manhood, exactly like military service for a Frenchman. Most young British students are introduced to the liberty of university life immediately after leaving the discipline of the boarding school. In this violent decompression, characters become revealed and demonstrative: it is with good reason that English biographers attribute so much importance to the years spent by their heroes at Oxford or Cambridge.

*   *   *

At the time when T.E. went up to Jesus, industrialisation had not yet encroached upon the boundaries of Oxford. The town was fresh and green, a sort of oasis where nature was just sufficiently kept in bounds to retain a well-bred air. The admission of women undergraduates had not yet (as happened after 1918) altered the atmosphere of the city, which remained a world apart, almost entirely masculine. No one was to be seen in Oxford or Cambridge except dons, pupils, servants and shopkeepers. The feminine population was tiny compared with the pullulation of young males: a few garrisons in the east of France, Saint-Mihiel or Lunéville, colonies that were almost entirely virile, were able to reproduce a similar state of affairs at that time.

In this nursery for the rulers of the empire there reigned a very definite *esprit de corps*, which was voluntarily archaic

and which though puerile in appearance was of great importance, since the reputations, the names, the friendships
and the enmities created in the great universities lasted
throughout the careers of those to whom they attached. To
have been ostracised by his fellow pupils for failure to conform to the niceties of a futile and complicated code was
capable thirty years later of preventing a man from becoming
a general, a bishop or an ambassador. Such institutions model
the personality according to standards that are not without
value, and above all create free masonries among men who
have the same attitudes and the same watchwords.

Lawrence was an Oxonian twice over: student of a college,
he was also a citizen of the town, where for a long time his
family was in contact with the small closed world of residents
and with the teaching staff. This artificial but in some ways
extremely exalting milieu left a deep impression on a man
who was meanwhile professing, to an inordinate degree, the
love of independence and a hatred of convention. All his life,
he was enormously proud of having been to Oxford, like some
Frenchmen who will boast through the worst vicissitudes of
life of having once been pupils of the École Polytechnique.

In the minds of many French people the great English
universities are institutions in which the only occupation is
sport. A quite inaccurate idea: beside the robust and slightly
unimaginative young men for whom physical achievements
are the most important, there are groups that carry on an
intense intellectual life. Some undergraduates turn towards
classical culture, others towards art, and in particular to
poetry of the most subtle kind (Byron was a product of Cambridge), and finally to politics, and politics that are often very
avant-garde since many English statesmen acquired extreme-
left socialist ideas at the university. In the citadel of the
England of tradition, scholars, poets and revolutionaries are
neither despised nor outcast, on condition that they adhere to
certain rules. It is a paradoxical miracle of the Anglo-Saxon
way of life which is not easily understood by the French, and
which explains the formation of strong personalities whose
originality and contempt for conventions is taken to an
extreme while remaining profoundly English.

This was the ideal environment for a man of T.E.'s

character, since it allowed him to develop without restraint. From now on every side of his character begins to appear: his intellectual gifts, his devouring love of study, immense potentialities in the realms of thought as in those of action, but also some strange defects; a pathological vanity that compelled him to be original and different at all costs, and a pettiness that is astonishing in a soul of this quality: a love of complicated and laborious jokes, paradoxes, poses, an unconfessed need for admiration and acclaim which he pursued by means that were somewhat tiresome. He took his jokes terribly seriously, said a companion of his youth, but would not allow himself to become the subject of pleasantry. A jibe, or shaft of wit wounded his touchy susceptibility and he would immediately shut himself up in his shell. In short, he applied himself a little too heavily to being an *enfant terrible* and it was a pose that people often found rather irritating: in this distinguished soul vanity was the vulgar element.

But despite his failings of character, Lawrence was popular among his companions, who could not help but admire him, the intellectuals for his wit, the others because they realised that this bookworm had an extraordinary physical courage and was always ready to run a risk if the enterprise was sufficiently amusing and exceptional. One or two spectacular escapades made him a celebrity. On one occasion he travelled with a friend through a subterranean watercourse which passed under the town, and which in Oxonion memory had never been explored, and was nearly drowned and asphyxiated in the attempt. Being twenty years old he amused himself greatly during this subterranean wandering by firing his revolver as he passed beneath the iron grilles of the manholes in the big streets of Oxford, in order to astonish the passers-by.

All his life he exercised a strange magnetism over certain people. Few of those who came in contact with him escaped from it. He had a feminine need to seduce, but he found a devilish pleasure in making enemies when his fancy took him that way, and it is not certain that he did not often try to wound and ridicule those whose superiority gave offence to a vanity that never slept.

As a scholar, he had in theory to live 'in' in Jesus College like the other students, in one of those dusty and hideously furnished rooms which are a classic part of English university life. But he found this hard to put up with. He never attended in the traditional torn and dirty black gown any of the meals taken in common in the great Gothic halls panelled in oak, with their open timberwork roofs, or indulged in the riots that were also traditional, beneath the indulgent eye of the senior members of the college. He did not live in college for longer than his first year, when he obtained leave to live at home. It was then that his parents furnished a summer-house for him at the bottom of their garden, in which he lived, passing the time in reading a wide variety of works in English, French and Latin. An omnivorous reader, he absorbed with unquenchable thirst the heroic exploits sung by the French mediaeval chroniclers, the Russian novelists, an infinite number of works on archaeology, the historians of the Crusades, the memoirs of the great captains from Xenophon to Napoleon (in particular the commentaries of Caesar, which he never ceased to reread for the rest of his life), and finally treatises on tactics, the ancients like Vegece, the moderns like Marshal de Saxe, Clausewitz and Foch.[1]

Attracted by anything that was bizarre and exceptional, Lawrence developed an infatuation for Charles Doughty, a strange author who satisfied at the same time his interest in travel and his complex literary tastes. Doughty had explored Arabia and had brought back a remarkable book about it, *Arabia Deserta*. Returned to a less dangerous life, he had written interminable historic poems in an archaic and sibylline language, but in which Lawrence found enormous aesthetic pleasure. *Arabia Deserta* was, as a student, his bedside book and he never ceased to extol the virtues of Doughty's impenetrable poetry.

We could wish to follow the young man in his immense voyage in the world of books. His precociously mature mind sought for works of originality: ancient chroniclers and

[1] Nothing in his letters indicates that he was ever acquainted with *La Tactique de la cavalerie au XIIIe siècle*, by Delpech. It is strange that this seeker after knowledge should not have discovered a classic without which the history of the Crusades is unintelligible and in which there is an exposition of the key ideas that were to guide him in the course of the Arabian war.

memoirs, much more than modern commentaries and com-
pilations. Like every inveterate reader, he opened a large
number of books, rejected many after one glance and hurled
himself voraciously on anything that could nourish his mind.
It is told how he would read lying on his stomach on the floor
of his room, surrounded with piles of books, how he would
fall asleep on the page and then almost before he had woken
up, once more plunge back into the book. It is not possible
to give enough importance to the vast store of knowledge
which he accumulated in this way during four or five years
of intense reading. His photographic memory enabled him
to remember the essentials. The capital of his knowledge was
amassed before his twentieth year and he lived on it throughout his career. His very active life in Syria and that in which
he was even more engrossed during the years of war would
not have allowed him to acquire his encyclopedic knowledge.

Travels in France

IN the midst of all this diverse reading, there was one subject into which Lawrence delved more deeply than the others, and which became the principal theme of his researches: the tactics and military architecture of the Middle Ages. It was this study that shaped the travels which he made in his youth.

From his childhood he had travelled around England to visit and photograph churches and mediaeval castles and he was particularly acquainted with the magnificent fortresses of Wales, sinister redoubts which appear to emanate from the mind of Victor Hugo. His studies of necessity took him to France. From the Conquest to the middle of the fifteenth century, the military history of England and of our country are indissolubly linked together.

In 1906 and 1907, before going up to the University, he went for two tours in France on a bicycle. On the first excursion in August 1906, he took his friend Beeson and they travelled from St. Malo to Fougères. The two young men had hardly any money and they were travelling through a France that was still not properly organised for tourists; however, Lawrence was enchanted, particularly by the chateau of Fougères and by the superb view which it gave of a plain that overflowed with beauty and richness. To feed the lyricism of his eighteen years, he had brought a copy of Ruskin with him. At the foot of the solid Norman towers he perused the subtle and tortuous arguments of the *Stones of Venice*. At the same time Marcel Proust was also enjoying the same aesthetic pleasure.

In August 1907 he again crossed the Channel and in the company of his father undertook a longer tour. They visited the regions of Les Andelys, Evreux, Beauvais and Gisors. Although impressed by the beauty of the churches, Lawrence was above all interested by the Château-Gaillard: the enormous fortress of Richard I became a part of the plan of

his studies; further, it belonged to the history of England.
He spent an entire day running around the ruins, climbing
on to the roofs, and edging himself into forbidden corners in
order to take photographs of the château from every angle.

Then leaving his father, he crossed Anjou and Brittany
and came to Mont Saint-Michel. This was a long-cherished
dream and his luck was in: a high tide completely surrounded
the Mount and he saw the water splashing against the foot of
the houses in the steep little street. His cup of happiness was
full: the sea was phosphorescent and Lawrence could watch
the glittering waves disporting beneath the moon.

*   *   *

For Lawrence the excursions of 1906 and 1907 were no
more than preparatory work. He was coming to know France
and the conditions of travel in this country better, he was
perfecting his knowledge (already excellent) of the language,
and working out in his mind his plan for the study of the
fortress châteaux of our country. With the minute attention
to detail which he paid to everything he did, he made out the
programme of another more extensive and more complete
tour of these monuments, using as his guide the works of
Viollet-le-Duc which he knew backwards. The itinerary which
he worked out cut across Burgundy, the Massif Central, the
Rhone Valley, Western Provence, the Languedoc, Quercy,
Poitou, Saintonge, Berry, in order to reach finally the district
of St. Malo.

This sort of travelling had its own brand of adventure: in
many places the roads were poor and the hotels primitive.
Having only a little money to spend, Lawrence travelled light,
put up in the most modest inns, and lived mainly on bread
and fruit. Wearing an old pair of trousers, and a crumpled
open-necked shirt over his sun-tanned skin, riding on a racing
bicycle with dropped handlebars, the solitary little figure
toiled across the broken countryside that he had chosen for
his route, feasting his eyes on novelties of every sort. And as
he rode he put together in his mind the basis of his thesis.
Whatever the distraction of the moment, he never allowed
himself to be deflected from the goal he had assigned himself.

At Vezelay he was enchanted by the sculptures of the

cathedral. The rich statuary of romanesque and Gothic
churches, with its wonderful lushness and its complicated
mysticism, has disappeared from most English churches since
the Reformation. The most beautiful sometimes seem cold
and naked to a Frenchman. Reduced to the nobility and full-
ness of their lines they no longer have the latent mysticism or
paganism, the slightly satanic touch which their ancient
builders imprinted upon them.

Having passed through Le Puy, Lawrence came to Crussol,
close to Valence, and standing five hundred feet above the
Rhone, he glimpsed the countryside of the South, something
that was entirely new to him.

Saint-Trophime at Arles and the portal of Saint-Gilles drew
from him a cry of joy: "It is absolutely unimaginably fine
with its sculptures and its proportions: all other architecture
is very nearly dirt beside this Provençal Romanesque." He
climbed up to Les Baux "perched upon a lonely olive
sandalled mountain" and from there he glimpsed for the first
time in his life the scintillating line of the Mediterranean
Sea. Lawrence, remembering his Xenophon, shouted like the
soldiers in the *Anabasis*: "Thalassa! Thalassa!" They are the
words of a schoolboy recalling his classics, but they contain a
genuine emotion, and the rather pedantic and turgid letter
which he wrote to his mother shows how much he was moved:
"I felt that at last I had reached the way to the South and all
the glorious East: Greece, Carthage, Egypt, Tyre, Syria . . .
they were all there . . . Oh! I must get down there——further
out—again. Really this getting to the sea has almost overturned my mental balance."

Beyond the plain of Arles whose beauty, although quiet
and restrained, has a certain heartrending quality, he conceived of a strange world with its poverty and its wealth,
anxious, complicated and tenaciously clinging to its pagan
beliefs. Saracen feluccas had landed on these coasts. Perhaps
he had a presentiment that in those countries, his soul in a
few years time would be ravished, transformed and then
destroyed.

At Aigues Mortes he bathed in the delicious lukewarm
water. He was devoured by mosquitoes and developed
malaria.

He continued across the Languedoc over rough roads, crushed by the heat of the sun. Carcassonne awaited him, the major work of his master Viollet-le-Duc. The visit to this fortress seems to have been the high-spot of the journey. Mad on mediaeval fortifications, he studied in detail and photographed from every angle a piece of restoration without realising its artificial nature. He was astonished by the size of the fortifications and by the beauty of the site. His letters are full of superlatives like those of the romanticists.

A few days later he passed through Toulouse, which he dismissed in his letters in two words: "a smoking industrial dung-heap". Tired or annoyed by some misadventure, and out of sorts, he had no wish to see the noble quays of the Garonne, or the cloisters of the Augustins, or the Narbonne Tower. He had a habit of making paradoxical and peremptory judgments in order to hide his secret antipathies for objects, ideas and men, though the reasons for them are often difficult to discover in this egocentric and temperamental soul.

He made his way back to the North by a zig-zag route through places that gave enormous stimulus to his erudition. At Cahors he saw the Pont Valentre and further on the extraordinary Château de Bonaguil, almost intact, and which raises above le Causse a dungeon shaped like a battleship; to Chalus finally he came half as student, half as pilgrim to seek the spot where King Richard I received his fatal wound at the beginning of the Hundred Years' War, a quarrel that is still not forgotten. In his wanderings between the Lot and Périgueux, he saw in the distance the Château de Biron. He knew, without doubt, that Lord Byron's family were descended from this French line; Byron's fate moreover has some subtle parallels with his own: scholar and aesthete, with a pride that was almost a disease, he sought like Lawrence to console himself for a physical handicap, in sporting exploits that were a little crazy. He also was bound by an intense devotion to the Mediterranean and sacrificed himself for the liberation of a people oppressed by the Turks.

By exhausting and very long stages he returned to Normandy and then to England. "I am as brown as a Jap and thin as paper," he wrote, and he brought back from

Central and Southern France the deep and false impression
of those who visit a country for the first time.

It must not be forgotten that this trip was undertaken by
Lawrence for the purpose of a study that had been most
systematically prepared, with a precisely defined object, and
that in the pursuit of subjects into which he was delving in
a spirit of pure scholarship this young man, who was usually
so sensitive to beauty, often forgot some of the subtle values
of the country through which he was travelling. Going too
fast, exhausted by the physical effort, absorbed by his
specialist preoccupations, he does not seem either in Attic
Provence, or in the country of the Albigensi, that Saracen
part of France still shaken by its ancient heresies, or in
Quercy which smacks of the Sabbath and of burnt corn, to
have fully understood the soul of a country so profoundly
original. In the Levant Lawrence, more mature, was to learn
how to forget his books and his erudition and to allow the
demons of the country to enter his soul.

It must be recognised that he had been through experiences
that were a little overpowering for an Englishman who had
never gone outside the British Isles and Normandy and we
must not be too hard on him if for instance he was horrified
by the food of Languedoc, which appeared barbarous to a
young islander brought up on eggs, bacon and custard. He
wrote to a friend: "I don't in the least know what I ate last
night! I fancy a plough-ox or two (is it nightmare?), some
potatoes (were they?), stewed infant or monkey . . . if you are
bored or overworn come to a Tarnais hotel for a week. For
3 francs a night one can have as many galvanic shocks as one
can support." Generations of the gastronomers of Cahors,
proud of their exquisitely prepared dishes, must have turned
in their graves on hearing such blasphemies. Besides, ten
years later the same man was to plunge without batting an
eyelid into the pyramids of greasy rice, surmounted by the
hideous and half-cooked heads of roast sheep, with which the
great Arab chiefs entertained him.

Who will know how much this first experience, with its
errors and omissions, contributed to forming in Lawrence's
mind the strange conception which he had of France? What
little setbacks, what humiliations, what incidents which he

has not related created in him, from his youth on, the strong enmity which he always had for our country? Although his mind was imbued with French culture, and although he spoke our language perfectly, he was never able to get on with the French.

This is a common phenomenon among the English, who are shocked by the casualness, the speech and the untidiness of the French, by the dirt of some of our provincial towns and by a thousand little details which they find all the more annoying because the civilisations, the customs and the ways of life of the two countries are on the whole so close to each other.

For most Englishmen France is the logical extension of England, a country that has rebelled, a sister that has gone wrong, a sort of larger Ireland, and as opinionated in her errors; the British admire her beauty but are irritated by her particularism and her inability to understand the absolute truth which is English.

The Garden of the Enchantress

MEANWHILE Lawrence was a student and the possessor of an exhibition, and he had to pass his finals before he could obtain his Bachelor of Arts degree. So much fantasy in the pursuit of his studies would have prevented him from passing his examinations in a place less liberal than Oxford. But the great English universities were ruled with an open-minded spirit that admitted of originality, and even encouraged it in exceptional pupils, and the dons of Jesus College were not too severe on the bohemian system of educating himself adopted by this student of whose remarkable gifts they were aware. Meanwhile they discreetly indicated to Lawrence that they would close their eyes to the irregular way in which he had worked, but that he must at the end of his studies present a work of a definitely substantial nature. He had been preparing this work, as we have seen, for some time, but his wanderings in France and in England as well as his extensive knowledge of the history of the Crusades showed him that he could not complete his thesis unless he went and studied, on the spot, the actual castles which the Byzantines, the Western Crusaders and the Arabs had built in Syria and Palestine. From their contact with the Orient the Crusaders, apart from certain diseases and vices, the taste for luxury and a few intellectual complications, had brought back ideas on warfare that changed the art of war in Europe. On the other hand they have also left, from Cilicia to the Red Sea, a number of monuments. Lawrence wished to research into the mutual influences which the builders of the East and of the West had exercised upon each other, by studying the castles of the Orontes, of Palestine and of the Lebanon. These ancient redoubts of the warriors of our race are for the romantically inclined traveller a wonderful sight. Maurice Barrès had been more moved by the feudal dungeons of Morea than by the Parthenon.

But Syria is far away and had the reputation of a country that did not welcome visitors; when T.E. announced to his family his intention of going to the Levant and, because of his meagre financial resources, of touring on foot, living on bread, milk and fruit and sleeping in the most humble abodes, one can imagine that his parents were not a little alarmed. They asked him to find out about the possibilities from people who had visited the Middle East, and in particular from Dr. Hogarth, the curator of the Ashmolean Museum at Oxford.[1] Hogarth had travelled much, having been in charge of excavations in Crete with Evans, in Cyprus, in Egypt and in Syria; besides he had known T.E. for a long time and had allowed him to help in classifying some ancient pottery.

Hogarth was very reticent. Lawrence's project did not seem practicable to him. In order to be more certain he advised the young man to write to C. M. Doughty, the traveller, writer and poet, for whom Lawrence had such an admiration. The reply was not very encouraging:

"Syria is a land of squalor where a European can find evil refreshment. Long daily marches on foot a prudent man who knows the country would, I think, consider out of the question. The population only know their own wretched life and look upon any European wandering in their country with at best a veiled ill will. . . . I should dissuade a friend from such a voyage, which is too likely to be most wearisome, hazardous to health and even disappointing."

It is rare for a man who has accomplished something of an exceptional and perilous nature to give much encouragement to another and much younger man who wishes to try the same experience. Lawrence must have reasoned like this, for despite his advice he persevered in the project.

He left in June 1909, with only a hundred pounds in his pocket, a Kodak camera, a large revolver and the things that

[1] The Ashmolean is a very fine museum whose imposing buildings are found in the centre of the University; it was founded by the endowment of a rich Oxonian, Ashmole, in 1683, and contains a variety of wonderful things: pictures, furniture, tapestries and Renaissance ceramics, etc.; the Cretan objects brought back from the excavations at Knossos are incomparably beautiful. It was partly in this museum that Lawrence's taste was formed.

a man who intends to travel on foot is able to carry (his Boy
Scout shirt, furnished with a quantity of pockets, had been
specially adapted by his mother according to his minute instructions). Most important of all for the success of his adventure, he had, through the intervention of Lord Curzon,
then Chancellor of Oxford University, obtained an *iradé* from
the Turkish Government, one of those passes which recom-
mends the owner to the local authorities, and which even in
these days when xenophobia is rampant, saves travellers touring in Eastern countries from many a misfortune. Lawrence
had also acquired at Oxford some elementary knowledge of
Arabic from a Protestant clergyman of Syrian origin, the
Reverend Odeh.

Thus equipped, he embarked aboard the P. & O. steamboat
Mongolia with Beirut as his destination.

*   *   *

These days one can quite easily travel—when there are no
revolutions—through Syria and Palestine by car. When
Lawrence undertook this journey nearly half a century ago,
there was no means of travelling in these countries, apart
from two railway lines, other than the bridle and foot paths.

The roads were not safe for a Western traveller; the iron
curtain which had been drawn between the Muslim world
and Europe had been breached in several places, but had
not been completely lifted. Islam was still defending herself
vigorously against the invasion of the infidels, her populations were distinctly xenophobic and it happened that
foreigners who ventured imprudently away from the beaten
tracks were apt to disappear mysteriously.

The Ottoman government did not object in principle to
this rather primitive means of getting rid of intruders, but it
feared that incidents of this sort might give an excuse to the
great powers for interference. In any case it did not encourage
tourism.

The country was unhealthy, it was scourged by fevers and
dysentery that were endemic, and the hotels were rare and
wretched.

Lawrence landed in Beirut in the height of summer, on the
19th of July, 1909. The town had not yet been touched by

Europe. It was an ancient Turkish port of the Levant, as the old prints show, with its caiques, the boatmen in their baggy breeches, the ragged Turkish soldiers keeping watch on the quay, its minarets and its muezzins.

Right away the young Englishman plunged delightedly into the native life. He did the round of the alleys and bazaars, dived into the sordid colourful swirl, rubbed shoulders carelessly with the Oriental mob with its robes, bare feet in Turkish slippers, and its sharp glances.

Above Beirut, he climbed the mountain from which one can see, between the harsh blue sea and the Lebanon, the narrow beach of red sand which runs down as far as Tripoli; he went to see the stream of Adonis, as it zigzagged through the pebbles.

The light of Syria stunned him; the hottest days in England and even the dog days in the French Midi could not have given him any idea of this dazzling vibrance. He gave himself to it avidly, soaking up the heat and the rays of the sun with his head, and emptying his mind. For the first time he was tasting the intoxication of dematerialisation with which he made himself drunk later on during the long periods he spent in the desert.

In the height of summer the Syrian climate is hard on a European. Lawrence suffered from the discomforts of the country more than the well-heeled traveller, since he was touring alone and on foot, by routes that were seldom used and with so little money that he was usually unable to make use of the rare hotels which he encountered. From the beginning he adopted the habit of lodging with the local inhabitants, and he has left a picturesque account of his experiences as a semi-tramp on the roads of the Levant; he knocked on the doors of the humblest native houses and was practically always given hospitality. Surrounded by the children, the goats and the poultry, he would seat himself even on the ground in order to eat the meal of bread and curdled milk; the women would come and wash his hands by pouring water over them from an antique pitcher; stretched out in some corner of the beaten earth floor, he slept among these peasants beneath a common blanket devoured by the family vermin. It was the sort of life which St. John the Baptist and Paul of Tarsus probably knew.

This method of travelling implied an ascetic contempt for comfort and an extraordinary resistance to fatigue and illness. He submitted himself to it meanwhile, except in the big centres or when some Anglo-Saxon mission gave him asylum. By means of this régime the reality of the country's atmosphere was impressed upon him. He began to talk a broken Arabic that was more or less intelligible to the ordinary people.

Leaving Beirut, he followed the coast as far as Sidon and then plunged into the mountains of Galilee, reached Lake Huleh (the Waters of Merom in the Bible), the first lake of Jordan before that of Tiberias. He visited the castles of Beaufort, Banias (Cesarea of Philippi), of Chastellet and Belvoir, thus covering the whole of Galilee. It is a region of rocky mountains and steep valleys, of ravines and precipices, and the paths which Lawrence had to follow in order to reach the ruined castles which he had come to study were rough and vertiginous. "In the day's march I went up and down hill the height of the Mont Blanc," he said referring to one day's journey. In this country brimming with history, the memories of the Crusades were not the only ones with which he was assailed. Brought up on the Bible, he rediscovered the settings of the stories related in the Book of Kings and the Book of Judges.

Lawrence thus crossed the heights of Carmel, some of whose slopes were still white with snow, from east to west, regained the coast near Haifa, and keeping along the sea, returned in the middle of August to Beirut, where he was able to draw breath. He had spent a month in Northern Palestine and nearly all the time he had profited from the hospitality of the natives. Among primitive people travellers are either received with generosity or else their throats are cut. Now the young man in the dusty clothes and hobnailed boots did not seem to the Arab peasants to be a very dangerous representative of trouble-making Europe. They took this none too fortunate visitor under their wing. All his life, Lawrence remained grateful to the poor people of Syria for the warmth of the welcome which they always kept for him since he first travelled among them.

* * *

The second part of Lawrence's journey, much tougher and more dangerous than the first, took him into Northern Syria, which he covered in August and September. He reached Tripoli, then Krak des Chevaliers, the key fortress of the Crusaders in Syria, a sort of Carcassonne but much more imposing. By Tortose, the castles of Margat and Gibelet, he reached Latakieh, whence he visited the ruins of Sahyun and of Harim. Plunging north-east, he found himself in regions that became increasingly dangerous, and in which there reigned a continual religious and political agitation. A foreigner touring by himself had every chance of being murdered (near Homs, a bandit had already shot at and missed him), and when Lawrence, drawn by the great names of Antioch, Aleppo and Edessa, announced to the Turkish authorities that he wished to continue his journey to the north, he met with some resistance. On the strength of the *iradé* obtained by Lord Curzon, the governor of Sahyun, afraid of allowing an 'Inglezi' to be murdered in his territory, supplied him with an escort of cavalry in order to pass through the defiles on the way to Antioch. Lawrence, who at twenty-one still loved to tease authority and to outwit the police, was amused to be accompanied, himself a ragged pedestrian, by a mounted guard, refused the offer of a horse and played tricks on his protectors who were constantly terrified of losing sight of this extraordinary traveller who hid behind rocks and dragged the unsporting Bashibazooks down impassable tracks.

In T.E.'s letters, which together with certain oral accounts that he gave to his friends form the only documentary sources for his first journey in the Orient, it is clear that from the time that he left Aleppo the young man was suffering from the fatigue induced by his travels. His stomach was upset by the primitive food, and he was tormented with malaria. He was driving himself to the limit. Between Sahyun and Aleppo he covered one hundred and twenty-five miles in five days, marching up to thirteen hours a day, his feet bleeding in boots that were completely worn out. But he was determined to reach Edessa, well beyond the Euphrates, the extreme point of Frankish colonisation, and he would rather have died on the road than give up his plan.

Between the Euphrates and Edessa he had an adventure that was very nearly fatal. While following a deserted track he was attacked by a Turkoman bandit who knocked him down and would have killed him had it not been for the intervention of a shepherd. In very poor shape, T.E. succeeded in crossing the Euphrates and reaching Birejik, where he alerted the police. Impressed by the *iradé* which he showed them, the Turkish police accompanied by the Englishman went to the bandit's village. In the end he was discovered and after a long palaver made to hand over the few objects with which he had made off.

The traveller, already very tired and his health undermined by fever, was quite exhausted by this adventure: he was cared for rather indifferently in the hospital at Halifat and was able to return to a less dangerous area. He came to Aleppo. The attack of which he had been a victim had caused quite a stir in a district in which Europeans were scarcely ever known to travel in so original a fashion, and an Aleppo newspaper had announced that he had been murdered.

Lawrence arrived at Aleppo about the 20th of September, seems to have reached Edessa by a native conveyance and then regained Beirut and England, where he landed in the middle of October.

* * *

It is difficult to discover the exact itinerary which Lawrence followed during the last part of his tour, between Aleppo and Edessa. He has himself surrounded the details of his first journey in the Levant with a certain mystery. It would not be impossible to suppose that, charged officially by his government to explore certain little known regions, he was therefore bound to be discreet. Is it not more likely that from about this time he developed a taste for the life of the dregs of the Orient, and that he was driven to dissembling that which in his journey could not be repeated? Either hypothesis could be considered.

Whatever the case, his journey and the conditions in which he undertook it constitute a very remarkable achievement. He had covered nearly one thousand two hundred and fifty miles on foot, in full summer, and usually well off the beaten track. He was probably the sole erudite European to have visited, studied, measured and photographed almost all the Frankish fortresses of Syria and Palestine. As well as all this effort, study and adventure, he had even found the time to collect some Hittite seals for Dr. Hogarth, thus assisting in a branch of archaeology which was up to then practically unexplored.

His exceptional mind had not stopped at the rather limited subject of architectural techniques: he had raised the question and attempted to understand the problems of how the Crusaders had organised the combined defence of this area as much by reference to the political and economic necessities of the different countries as by the nature of their geography. So broad a sweep in a man of twenty-one shows, apart from a profound knowledge of the history of the Crusades, a rare gift for strategy. Certain passages of letters which he wrote in the course of his tour could serve as a vade-mecum for the modern military student interested in the possibilities of a campaign in Palestine and Syria.

* * *

Lawrence returned to England exhausted, ill and enraptured. He was enormously enriched. He had got together the basic elements of an excellent work of erudition; he had made contact with regions that tingled with a secret life and whose countryside, inhabitants and entire atmosphere had captured his heart for ever; he had studied Syro-Palestine in all its aspects: its exalted past, and the burning questions raised by its hazardous present: the political, religious and racial situation, its military possibilities—he had meditated on all this during his long solitary marches. Finally—and this was perhaps for him the most important—he had been able to measure how far his tenacious will-power could drive his puny body and the journey satisfied his vanity as much as his pride.

* * *

In the course of the year 1910 Lawrence wrote his thesis "The Military Architecture of the Crusades" (since published as *Crusader Castles*), and passed his final History examinations brilliantly, obtaining a 'first'. His studies finished, the young man had to choose a career. He had always been attracted by archaeology, and after this first journey which had filled him with enthusiasm, he wished to return to the Levant. Dr. Hogarth recommended him for a research demyship at Magdalen College, which would assure him of the vital minimum of a hundred pounds a year, and thus enable him to join the archaeological mission which under Hogarth's direction was carrying out some excavations for the British Museum at Carchemish on the Euphrates, as an unpaid assistant.

In December 1910, Lawrence embarked on the steamship *Saghalien* of the Messageries Maritimes Line, and for the second time sailed for the Near East.

* * *

On his way out to this turbulent Orient to which he was so compellingly attracted, he was given the opportunity to visit the centres of a more restrained culture and art, since his boat put in at Naples and Athens. The Parthenon roused his refined mind, but his joy was full of reserves, for he wrote to his mother: "There will never be a great book on Athens unless it is one by an enemy: no man who knew it could resist its spell, except by a violent attack upon its spirit, and who can attack it now of artists, when Tolstoy is dead? He, and he alone, could have uprooted Greek culture in the world." A subtle if debatable view, and unexpected in a boy who had just come down from the university. It is interesting to note that here Lawrence met Maurice Barrès of *Voyage de Sparte*. These two men with their Nordic ideals were in revolt against classical culture, with which they were, however, whether they liked it or not, thoroughly imbued. "In asserting the perfection of Greek Art, I deny myself," said the Lorrainian. Had T. E. Lawrence, who had read everything, read the *Voyage de Sparte*? The young Oxonian and the intellectual dandy of *Culte du Moi*, men so different in other ways, had their points in common. With minds that were almost too gifted, they loved to debunk preconceived ideas and to strike paradoxes in order to astonish their audiences, but their desire to be original at all cost often led them astray.

*   *   *

On the 15th of December, 1910, Lawrence landed at Constantinople and at the end of the month found himself at Aleppo. He did not go immediately to the site of the excavations at Carchemish, as he wished before starting work to perfect his knowledge of Arabic. He installed himself in the school of the American mission at Jebail in the Lebanon, near Beirut. At the end of February Dr. Hogarth came to Syria to look for him.

Carchemish

DURING the years which preceded the first world war, England indulged in a grand Arabic dream. As the ruler of Islamic India she conceived the project of linking this colony with the Mediterranean, and of bringing under her political influence the whole chain of Arab or Arabianised states constituted by Afghanistan, Persia, Mesopotamia, Syro-Palestine and Arabia.

She prepared for this vast enterprise with patient underground work. Her agents were scattered throughout these semi-savage countries, all profoundly xenophobic and anti-Christian. The Intelligence Service, the Colonial Office, the Army and the Admiralty all worked together: consuls, travellers, merchants penetrated these coveted lands by way of the frontier of India, the Persian Gulf or the Mediterranean coast, and with an enormous degree of skill, tact and generosity they attempted to win over the shy and backward peoples and the chieftains of a world that in many places had not progressed beyond the anarchy of feudalism.

In the more centralised and relatively more evolved countries such as Persia or Turkey, the work was of a very delicate nature. It went from the subscribing of national loans to the financing of revolts in the areas where religious and ethnic minorities had always some good reason to rebel and where shots are of little consequence.

Moreover, in this colonial enterprise, the English had not only to take account of the resistance of the natives. In Persia they were in competition with Russia, and in the Turkish Empire with the Germans who had become the friends and official advisers of the Young Turk government. In this country they had such first-class observers as, for example, Shakespeare in Arabia, the extraordinary Gertrude Bell in Iraq, and scores of other agents. It would be inaccurate and rather coarse to describe such people as spies in English pay. Usually disinterested and passionately believing in the greatness of their country, they worked with an idealism that was inspired by the conception of a large-scale English expansion and of the foundation of a *Pax Britannica* in Western Asia, a project which had great nobility even if the means employed did not always match the moral tone of the intentions.

There is no evidence for stating that Dr. Hogarth belonged in any way to the network of propaganda and information services which executed the requirements of British policy in Asia. Those who knew him well believe that such an activity would not have fitted in with his direct and abrupt nature, but there is a strong temptation to think differently: his entire archaeological life was spent at the nerve points of the Mediterranean chessboard, in Crete, Cyprus, Egypt and Syria, and during the war he took his place quite naturally in the Arab Bureau: he must at least have given gratuitous information and advice to the members of English political circles in which he had friends.

This necessarily leads the historian to pose the same question about Lawrence. It seems extremely probable, although there is no known document to prove it, that for a long time before the war T.E. had contacts with the British Secret Service and was employed by it, and one is led to think that Hogarth played Lurgan to this Kim, whose potentialities he could guess. It is difficult otherwise to explain Lawrence's mysterious comings and goings in Syria or the virtuosity which he exhibited in Egypt from the beginning of 1915 in organising the network of allied espionage in Turkey. Passages from his letters in 1910, 1911, 1912 and 1913, are revealing: "For some reason Dr. Hogarth is very anxious to make me learn some Arabic," he said, and elsewhere: "It strikes me that the strongly-dialectical Arabic of the villagers would be as good as a disguise to me. . . ." How else can these remarks be understood unless one supposes that Hogarth, like Lawrence, was occupied with secret activities, or was preparing to be?

A portrait by Augustus John shows Hogarth with his socratic goatee beard, his eye sparkling with intelligence, his clothes neglected. This fine well-balanced scholar, not wishing to assert himself, hid a rare energy beneath his mildness. Ever discreet, and in the background, he controlled and

shaped the career of T.E. whom he had known since childhood. Without doubt Lawrence found in this robust pagan
character the stability which he himself lacked. Hogarth was
practically the only person whom he always admired and
respected unreservedly. "I owed him everything I had since
I was 17, which is the age at which I suddenly found myself . . . ," he said somewhere. Any study that did not lay stress
on Hogarth's personality and the major influence which he
exerted on Lawrence's life would be incomplete.

*   *   *

At the end of February 1911, as has been said, Dr. Hogarth
came to look for Lawrence at Jebail, in the Lebanon. He
wished to get his pupil to make a reconnaissance of Syria
under his direction. He was accompanied by a Cypriot,
Gregory, in whom he had great confidence and who acted as
foreman on the site of his archaeological excavations. The
exact object of this journey remains rather mysterious. The
three men reached Haifa by sea, visited Mount Carmel,
Nazareth,[1] the village of Yarmuk and its vertiginous viaducts. At Deraa, at the limit of the Druze country, they took
to the railway line which brought them to Damascus, then to
Homs and Aleppo. At the end of March, they were in camp
at the Carchemish excavations. Such a trip which at this time
was in no way an exploration had all the same no lack of difficulty and danger: the line from Asia Minor to Medina, although a modern railway, was none the less a religious route.
Many of the travellers who used it, fanatical pilgrims, were
not at all pleased to see Christians, and above all Christians
who did not belong to the country, mingling with themselves.
For Europeans this kind of tourism had a strong tincture of
adventure.

The journey filled Lawrence with wonder. He was re-
discovering this country which a year before had captivated
him, and he penetrated further into it than he had done before. He was able to see for the first time the ancient route of
the Hadj that leads to the holy places of Islam. Above all, he

[1] "Nazareth is no uglier than Basingstoke or very little," said
Lawrence cynically, and one cannot say that he was altogether wrong.
It is the same sense of humour as Byron's ("The Parthenon looks like
the Mansion House," said the latter).

was visiting these countries at the side of his admired master,
who enriched them with his immense learning. Hogarth knew
all about the past and the present of the areas through which
they travelled, he spoke Arabic, Turkish, Greek, French,
German and Italian, his views on both the short- and long-
term politics of these troubled countries—the Balkans of the
Near East—were profound, and it is legitimate to suppose
that during the long days spent on the roads of Palestine and
Syria, he devoted himself to moulding this disciple for the
missions with which he intended to entrust him.

*   *   *

In 1878, a certain George Smith had discovered near the
little village of Jerablus, on the Euphrates, about sixty miles
to the north-east of Aleppo, on an acropolis that stands above
the river, some strange sculptures that did not seem to be
either Roman, Greek or Assyrian; the British Museum had
started excavations whose direction they had entrusted to a
certain Henderson, the British Consul at Aleppo. But the
place was not easily accessible and the country was rather unsafe; the work yielded but slender results and was abandoned.
In 1910 the British Museum's interest in Carchemish was
re-awakened. The site had been identified as Hittite, and
the attention of scholars was attracted to these little-known
people, whose language even to-day has not been completely
translated, but who played a major rôle in the early history of
the Levant. These warriors, mounted on the same chariots
that carried the Achaeans of the Trojan War, were installed
two thousand years before the Christian era as a conquering
aristocracy on the Upper Euphrates, occupying acropoli
similar to those of Mycenae or Tyrinthia. It was hoped to
find among these Hittites the first examples of the blonde in-
vaders of South-East Europe, the prototypes of Menelaus and
Achilles. Carchemish had been one of their centres, and after
having abandoned the work for a quarter of a century, the
British Museum decided to start it up again: Dr. Hogarth was
put in charge of these new excavations.
It must be remarked that the great British Museum underwent a sharp revival of interest in Carchemish at the precise
moment that the Berlin to Baghdad railway, which was being

built by the Germans and which represented so great a menace to the political and economic undertakings of the English in the Orient, reached the Euphrates. The Germans were engaged in throwing a bridge over the river and their works' site was only a few hundred yards from the Tell of Carchemish. How can it be doubted that the archaeologists whose task was to carry out the excavations had as a subsidiary task to keep an eye on the activities of the Germans?

*   *   *

The life of the English scholars was full of activity and of the unexpected. They had to be contemptuous of comfort, hardened in spirit, and fond of adventure. The regions of the Upper Euphrates could not be considered to be well policed and civilised: the Turkish administration, always rather feeble and relaxed, had some authority in Anatolia and the big cities of the Empire only, but in the remote lands, inhabited by nomads and a primitive agricultural people, it was practically powerless. Beyond the Euphrates the country of the Kurds was almost independent, and given up to the authority of the tribal chieftains, who were often at war with each other: the Kurds and the Arabs murdered each other gladly, either out of clannish rivalry or simply because they enjoyed being brigands. At this time, moreover, the Ottoman Empire, despite the rise to power of the Young Turks in 1909, was beginning to dissolve: after the loss of Egypt in 1888, there followed the amputation of Tripolitania, occupied by the Italians. The tension in the Balkans and the preparations for the war which was to break out in 1912 did nothing to improve matters, and the government had other preoccupations without having to restore order in outlandish countries of no great political or economic interest.

Let us imagine then in the midst of this anarchy two groups of Europeans: the Germans of the railway line and the English archaeologists left almost entirely to themselves and living as they would have done in some negro kingdom in the centre of Africa. In this state of insecurity the Germans relied on a considerable guard of Ottoman soldiers and on their own weapons: as for the English, they had recourse to their diplomacy and to their traditional skill in dealing with the natives of primitive countries.

Even so it is astonishing to think how much they behaved at times, in a country that was theoretically independent and subject to its own administration and laws, as though in a conquered land. Leonard Woolley, who directed the Carchemish excavations in 1912 and replaced Dr. Hogarth, relates in his memoirs,[1] in all simplicity, that he twice and in open court menaced with his revolver the Turkish judges who would not give him satisfaction on some question of land ownership. He tells also how the watchman of the British Consulate at Aleppo amused himself by firing at the passers-by, but that the Ottoman police did not dare arrest a man who was in the service of the English.[2]

* * *

On the western bank of the Euphrates, around Carchemish, the countryside, by comparison with the rest of those arid, dried-up regions, is fairly pleasant. Near the native villages there was some cultivation but beyond the Euphrates extended the Kurdish steppe, flat and treeless, the northern extremity of the great Syrian desert, scarcely less sterile, mysterious and disquieting and, like all deserts, devastatingly attractive to some individuals.

The site of Carchemish in itself had everything necessary to excite the imagination of scholars and dreamers alike: the atmosphere was charged with history. Beneath the Arab buildings were found Byzantine walls, then Roman cement, lower still some Greek and Assyrian remains, and finally those of Hittite origin. But beneath even these remnants the diggers found the traces of forgotten civilisations and even implements of stone cut by the first occupants of the ancient city. Myth and history, in a country haunted by humans since the earliest times, were mingled together. Quite close to Carchemish on the Euphrates was Doura Europos, the ford of Europa. Does this name have any connection with the virgin of legend who was ravished long ago by the sacred bull,

[1] *Dead Towns and Living Men*, pp. 156 and 171. See also the note, p. 229. If the same book is still to be believed, the methods of the French residents in Turkey were not very different (*idem*, p. 258).
[2] *Idem*, p. 97.

4

or more simply did it indicate one of those fords essential in these bridgeless lands, by which the armies of Asia were able to roll out into Europe? Seventy miles further to the south, at Thapsak, the Ten Thousand had crossed the Euphrates on foot on their way to Cunaxa.[1]

These countries which are at the junction of regions that are semi-European, of the desert and of the high Caucasian mountains, have a strange climate. Their winter is harsh and they are swept by an icy north wind that comes from the Taurus or from the Elburz. Spring is charming: the Orontes and the Euphrates reflect the poplars as though it were Normandy, and the steppes are covered with grasses and flowers. Summer is torrid and the sand-laden winds of the evening crush one like the blast of hot air from an open oven door, making Bidon V, Jibuti and Aden sometimes uninhabitable.

The archaeologist's house, a cabin made of puddled clay of less than primitive comfort and "alive with cats and fleas", was six or seven hundred yards from the site. Hogarth, his deputy Campbell Thompson and their young assistant led a life that was austere but free, healthy and unbuttoned in the way of celibate camps. In return for a modest salary of fifteen shillings a day, Lawrence was put to work collecting and classifying pottery, taking notes on the finds, and developing photographs, but above all his job was to oversee and direct the gangs of native labourers.

The basis of every archaeological excavation is an enormous amount of navvying. In order to find the delicate objects that decorate the show cases of museums it is necessary to move as much earth as in digging a canal. The scholar becomes the entrepreneur of public works and the English must have taken on a hundred and fifty or two hundred Arab and Kurdish workmen for these excavations. Such gangs are usually composed of fairly moderate elements: wanderers, tramps, outlaws and good-for-nothings, always difficult to handle. Hogarth, who had a long experience of this sort of work, knew however how to do his recruiting, treated his workers with firmness but with strict justice and found in Lawrence an excellent assistant.

[1] *Anabasis*, 1–4.

The young man proved to be a leader of men: he had authority and gave proof of an extraordinary judgment in the employment of this labour force. In agreement with Hogarth, he had instituted, to encourage the workers, a system of rewarding every discovery of an antique object, with a certain number of shots. This method filled the Arabs and the Kurds with enthusiasm, and Lawrence has been described dancing with joy in the middle of his workers, shouting and firing his revolver into the air whenever a bas-relief or a good piece of pottery had just been dug out of the earth.

Whilst on this work he learnt to speak Arabic fluently and acquired considerable experience in the handling of Orientals. He plunged with delight into native life. In the diggings he spent hours listening to the stories of the workmen, mixed with them, played with them, and managed to drop the barrier that separates the Westerner from the little folk of the East: the Syrian navvies accepted this small sunburnt man, naked from the waist up and covered with dust, almost as one of themselves; he wore an old pair of khaki shorts with a large Kurdish belt, the largest that he could find, and it looked a bit ridiculous on his childish body. Lawrence's necessities were no greater than those of his workers, and he did not despise them: sometimes even he took their clothes, and wandered around the site and in the village in the robes of a Bedouin. A Roumi of this sort had never been seen in Syria before.

*   *   *

> "Sometimes, a soldier smuggled in a
> pretty child or a beautiful woman with
> whom he had become enamoured."
> (Anabasis, iv. 12.)

To plunge so completely into the atmosphere of the Orient is not always without danger for a European. Microbes against which he is not vaccinated pullulate in the moulderings of very ancient civilisations. In the garden of Armidia, the enchantress, the serpent is not a symbolic animal, but a perennial and venomous beast found beneath every stone. Perhaps Lawrence was ill protected against some of the perils of the country.

A little time after his arrival at Carchemish, he contracted a very tender friendship with a certain Sheik Ahmed, sur-named Dahum, the Black.[1] This lad of fifteen years was in-telligent enough, restrained, kind and very handsome. One finds sometimes in these lands men who have a beauty of body and face that is not of our times, and who instead of the full nose, the thin legs, and the large flat feet of the Bedouins have the straight nose and the long muscular and delicately jointed limbs of a classical Apollo.

Dahum had been a donkey-boy in his village, then a servant on the German work-site, and finally he had become a 'boy' for the English. Lawrence conceived a very great affection for this beautiful human animal. He helped the young Arab to learn to read and write, and gave him enough idea about photography to enable him to act as his assistant. The Arab became his habitual companion, "his kindred spirit", as David Garnett rather curiously says. The two men never left each other, went for long trips in the semi-desert countryside, bathed together, and played like puppies in the water.

This intimacy did not go unnoticed. The English silently disapproved of it, the natives made ribald jokes. They were not particularly shocked by this kind of friendship, but they firmly disapproved when Lawrence sculpted Dahum, in the soft stone of the country, and produced a statue of him in the nude. Moslems are prudish on this point: "Whoever shows himself naked dishonours himself", and the joking became hostile despite the young Englishman's popularity. Lawrence seemed to take pleasure in scandalising the natives as well as his own compatriots, overdid it and advertised his affection. A childish sense of humour, the desire to defy public opinion, was Woolley's verdict, and he makes out that there was nothing culpable in the friendship of the two young men. The whole story is slightly ambiguous, and one cannot help thinking of such paragraphs from his memoirs of the war as the complacent:

[1] Woolley imagines that Dahum is the translation into vulgar Arabic of the Semitic word *tehom*, meaning obscurity, the dark chaos which according to the Bible covered the waters before Genesis (*Dead Towns*, p. 142). He remarks that Dahum's family, which had lived at Carchemish since time immemorial, was probably Hittite in origin and not Semitic.

"Our youths began indifferently to slake one another's few needs in their own clean bodies—a cold convenience that by comparison seemed sexless and even pure. Later some began to justify this process, and swore that friends quivering together in the yielding sand with intimate hot limbs in supreme embrace, found there hidden in the darkness a sensual coefficient of the mental passion which was welding our souls and spirits in one flaming effort."

In any case there were troubled echoes of these things within his complex soul.

There was another native with whom Lawrence was very friendly. This was the foreman on the diggings at Carchemish, a certain Sheik Hamoudi, surnamed the Hoja, a character of the most picturesque type. Though still young, he had led a not very edifying life, he had run loose in the desert to rob travellers and had committed a number of murders. Grown steadier as he grew up, he was about thirty when Lawrence met him, and had married and settled at Jerablus. Hogarth took on the ex-bandit, and as, despite his past sins, he was energetic and honest, he made him the boss of the site. The Hoja during his rackety youth had learnt everything about the life of the desert nomads, so much in fact that Lawrence took him as guide and mentor on the trips which he made to the least known corners of the country.

To treat the native as friend and equal was not to conform to the traditions of the British, but through this intimacy with two Arabs, Lawrence acquired in a few years in the Orient a knowledge of things which many men never discover in a lifetime spent there.

* * *

The English did not entirely isolate themselves on their excavations. They entered into fairly cordial relations with the Germans, who from time to time came to drink a glass of beer or even to dine at their camp. T.E. had made friends with Mrs. Fontana, the wife of the British Consul at Aleppo, and carried on a sort of intellectual flirtation with her which was not without a certain irritating effect on the husband, and which the young wife found touching. A few visitors also came to Carchemish, officials, tourists and scholars, and it was thus that T.E. met the already famous Gertrude Bell.

This elderly lady, lacking in grace and slightly ridiculous, had led an extraordinary life in the Orient. Alone with her native guides she had crossed the deserts of Syria and Meso-potamia, and regions that were almost unexplored. Installed in Baghdad in a city to which Europeans were with difficulty admitted, but whose freedom she had received because of her generosity, courage and diplomacy, she created there a kind of centre for British propaganda. She has been compared by some people to Lady Stanhope, but there was nothing in common between this mature, ugly, prudish woman, high-minded, charitable and full of Victorian ideals, and the proud, eccentric aristocrat who dreamt of becoming queen of the Lebanon, kept up an armed guard and an Oriental court, and slept with her native servants.

It is amusing to imagine the meeting between Gertrude Bell and Lawrence, the one already a celebrity on account of her explorations in Arabia, the other an unknown young man who had already seen much of the Levant, and who dreamt of discovering more. These two strongly divergent characters greeted each other without much warmth. In her letters Gertrude mentions the young archaeologist but briefly, and from the height of her experience and reputation she slightly snubbed the badly dressed student. As for T.E., he had some amusing and biting comments to make on the explorer, who in order to dine in the mud hut, unpacked from her luggage an unlikely evening dress, and annoyed the English searchers who were doing their best at Carchemish, without great re-sources, and making use of the means that lay to hand, by praising over and over again the methods employed by the Germans who were then engaged in excavating Kalaat Shirgat.[1]

[1] Later Lawrence made friends with Gertrude Bell, but it is clear that these two specialists of Arabia did not have an unreserved affection for each other. In 1927, Lawrence, after having read Gertrude Bell's letters which had just been published by Benn, wrote (4th October, 1927, from Karachi): "Gertrude was not a very good judge of men or situations, and was always the slave of some momentary power: at one time Hogarth, at another Wilson, at another me, at last Sir Percy Cox. She changed her direction each time like a weathercock: because she

Lawrence, who when bitten by a fly could be extremely disagreeable, would willingly have put the old girl in her place, but he was obliged to draw in his horns, as Gertrude was powerful in London, and had the ear of governmental spheres and of the directors of the British Museum. Besides, the excavations were not going very well: Thompson and Lawrence were still struggling with the cement foundations of the Roman fort which covered the remains of the palace of the Hittite king Sangara. They had not found much of any great importance and a bad report from Gertrude Bell, added to this relative lack of success, would risk putting an end to their work. And Lawrence was anxious to remain at Carchemish, as he liked the life that was at once studious and romantic. He employed all his charm for Gertrude's benefit, but was happy to see the intruder depart.

*   *   *

Thompson and Lawrence remained at Carchemish till the end of June 1911. When the heat obliged them to stop work, the two enthusiasts did not immediately return to Europe. They went first of all to have a look at Tell el Hamra, the other Hittite township on the Euphrates, twenty miles to the south of Carchemish; then, whilst Thompson returned to the coast, Lawrence prepared to carry out a project which had been near his heart for a long time.

He dreamt of visiting again that region of Aintab, Birejik and Uofa (the Edessa of the Crusaders) where two years before, a newcomer to Syria, he had travelled protected by his guard of Bashibazooks and had been nearly murdered. On the 12th of July he left alone, reached Edessa and spent three days in visiting the town. There are there a powerful Frankish castle, and some purely Oriental monuments belonging to an Orient almost untouched by Europe: a charming mosque, all with domes of ceramic and delicate little pillars is reflected in a pool in which the sacred fish, worshipped since time

had no great depth of mind. But depth and strength of emotions—oh! Lord yes. Her life had crisis after crisis of that sort, and they are all missing from the book. Very probably they were missing from her letters home." It is a harsh comment. Was Lawrence annoyed by the tiny place he occupied in the explorer's correspondence?

immemorial, glide amid the water-lilies. Astarte stretched out
her hand to Islam. This was all very exciting for a man who
was taken with the picturesque and with humanism, but
"Always his soul hungered for less than it had" and fleeing
beauties that were too facile, he left the Persian charms of
Edessa in order to launch himself at hazard across countries
increasingly forbidding, towards Haran, Birejik and Rum
Kalaat.

It took him more than a week to reach his goal. After such
a trip he began to show signs of fatigue, and when, on the
24th of July, he arrived at Rum Kalaat, he was sick and
suffering agonies from a dental abscess. Meanwhile he was
supported by the joy of having reached this town that was
almost unknown in Europe: it is an enormous ruined
fortress that stands on a promontory, three hundred and fifty
feet above the Euphrates. Beneath Turkish and Arab accre-
tions are to be found the machicolations and the underground
vaults of the Frankish builders and the ancient Byzantine
walls. Lawrence studied and photographed Rum Kalaat for
two days, then returned to the south. In three mortal stages
he reached Jerablus on the 28th of July. He was exhausted:
he was eroded by fever and above all dysentery. He collapsed
but the Hoja took him into his house and looked after him
devotedly. The Arab deserves much credit for taking in a
European who was in such bad shape, for if Lawrence had
died under his roof he could well have been accused of
poisoning his guest and have been in trouble with the
Turkish police; the whole village advised him to put the sick
man out of his door. Lawrence gradually recovered, but he
needed a week before he was in a fit state to undertake the
journey, first by horse and then by car, which brought him to
the station at Aleppo. On the 13th of August, he embarked at
Beirut for England.

Although Lawrence's later travels through Syria are little
known and rather mysterious, we have the complete journal
of the July 1911 journey from his own hand. This brief and
simply written diary deserves to be read, for despite its scanti-
ness and telegraphic style, it reveals the profound nature of
its author. The terse pointed notes which affect to describe
visits to ancient fortresses and the crossing of deserts are in

their pretended objectivity purely subjective and betray the tormented sensibility of a mind that was completely turned inwards. Lawrence is less interested in unknown cities than in his own exhaustion and suffering, and mercilessly tests his own capacity to stand pain. It was in this slightly sadistic game that he took his pleasure, while daily life on the physical and intellectual plane filled him with horror.

* * *

Lawrence returned to Oxford at the end of August 1911. He was very sick. "Doctors dispute over my carcase, they seem to agree that I must not go to the East again for three months," he wrote at the end of September. But he learnt that the British Museum had decided to start the excavations again. "I am in the seventh heaven or there about . . ." cried the man who a few days before had been too exhausted to see his friends. At the beginning of December he left again for the Levant.

The work at Carchemish could not be put in hand again for several months, and in order to avoid leaving Lawrence with nothing to do, it was decided to send him to Kafr-Ammar, in Egypt, where the celebrated Sir Flinders Petrie was making some excavations. When Petrie saw a strange urchin figure arriving dressed in shorts and a blazer, he was a little taken aback. "This is not a game of cricket, young man," he exclaimed. But he soon became accustomed to Lawrence's peculiarities and learnt to appreciate his intelligence and competence. He was himself an overbearing character, unmethodical and eccentric, and Lawrence's letters recount the picturesque life which they led in his camp. But Egyptology, already an advanced and highly developed science, did not contain for a man like Lawrence as much of the mysterious attraction as that of the still almost unknown Hittite civilisation. His beloved Syria called him: at the beginning of April he was back at Carchemish.

Leonard Woolley, who had replaced Hogarth at the head of the expedition, and Lawrence built, close to the Tell where they were carrying out their researches, a house that was big enough and more comfortable than the old mud hut. It had a central room heated by a vast fireplace and completely lined with books: the floor was paved with a fine Roman mosaic which the archaeologists had found nearby. It was here that they worked, took their meals and received their guests, offering them tea in Hittite cups four thousand years old.

Visitors saw a small, rather gauche young man, atrociously dressed, in large boots and scanty clothes. Silent and secretive he came in and out without noise and took very little part in the conversations. Many took this strange boy with an Oxford accent, who could scarcely hide his contempt for everybody and his personal conviction that he knew a great deal more about everything than the people he spoke to, for a rather irritating poseur. But if he irritated he also interested, and few men or women could resist the desire to win him over at the risk of incurring a snub.

One day a traveller sought hospitality from the archaeologists. He was a lieutenant in the Indian army called Hubert Young, who during a period of leave had come to study Arabic in Syria. Lawrence was very cool towards him at first. From this time on he had a violent prejudice against professional officers, but he quickly saw that Young, although he was apt to put on the airs of an old soldier, was cultivated, very shrewd, and understood admirably the countries of the East. The two young men found that they were sympathetic and conversed long together; on returning to his Indian garrison this officer remarked to his friends: "There is a little man at Carchemish of whom more will be heard some day...." Five years later Young was to fight the Arabian campaign with the "little man" whose personality had so struck him, and he was to write one of the most interesting accounts of him that we have.[1]

* * *

After the disappointments of the year before, the excavations in 1912 yielded a rich harvest not only in pottery but in sculpture of a high quality. "We have one piece of Hittite sculpture more realistic and artistic than anything Egyptian. It suggests a flood of light on the development of early Greek art . . ." wrote Lawrence in May 1912.

Meanwhile the life at Carchemish was not quite so calm

[1] *The Independent Arab.*

as the year before. In June cholera made its appearance around the Upper Euphrates and was ravaging Aleppo. It was threatening Jerablus and the German and British camps, and was capable of stopping the work in progress and of course of endangering the lives of the two Englishmen, who, Bohemian and negligent in their ways, never took any precautions, and ate and drank whatever they liked. Above all, friction occurred between the archaeologists and the railway engineers. Some of the Germans were brutal, full of themselves, and behaved as if they owned the place; they treated their people badly, and were in constant conflict with them. Lawrence, made furious by the German invasion which had entirely changed the atmosphere of Jerablus, did his best to put spokes in the railway-builders' wheels. He stirred up the Arab and Kurdish workmen against their employers, schemed, had the works boycotted, and organised strikes and brawls. The little man was a born agitator and he had a diabolical love of intrigue.

In the summer of 1912, Lawrence went for a rest to Jebail, in the Lebanon, with his friends of the American mission, and Woolley returned to England. The Germans took advantage of this in order to lay their hands on the Tell of Carchemish, under the pretext of wishing to use the stones for their embankment. The native watchman, Hadj Wahid, left in charge of the camp on the site, held his ground with a rifle, and was able to warn Lawrence by telegram. For several days the German engineers did not dare go near the old city where a madman, armed with two revolvers and an old musket and completely inebriated with raki, threatened to damage anyone who touched a stone of the Tell. Lawrence's arrival with a representative of the Turkish Minister of Public Education put an end to this heroic-comic incident.

The Turkish Administration came down on the side of the English, and the Germans were made to look foolish. War was now declared between the two camps of Europeans that were four hundred yards apart. One day a German official for some futile reason ordered the Englishman's 'boy' to be whipped. The indignant Lawrence provoked a scandal and demanded a public apology. The war became a struggle for prestige between the English and the Germans, while the inhabitants looked on and jeered, though they favoured the English, who were more just and more generous. But in playing this game the Europeans were to lose all the Arabs' respect. It was the old story.

Lawrence, who had spent the summer of 1912 in the Levant, had no further desire to return to England. "It's a place where one eats lotus nearly every day and you know that feeling is bad for one's desire to do something worth looking at," he wrote to a friend. It is clear that he no longer wished to live in the West. At Christmas he made a brief appearance in Oxford, but only stayed there for a few days. Syria held all the strings of his heart. Meanwhile the country was in a state of anarchy; the war in the Balkans, which had broken out in the autumn of 1912, monopolised all the Turkish forces, and the outlandish regions of the Upper Euphrates were more or less abandoned to themselves. The Kurds were in open revolt. The Arab peasants on the right bank of the Euphrates lived in constant fear of being raided by the nomads: a Kurdish attack on Aleppo and pillaging of the bazaars were even spoken of. In this chaotic situation Lawrence was in his element. Running hither and thither he spread alarming rumours: he organised the defence of the Consulate at Aleppo with rifles borrowed from an English gun-boat stationed at Beirut; one wonders whether he was serious or whether he was indulging in a huge practical joke.

Despite the restlessness of the country, Lawrence went on long excursions into the interior, during the leisure which the excavations allowed him. He travelled as much by the river as by the tracks; he had brought back from England a dinghy which he had fitted with an outboard motor and with which he went up and down the Euphrates. (He loved using this motor, being gifted with that mixture of sense, intuition and dexterity which provides some men with an understanding of things mechanical and means that an engine becomes alive beneath their fingers.) He spoke Arabic better and better,[1] he had taken the habit of wearing Oriental clothes, was hardened to the discomfort of the life of the inhabitants, and accompanied by his two friends, the Hoja and Dahum, he managed to pass unnoticed to the unknown corners of Syria. This part

[1] Though he could never read or write it.

of his life has remained full of mystery, and it is doubtful whether it is possible to piece it together. He has always kept it jealously secret and he has scarcely left us any light on his peregrinations. "I liked the things underneath me and took my pleasures and adventures downward," he said at one point. He has spoken to his friends of a day when, alone in the desert with the Hoja and Dahum, he nearly died of thirst, and he has told how the three exhausted men quarrelled among themselves. In some corner of Syria which he has left vague, and in which he was wandering with Dahum, he speaks of having been arrested and enrolled by force in the Turkish army. He got away by bribing the sentry, and fled by night.[1] He also talks of the weeks which he spent in Port Said mingling with scum of the port, sleeping with the dockers and employed in unloading the colliers. What truth there is in these stories no one will ever know. They certainly have a basis of authenticity: Lawrence, like all the best liars, never lied completely.

When the summer of 1913 came and the site was shut down, Lawrence remained alone at Carchemish for more than a month before deciding to return to England. When he left in the middle of July, he was accompanied by his two friends, Dahum and the Hoja, from whom apparently he could not be parted. He brought them to Oxford, introduced them to his family, and put them up in the summer-house which his parents had had built for him in the past.

It was a strange and rather scandalous idea. Lawrence took pleasure in outraging the racial prejudices of his fellow countrymen, to speak of nothing else, and for several weeks he paraded the two Arabs in their desert robes, arousing the curiosity and the mild disapproval of the prudish and traditional university city.

Dahum and the Hoja behaved like clowns. Lawrence taught them to ride a bicycle (ladies' bicycles of course on account of their Bedouin robes) and crowds gathered as they rode through the centre of the city: there was an incident between these primitives and an Egyptian student: the English frowned, and Lawrence at the end of August, having produced the desired effect of curiosity and scandal, and

[1] Liddell Hart, *T. E. Lawrence*, p. 27.

having astounded the two Arabs, returned to Carchemish, where the excavations were started up again at the beginning of October.

In October, one of Lawrence's brothers, Will, who had obtained an appointment as a professor in India, passed through Carchemish in order to see T.E. The free and adventurous life of the archaeologist filled him with enthusiasm and the stories which he heard turned his head, for he wrote to one of his friends a curious letter:[1]

"My Bedawi brother showed me Aleppo well, taking me on calls to houses in the Moslem quarter, so bigoted still that he's the only European who knows it owing to his habit of going in Arab clothes. . . . Then I went over to the Euphrates and lived in my brother's village and swam the great river three times in the day, and practised pistol shooting and looked at his excavations. Greater things were to follow.

"One of his chief friends is Busrawi Agha, the chief of the Melli Kurds, and the greatest man in Kurdistan, since the Young Turks poisoned Ibrahim Pasha. Busrawi is the man who carried out the massacres at Urfa, 8,000 people, and Adana and Nezib just four months ago. At the last my brother was actually on the spot in disguise, and during the late war he and a Kurd planned the sack of Aleppo, actually arranging which should have the loot of which house, and apportioning two bankers' houses, great collectors of *objets d'art*, to Ned [T. E. Lawrence]. They gave him a bodyguard of 200 Kurds whom he put up for some weeks. The failure of the Bulgars before Istamboul checked their plans which still simmer. . . ."

This letter is obviously highly imaginative: the massacres he mentions took place in the spring of 1909, before Lawrence had arrived in the Orient; it is difficult to see the Englishman standing by at the massacre of Christians or at the sack of a town; as for the guard of two hundred Kurds, how could T.E. have provided their pay on fifteen shillings a day?

There is something rather disquieting about this document. One wonders what Lawrence could have told his brother to dazzle him to such a degree. As a result of his visit to Carchemish, Will wrote a poem which reveals that the young man had a heated imagination:

[1] To be found in the *Correspondence*, p. 158.

To T.E.L., February 18th, 1914[1]

I've talked with counsellors and lords
Whose words were as no blunted swords,
Watched two Emperors and five kings
And three who had men's worshipping,
Ridden with horsemen of the East
And sat with scholars at their feast,
Known some the masters of their hours,
Some to whom years were as pressed flowers:
Still as I go this thought endures
No place too great to be made yours.

*   *   *

In this year of 1913, the East, shaken by the effects of the Balkan War, was suffering from a growing malaise, while in Europe the fever mounted. Kitchener, the English Resident in Egypt, aware that Turkey, which was under the aegis of Germany, would probably, in the event of war, be on the side of the enemy, was preoccupied with the protection of the Suez Canal, the essential artery.

The Sinai peninsula, an almost uninhabited and in fact uninhabitable desert, is a natural bastion for the defence of Egypt. Now it was under Turkish control and almost unexplored. It was necessary to make a reconnaissance, draw up an outline map and discover what dangers lay hidden in its disquieting solitudes.

At a time when in Europe and the Near East the finger was on the trigger, and when the slightest incident was capable of unleashing catastrophe, there could be no question of sending an armed reconnaissance into Sinai and a disguise had to be found. The officer to whom this mission was entrusted, a sapper called Captain Newcombe, found himself joined by two archaeologists, Woolley and Lawrence, and he set out officially on a scientific expedition. The Palestine Exploration Fund was brought into the plot and the three men were gravely instructed to go and look for "the itinerary followed by the Israelites in the course of the famous forty years which they spent in the Desert".

At the beginning of January 1914, Woolley and Lawrence

[1] *Lawrence by his Friends*, p. 104.

were taken from their work at Carchemish and instructed to go and join Newcombe at Beersheba. Lawrence went immediately and presented himself to the Egyptian map-making department, whose chief, Mr. Dawson, has described his first meeting with the future hero of the Arabian war. There appeared at the door of his office a little "pipsqueak", incredibly badly dressed, who "almost danced into" the room, and who with an expression that was at once mocking and embarrassed, explained what he had come for. After he had gone, the officers of the department asked dumbfounded "whether the visitor was real or pretended clown".[1]

Newcombe waited with some anxiety for the arrival of his companions, and imagined without much pleasure that he would be hampered by two grey-bearded scholars. He was relieved when he saw the energetic and optimistic Woolley arrive with the peculiar young man who seemed to be about fifteen, but who could speak Arabic like a Bedouin, and was thoroughly acquainted with the life of the desert. He was furthermore surprised to find himself confronted by a boy whom he had already met. His family in fact lived in Oxford, and had ties of friendship with the Lawrences. Newcombe was a regular officer in love with his career, and came from an old military family (one of his great-uncles was killed at Waterloo); he had in fact every reason to displease Lawrence whose prejudices against professional soldiers we know; however, the two men understood each other very well, perhaps because of the former friendship, or more likely because it was difficult to resist Newcombe's dynamic character, his direct intelligence and good humour and the competence of the Engineers captain who had a thorough knowledge of the Near East, in which he had been for several years, drawing up maps and delimiting frontiers.

Newcombe, Woolley and Lawrence with a few Arabs (Dahum came with his friend on this expedition) combed the Desert of Sinai for six weeks, surveying the tracks and the water points and paying but scant attention to the halting places of Moses and Aaron. At Aqaba, the worried Turkish authorities tried to hinder Lawrence's activities, since in his usual fashion he was making fun of the Ottoman police and

[1] *Lawrence by his Friends*, p. 132.

disobeying orders. He was dressed as an Arab, and indulging with delight in "the great game" of spying in enemy territory.[1]

* * *

Histories and biographies being written after the event, it is possible to introduce some logic into the tissue of accidents, absurdities and inconsequences which constitute human life. No one at the beginning of 1914 could have foreseen the events that were about to follow, nor the way in which they would take place. How could Lawrence have imagined that one day he would enter with five hundred camelmen the verminous village of Aqaba, where alone with his donkey-boy he had played tricks on a Turkish official? He could not have known how, when or where he was to make use of the enormous store of knowledge which he had accumulated from the Arabs. Europe and the Levant were troubled with obscure presentiments of the catastrophe, but life continued and men who were about to cut each other's throats were forced to treat each other correctly and sometimes cordially.

Woolley and Lawrence, after six weeks of scientific-military work, had only then to return to Carchemish and take up their tasks as archaeologists; they took the pilgrims' route and by way of Maan, Damascus, Homs and Aleppo they reached their camp. There they found everything in complete disorder.

The Germans from the railway line had made mistake after mistake with their workmen. They paid high wages, but treated their men hard and left the recruiting and the settling of salaries to Greek and Armenian sub-contractors. Lawrence's intrigues had probably contributed to increasing this tension between them and their men, for it had reached such a pitch that the engineers had to live under the constant protection of a Tcherkessian guard.

The very day that Woolley and his assistant returned, the explosion occurred. While the men were being paid, a dispute arose between the German accountant and a Kurdish workman. The accountant, irritated, said to the Tcherkessian

---

[1] The details of their wanderings in the desert can be found in a report that Woolley and Lawrence wrote later, and which was published under the title of *The Desert of Zin*.

5

guard, "Hit him!"; the Kurd replied to the blow of the whip by throwing stones and called to his assistance a hundred of his friends who were standing nearby waiting for their pay, and immediately the battle was joined.

The six or seven Germans assailed in their office with volleys of stones defended themselves with their rifles, and the Tcherkessian guard following suit, they wounded several inoffensive workmen and killed one of the Kurds. In their panic they even fired on one of their own engineers who was working on an island in the river.

Enraged, the workmen and the village people seized every weapon that came to hand and running completely mad they fired in every direction; they entrenched themselves behind the old Hittite wall on the Tell of Carchemish in order to spray the offices of the railway with bullets; the position of the Germans was rapidly becoming extremely dangerous.

Hearing the fusillade, Woolley and Lawrence came to see what was happening. The natives, wild with excitement, were shouting, "Death to the Christians!" It was all very well for them to say that the English were not Christians, the position was very delicate and the archaeologists deserve credit for not losing their heads. Their sangfroid and their influence with the natives avoided what would probably have been a massacre. They intervened, calmed the Kurds, the Arabs and the Germans alike, and in doing so ran a considerable risk of being killed by a stray bullet. After hours of firing and excitement they succeeded in restoring peace.

The affair caused a sensation. The next day, "consuls, valis, kaimmakans, mustasarrifs and commandants" were on the spot to listen to the frantic complaints of the Germans and the natives. In the imbroglio of an extremely complicated quarrel, in which the two parties threw in each other's faces grievances both true and false, old and new, the Turkish officials did not know which way to turn, and wisely did nothing. Meanwhile all work on the line was interrupted, and the Germans demanded more soldiers to ensure their own safety. No one knew how to sort out this business.

It was the English who in the end put everything straight. They brought together the adversaries, persuaded the Ger-

mans to pay the blood-price for the Kurds who had been
killed or wounded, and established a veritable peace treaty
between the engineers of the railway line and their workers.
Lawrence was exultant, and one can just imagine him going
round the village and up to the German camp, not strutting
about, but with that affectation of simplicity and indifference
of which he had the secret, in order to hide the victories that
caused him to rejoice.

One ought of course to discover the German point of view
on these incidents; all their engineers were not necessarily
fools and blunderers and it would be interesting to have the
story from one of them. They were working in a country that
was semi-savage, they had to deal with the Turkish government whose inertia was proverbial, and at their door they had
an Englishman who was ready to think of anything in order
to impede their work. Their task cannot have been easy.

*   *   *

Lawrence continued to work on the excavations, and to
travel round Syria with his Arab friends; apart from this he
read much and even started to write.

From his letters we know his literary tastes. His favourite
writers seem to have been the authors of the 1900 school,
with a marked leaning for lengthy works: William Morris,
Ruskin and the very flamboyant Doughty; he loved Tolstoy,
Dostoyevsky, Melville and his unusual *Moby Dick*. He read
numbers of French authors, and admired Mérimée, Flaubert,
Heredia, Anatole France, Paul Fort, Jules Laforgue, Regnier
and Samain. All his life he adored Rabelais. This is surprising in a man who had none of the truculent vitality of
the native of Touraine. Reserved and secretive, he doubtless
found relaxation in a work which without loss of subtlety is
materialist, broadminded and full of joy. He tried his own
hand at literature, and started work on a book on seven great
cities of the East: Cairo, Baghdad, Damascus, Smyrna, Aleppo,
Constantinople and Medina. He had entitled this work *The
Seven Pillars of Wisdom*, which he had taken from a verse in
the Book of Proverbs: "Wisdom hath builded her house, she
hath hewn out her seven pillars" (Prov. ix. 1).

This book would doubtless have revealed his adventures

and his impressions in some of those beautiful shimmering cities. But it must be observed that he never visited Medina; drawn like every enthusiast of the East to the forbidden city, he made plans for entering it, by following as a donkey-boy a caravan of pilgrims, but the war prevented him from achieving this project. We know nothing of this work, as T.E. never finished it and burnt the manuscript in 1914 at the time that he joined up; he was to make use of the title again for his memoirs of the war.

* * *

Lawrence was living his last months at Carchemish: less than a year later, he was to be sucked into the whirlwind of the war. These four years in Syria have a place of capital importance in his life. They are the *Wanderjahre* of Wilhelm Meister; neither the devouring curiosity nor the discovery of exotic lands are lacking, nor Mignon. Like Goethe's young hero, he "has eaten at the table of the Greeks his heritage as a child of the North". He knew Arabic, from Northern Arabia to the Upper Euphrates he knew the country backwards, and he had made a host of friends at every level of society, among the rulers as among the lowest; through his intimate friendship with two natives, he had acquired to a certain degree the ways of thinking and feeling of an Arab.

From this time also were formed in him the two political passions that filled his soul: hatred of the Turks and of the French. Woolley, who had passed long months living with him, analysed these sentiments in his precise fashion:

"He liked France and often talked of the pleasant time he had had there and I think he was even fond of the French people. But, especially after a long stay in the Lebanon, he felt a profound jealousy of the part they played or wished to play in Syria. That French politicians should aim at a control of the country he had come to love infuriated him. He hated the Turks because they were masters of Syria and treated the Arabs as inferiors; that their place should be taken by a non-Arab power was monstrous. Long before the Sykes-Picot agreement drove him into a deliberate policy of frustration Lawrence was an enemy of France."[1]

[1] *Lawrence by his Friends*, Essay by Leonard Woolley, p. 94.

Thus his impressions of Syria were to determine the course of his life.

* * *

In June 1914, Woolley and Lawrence came back to England. They were being pressed to write their report on the exploration of Sinai, and this for political reasons: the international situation was becoming more and more tense, and incidents had to be avoided.

"Turkey was not in the war but was sore about the Sinai survey, which it felt had been a military game. K. (the only begetter of the survey) insisted on the Palestine Exploration Fund bringing out its record of our archaeological researching p.d.q.[1] as whitewash. Woolley and I had instructions to get it done instanter," said Lawrence later to one of his biographers.

The two archaeologists were thus occupied in making maps and in producing their report in the rather formal style required by the Fund when war was declared.

[1] pretty damn quick.

PART II

The War

WAR precipitates us into an unknown world. For many men its enslavement is also a liberation. It reveals them to others and to themselves in an unsuspected light, and then generally destroys them. Many of the survivors have great difficulty, when peace comes, in reintegrating themselves into a society in which there is neither brutality nor licence.

But while it lasts this Kali gives, in the midst of wastage, improvisation, chaos and danger, extraordinary opportunities to young men. She leaves to leaders of twenty the free ordering of the sacred things which in time of peace are in the care of old men: the lives of men, the secrets of State. The second lieutenant, because he is around when the colonel is on leave or has 'flu, assumes the responsibilities of an emperor.

England was as poorly equipped as possible to fight a war which her diplomats and information services had seen coming for so long but for which her rulers had not dared to prepare the country. She had at her immediate disposal a hundred thousand men which she hurled into the inferno, and while the First Hundred Thousand were getting themselves killed with prodigies of courage, she could do no more than create an army out of nothing, whilst praying that the French front would hold.

The storm shook Lawrence and Woolley, as it threw all the English into confusion. The two archaeologists hastily finished their work for the Palestine Exploration Fund, and then looked for a place in the Army or in Government service. It is said that, wishing to join up, T.E. was turned down on account of his small stature, but it is not certain. Whatever the case, he and Woolley attempted to enter the employ of the War Office, with a recommendation from Newcombe. They were given promises on this subject, but no assignment reached them, and tired of waiting Woolley asked for and obtained a brevet commission in the Artillery and was posted to

a unit with the hope of being sent before long to the French
front. At the same time three of Lawrence's brothers were
under arms and about to depart for the front: Robert the
eldest as a doctor, Frank as an infantry officer, while Will was
being trained as an air observer. T.E., bored with nothing to
do, asked Hogarth for his help, and thanks to his recom-
mendations managed to get himself taken on by the Geographical Section of the General Staff, which was then ill
provided with competent personnel. The young man was
very rapidly made a second lieutenant, and spent the last
months of 1914 drawing up the maps of Sinai and writing a
guide of that area for the use of troops that might be engaged
in a campaign there. He made use of his memories of the
expedition of January and February 1914, and, so he said,
invented the rest. "A Nemesis may be awaiting him," he
wrote of himself, "He will be served out a copy of his own
book and told to find his way about the country with its help."
In fact he must have done his work with the rigorous care
with which he did everything of importance.

At the end of the year, the War Office was looking for
officers with a knowledge of the Near East to strengthen the
Information Service of the Headquarters in Cairo. Although
his work in the Geographical Section was very much
appreciated, Lawrence was posted to the Levant. He was
accompanied by Newcombe, recalled from France where he
had been fighting, and by Woolley. The three men arrived in
Egypt in mid-December 1914.

*　　*　　*

In order to understand Lawrence's life and activities
during his stay at the Headquarters in Cairo in 1915 and
1916, we must recreate the strange atmosphere that existed
in Egypt when he arrived.

The war had thrown this country into a fever of worry, and
her English rulers were still at sixes and sevens in a State
whose political equilibrium had always been fragile. Turkey
had hesitated several months before taking part openly in the
conflict. When on the 30th of November, 1914, she entered
the war she closed to the Allies their access to the Black Sea
and at the same time threatened the Suez Canal, England's

indispensable artery, both militarily and economically, and the English were obliged to create a bastion for their Empire out of this Egypt of whose population they were by no means certain and many of whose governing classes were pro-Turk and anti-English.

Turkey was in fact theoretically the suzerain of Egypt, and was paid by her an annual tribute; the Khedive, Abbas Hilmi, who was on the side of the Turks, had stayed on at Constantinople since the commencement of hostilities, and refused to return to Cairo; England was compelled to depose him, to nominate in his place, with the title of Sultan, his uncle, Prince Hussein, proclaim martial law, and put the country under a British protectorate. To maintain order and defend the Canal nearly a hundred thousand men had been collected in the area, but these troops were recent recruits and still untrained, the units of the old professional army which had up to then occupied the country having been sent to France.

In this troubled environment, the soldiers and administrators charged with the defence of Egypt felt that they were being attacked from both inside and out, and lived in a state of constant anxiety and in fear of political intrigues. Their distrust was not reserved for the enemy and for those suspected of being in collusion with him; it extended to the allied nations, France and Russia, with whom these soldiers and officials, for the most part trained in India or the Near East, had always thought of England as being in open or suppressed conflict.

While on the front in France a danger that was immediate and obvious welded the Allies together, it was quite different in the Oriental theatres of war, where old political and commercial rivalries, ancient conflicts and bitterness caused England, Russia and France to forget the necessity to devote themselves without hind-thought to the struggle with the central empires. Their co-ordinated action was often hampered by the desire to retain privileges and to acquire fresh bases for future rivalries. In the East the allied front was constantly divided, with results that enfeebled it and led to a criminal expenditure of human lives.

Such an attitude on the part of nations engaged in a

struggle for life can have no justification, but it can on the other hand be explained historically by the long succession of events which led up to it and which we must recall.

*   *   *

The Levantine coast, from Constantinople to Alexandria, controls all the commerce with the East. Through the Bosphorus passes all the traffic of the Black Sea; the old caravan routes terminate in the ports of Asia Minor and Syria; the Suez Canal provides communication to India and the Far East. Within a compass of six hundred miles are found all the most sensitive points of the commerce between Europe and Asia. Now this Asiatic trade has been disputed by the nations of the West for centuries.

The pious expeditions of the Crusades were not entirely devoid of colonialist and mercantile ambitions, and they degenerated into struggles between the English, Germans, Byzantines and French. Their unhappy issue did not put an end to this rivalry. François I obtained from the Sultan of Constantinople the Capitulations of 1535 which gave France the advantage over the other Powers and made her the official protector of the Holy Places. All Christian ships had to fly the French flag in order to gain access to the Turkish coast. Such concessions to our country gravely damaged the interests of the rival nations and wounded their *amour-propre*. They joined in denouncing the scandal of an alliance "between the Crescent and the Fleur de Lys", and the English king, concluding in his turn a treaty with the Porte, was not long in freeing himself from the humiliating obligation to fly a French pennant from the masthead of British ships.

Throughout the seventeenth and then the eighteenth centuries the struggle continued. To all the Asiatic products for which Europe was clamouring, there was added one for which an enormous demand arose very rapidly, and which became the object of a very active trade: coffee, the produce of Arabia. In 1775 the English obtained from the Egyptian Beys, who were almost independent of Turkey, facilities for the passage of their caravans, thus creating the 'overland route'; ten years later the French managed to gain the same concessions. The essence of this bitter conflict is fairly adequately distilled in the instructions which the Directory gave Bonaparte when he left for Egypt in 1798. His mission was to "kick the English out of all their possessions in the East as far as he could go, to destroy their trading stations in the Red Sea, to cut the isthmus of Suez, to ensure the free and exclusive possession of the Red Sea to the Republic, and to ameliorate the lot of the natives of Egypt by every means in his power".

Napoleon had entered Cairo in 1798, but in 1802 not a single Frenchman remained in the East. The Emperor meanwhile did not abandon his project of striking at England in India. He entered into negotiations with the Tsar Paul I, and resolved in agreement with him to invade India by the old' route to the south of the Caspian and the Oxus. The assassination of Paul I altered Russia's plans, but Napoleon persisted in his design. Deprived of Russia's assistance, he attempted to obtain that of Persia. General Gardane was sent off to this country to solicit an alliance and to reorganise its army. When the Empire crumbled, all these plans naturally went up in smoke, but the English stood fast, haunted by the fear of an attack on India by Russia and France from the interior of Asia, and keeping as their base for operations the eastern end of the Mediterranean. Henceforth one of their essential principles was to push the French out of Egypt and Syria, and to close to Russia her access to the Mediterranean, through the area of the Straits, or through Persia and Afghanistan.

It was England's concern with keeping the Russians out of Constantinople that was the cause of the Crimean War. When later, in 1869, the French pierced the isthmus of Suez, threatening the monopoly of the English overland route, the English made every effort to gain control of the Canal. They achieved this in 1875 when they bought the Khedive's share in it.

In Syria there was the same rivalry, and the same struggle: the French pretended to play their traditional rôle of protecting the Holy Places and the Christian subjects of the Ottoman Empire and maintained close relations with the Sultan. The English watched French infiltration with not a little anxiety. Since France was supporting the Maronite

Christians, she developed a friendship with their traditional enemies the Druzes and the Moslem Arabs. When in 1860 the Druzes massacred seven thousand Lebanese Christians and quite a number of European Christians, it was claimed in Paris that the English had encouraged the slaughter, and the accusation was repeated when the massacres of Damascus took place a few months later. European opinion was moved by these atrocities and France was charged by a conference of the Powers (England, Austria, Prussia, Russia and Sardinia) with restoring order in the Lebanon. A force of six thousand, commanded by General Beaufort de Hautpoul, disembarked in the area of Beirut and restored a certain degree of calm, but an alarmed England demanded the withdrawal of the French forces as soon as possible. Syria was already setting the two countries against each other, and the historian and polemicist Poujalat could write in 1861 lines which might have been published at the time of the Druze revolt in 1923:

"England is a great nation at home, and I admire her for the dignity of her institutions, but abroad she is shameless in the means of influence which she employs. The spirit of evil is her Prime Minister: ... she strikes the ground to bring forth revolutions and speculates in the destruction of peoples. ... In Syria, repulsed by the Maronites who were devoted to France, she appealed to the Druze nation, a race without faith or laws, protected her, demanded power for her, and finding that the cult of the Cross would not further her ends, she turned towards the Brazen Calf. ..."

France's rôle in the Near East was spoken of in the same tone and with the same conviction on the other side of the Channel.

Political rivalry was not, however, limited to these two nations. At the end of the nineteenth century, Russia had insinuated herself into Armenia and the Caucasian countries and obtained from the Ottomans the privilege of building railways in the north-east of Turkey. She dreamt obstinately of conquering Constantinople. Germany also had considerable ambitions. She wished to develop Mesopotamia and turn it into a 'German India'. She hoped to make Turkey into a protectorate and to achieve this she had created across

Austria-Hungary and Bulgaria a bridge of influence to put her plan on a workable footing.

A German mission was reorganising the Turkish army; Germans were building the railway from Constantinople to Ankara and Koniah and they had obtained in 1909 the concession for the Koniah–Baghdad–Bassorah line.

Then oil: the English, pioneers in the matter of oil, had understood the importance of the immense deposits of mineral oil in Mesopotamia and Persia before their rivals. In 1914 they obtained the exclusive concession for oil exploitation in the area of Mosul and Baghdad.

In 1914 the position of the Great Powers was broadly speaking as follows: in Turkey, the Germans were posing as friends and protectors; they were in complete favour with the Young Turks, they were reorganising the Ottoman army, and they had seen to it that they had been given the concession for the construction of the principal Turkish railway lines.

The English were considered by the Ottoman government with a respect that was full of apprehension. They had submitted the Turks to a sort of double dealing, supporting them or despoiling them at the whim of their changing and complicated politics. Sensing their hold on the country diminishing to the profit of their rivals (especially the Germans and the Russians), they turned to the minorities of the Ottoman Empire and in particular to the people of the Arab race over whose separatist tendencies they sought to establish a sort of unofficial protectorate. They had, besides, been conceded advantages, as we have said, in matters concerning oil.

The moral and economic position of France in Turkey was very strong: French was the language of culture throughout the Near East (nearly all administration in Turkey—public or private—including the German railway line and the Deutsche Orient Bank used it as the official language). In the Ottoman Empire there were a large number of French schools, in which the élite were educated.

Their economic interests were not less and were of greater importance than those of any other Western nation. Banks, monopolies (such as the control of tobacco), dock concessions, the supply of electricity, telephones, railways, mines had all been financed by French capital. France had invested in Turkey more than one thousand million gold francs.[1]

Despite the pacific aspect of this penetration, we should not at the same time ignore its deeper objectives. It was indeed a question of colonisation and the solicitude of the Powers for the Sick Man had no other cause. Each of the European rivals was only checked in the brutal conquest of Ottoman territory by the opposition of the other interested parties. After each squabble between the would-be colonisers, they all loudly declared their intention of maintaining the integrity of the Ottoman Empire, but not one of them had the slightest illusion about the hypocrisy of such a statement. One day would come the scramble for the spoils. Just as in 1907 the English and Russians had agreed on a disguised dismemberment of Persia, the German–Russian agreement of 1911, and that concluded the same year between the English, the Germans and the French, on the subject of Turkish railway lines, constituted a sort of anticipated sharing of the skin of the Ottoman bear, whose death, though still relatively lively, was now being discounted.

The war made allies of three of the competitors, England, Russia and France. Could these three nations forget from one day to the next, however, that they had for centuries kept their fingers on the trigger in the Near East? Could the English officials in Egypt and India, reared in a violently anti-Russian and anti-French tradition, so quickly forget past history? Kitchener, the English Minister of War, had spent his life manœuvring and meditating on the Eastern chessboard; great though his character may have been did nothing remain in his policy of his old habits of thinking? For his old subordinates in any case, Fashoda was a reality that was much closer than the battle of the Marne, and the mere presence of Frenchmen in the Eastern Mediterranean and within reach of Egypt made them bristle with mistrust.

*   *   *

[1] See Henry H. Cummings, *Anglo-French Rivalry in the Near East* (Oxford University Press).

All this explains the distinctly anti-French atmosphere
which reigned in Egypt when Lawrence arrived there. It
encouraged and excited the ideas which he had acquired in
Syria. He who was to shock the rulers of Cairo on so many
subjects would at least be in full agreement with them on
this point.

The Intrusives

THE Egyptian army was commanded by General Maxwell. He was a straightforward hard-working man, who knew the East well, but who it seems lacked inspiration. He was overwhelmed by the multiplicity of his political, administrative and military tasks, and allowed himself to be overtaken by events. In order to defend the Suez Canal and maintain order in the country he had created a heavy and complicated organisation. A hundred thousand men stamped the narrow land of the Delta. These troops were composed of youthful elements, recruited in England, India, Australia and New Zealand, excellent but not yet trained; the Headquarters and higher formations came from the professional British army, and comprised, together with some very brilliant, officers, others who were tolerably sclerotic.

In every war an army must change its skin, but the old one takes a long time to fall. In England, as in France at this time, the staff was encumbered with ageing men who thought much more about creating comfortable niches for themselves than about training the units for warfare. In Egypt staff officers proliferated; all the hotels of Cairo were requisitioned and crammed with administrative organisations, secretariats and telephones. Ambitions, intrigues and the pursuit of gold lace were unleashed, and behind too many desks were to be seen caricatures of colonels and majors, old fighting cocks with bloodshot eyes who lived with the *Army Almanac* and the *Aldershot Regulations* on their tables.

The group appointed by Kitchener and which, apart from Lawrence, included Newcombe and Woolley, a journalist Philip Graves, formerly the *Times* correspondent in Turkey, and two Members of Parliament, George Lloyd and Aubrey Herbert, was not made very welcome by these extremely traditionalist professional officers. Regular soldiers are not fond of civilians who teach them new ideas and systems, especially when these civilians are politicians, intellectuals and journalists, men whom they instinctively abominate. Certain groups in the Headquarters were rather hostile to the newcomers, but they took it philosophically, referred to themselves as "the Intrusives", put up with being treated as eccentrics and remained as foreign bodies in the heavy military organisation of Egypt.

It would not be true to say that they were boycotted, since General Maxwell was not hostile to them and put them under the orders of a remarkable man, Gilbert Clayton, who knew exactly how to make use of them. Clayton was an Artillery officer, seconded to the army of the Sudan, who had entered the Civil Service of that country and was intimately involved in the politics of the Moslem world. He was thirty-nine years old when at the beginning of the war he was sent to Egypt. His functions became rapidly very important, since to those of chief of the Intelligence Service both civil and military were added those of liaison officer with the government of the Sudan. He was thus in direct contact with the three most influential men in the Near East: Sir John Maxwell, the Army Commander in Egypt, Sir Henry MacMahon who was at the head of the civil power in that country, and Sir Reginald Wingate who governed the Sudan with the title of 'Sirdar'. This alert, restrained, dogged and secretive man, with a capacity for work that seemed limitless, realised at once the part that he could exact from these independent spirits that were put at his disposal. He also understood that civilians who are accustomed to liberty and responsibility will not give of their best unless they are allowed their head. He guided and influenced rather than gave orders. Always in the background he had a profound influence on their activities. He was the instigator of much that was to happen in Arabia, Palestine and Syria during the course of the war.

*   *   *

The team of Intrusives was immediately put to work. They were given offices in the Savoy Hotel, where the excitement, with all the comings and goings, the bustle, the crowd and the noise, was such that Aubrey Herbert compared it to an Oriental railway station on a busy day. Newcombe

organised the spy service, Woolley propaganda, Aubrey
Herbert was in charge of the political police, and as for
Lawrence he was in theory the cartographer, but he had
many other activities: in particular, he established for
Clayton the enemy's order of battle and drew up a manual
for the use of officers on active service. To obtain the necessary information for his work, and to pinpoint the Turkish
units, he made it his job to interrogate the prisoners and
suspects personally. "Lawrence and Graves spent most of their
time among the Turkish prisoners and came to know more
about the Turkish Army than the Turks themselves," said
Newcombe later. T.E. was helped in performing this task by
his knowledge of the countries of the Levant, which he had
previously travelled through in every direction. He had a
memory for minute detail, and when this English officer spoke
to a Turkish prisoner about his village, quoted the names of
the local notables, mentioned the scandals that concerned
their families and relations, the wretched peasant was so
flabbergasted that he did not dare remain silent or tell lies,
and told everything he knew.

More important was the fact that, hardly arrived in Egypt,
Lawrence had managed, it seems, to regain contact with the
friends and agents that he had left in Syria. We have very
little information on his work as the organiser of a network
of espionage and of a resistance movement against the Turks
in the Arab countries. Although this is something in which
he showed his most marked characteristics, his biographers
have laid very little stress on this part of his career: for
obvious reasons he said very little about these activities himself. It seems certain, however, that he devoted much time
and effort to it. As early as the 15th of January, 1915, less than
a month after his arrival in Cairo, he was in a position to be
able to indicate in a letter to Hogarth the exact appointments
which the German archaeologists whom he had met in Syria
had been given in the Turkish Army, and he was informed
on the smallest details of what was happening at Carchemish,
knowing even the names of the native workmen who were
guarding the abandoned site; thus he must have been
receiving precise information from a number of agents.

*   *   *

In the Headquarters in Cairo the strange boy had not gone unnoticed, and his originality and offhand manner had caused astonishment. One would have expected to find this second lieutenant of twenty-seven, who without military experience had suddenly arrived in a vast and very hierarchical organisation, with its own routines, prejudices and important figures, keeping quiet for a time, watching and adapting himself. But from the very first day Lawrence summed up the situation, made his plans, schemed and asserted his strong personality.

He obstinately refused to submit to the customs and the taboos of the milieu in which he found himself. He had always, though it is not quite clear why, detested professional officers, and he took a perverse pleasure in shocking the soldiers of the old school with his opinions, his manner, his behaviour in public, and above all by a constant criticism of everything that went on in the army. He had a way all his own of exasperating his superiors with an exaggerated respect, belied by an expression full of sarcasm and irony. He dressed abominably, forgetting when he went out into the street to put on his belt and equipment, a mortal sin in the English Army, and he rode bare-headed and at top speed between Cairo and Boulak on the biggest and noisiest motor-cycle that he could find.

Seated behind a screen with Aubrey Herbert in the lounge of Shepheard's Hotel, he would count with shouts of laughter the number of colonels who were there at tea-time, and the apoplectic and pot-bellied senior officers, knowing full well that they were being mocked by a subaltern, vowed revenge.

Lawrence and the Intrusives met then some opposition in some parts of the Cairo Headquarters, but they were also able to find worthwhile support for themselves. Their service was part of the connection between the civil and the military administration, and in consequence they were in constant touch with the Residency. They were in favour with Sir Henry MacMahon and had made an important ally in the person of Ronald Storrs, the Oriental Secretary to the High Commissioner for Egypt.

His friends like his enemies said of Storrs that he was the most brilliant Englishman in the Near East. Formerly assistant to Kitchener, he had remained, after the latter's departure, at the head of the political services in Egypt.[1] He had a complex character full of unexpected depths. Engaging and witty, he cut with some the figure of an aesthete; he loved Debussy, could improvise on the piano, admired modern French literature and the Russian ballet; during his travels in France he had made friends with Madame de Noailles. In fact, however, he hid beneath the appearance of an amateur an acute intelligence, a vast and solid culture, a profound belief in the greatness of the British Empire and much courage. He knew every angle of Levantine politics, read, spoke and wrote both vulgar and literary Arabic; he was one of the few Europeans who could penetrate the Oriental mind, and what was even rarer he was capable of convincing the Orientals with the subtleties of his arguments.

Storrs watched with sorrow as Headquarters, composed to a large extent of officers who were utterly ignorant of the Near East, piled error upon error and destroyed the subtle edifice which in less troubled times English diplomacy had built with such care in the hypersensitive countries of the Eastern Mediterranean. Clayton and his assistants were renewing a tradition of delicacy and tact which was in danger of being swept away by the incomprehension of the military. Storrs was drawn to these men with whom he could at last talk and work usefully. He co-operated closely with the Intrusives. He was involved in all their transactions, as he was in all English policy in the Levant. It was he who two years later was to take Lawrence to the Hejaz and to support his collaboration in the Arab Revolt.[2]

[1] Officially what was in fact the English protectorate of Egypt was known as the "British Agency". Kitchener had been its chief. Storrs was the "Oriental Secretary of the British Agency". He had entered Egyptian service in 1904.
[2] I have asked Sir Ronald Storrs a number of questions during the course of the preparation of this book, and I have made wide use of the information which he gave me verbally, and of his book *Orientations*. I also have the annotations which Sir Ronald Storrs made on the pages of the present work, of which I sent him one of the first copies.

The First Turkish Attack on the Suez Canal

February 1915

LAWRENCE'S opinion of the military machine was irritating enough on the part of so young an officer, but it must be stated that many of his criticisms were justified, and that the first actions on the Eastern front in Egypt showed that the High Command did not make the best possible use of the considerable forces put at its disposal for the defence of the Suez Canal.

The entry of Turkey into the war on the 30th of November, 1914, had immediately confronted the Allies with anguishing tactical problems. The closing of the Straits had interrupted all rapid communications between Russia and the Western bloc. England was cut off from her supply of meat and grain from the Ukraine, and the Russians lost the imports of munitions which they needed. Besides, the Ottoman armies menaced the Suez Canal, the artery indispensable to Britain for keeping in contact with India, the source of her recruiting and provisions. The Canal once cut, traffic between India and the West would have to be re-routed round the Cape, and this would have necessitated two or three times the number of ships.

The Germans, eager to profit from such a situation, feverishly pushed the Turks on to attack the Canal, and supplied them with equipment, guns and military advisers. Jemal Pasha, one of the leaders of the government of Young Turks and the Minister of Marine, himself took command of the expedition: he hoped not only to interrupt the flow of traffic through the Canal, but also to reoccupy Egypt, considered as an irredentist territory of the Ottoman Empire. To organise this operation, he had to help him the Bavarian colonel Kress von Kressenstein, chief of staff of the 8th Ottoman Army Corps.

Two army corps were concentrated at Beersheba, on the eastern confines of the Desert of Sinai, one composed of Anatolian Turks and the other of Arabs, in all about twenty thousand of foot, to which were added nine batteries of field artillery, a heavy howitzer drawn by teams of oxen, bridging equipment, a camel corps and Bedouin auxiliaries. The expedition set out towards the end of January and took ten days to cross the one hundred and fifty to two hundred miles which lay between it and the Canal Zone. They advanced by night, so as not to be observed, and each day's march must have been very carefully planned, since Kress von Kressenstein claims that they did not lose a single man or animal on the approach march.

The army was split into three columns: two detachments, one following the coastal route, the other the most southerly caravan route that ended at Suez, were designed to act as diversions. The largest corps, destined for the principal attack, used the central route through Aujaa and Hassana, and on the 2nd of February, 1915, it appeared in front of Ismailia.

Jemal attacked at dawn on the 3rd of February, sending in first the 25th Arab Division. The dispositions which the English had taken to defend the Canal were not the most distinguished. Major-General A. Wilson, who was in command in this sector, had massed all his forces to the west of the Canal, leaving only a few light detachments on the east bank. It was jokingly remarked at Cairo that it was not the English Army that was protecting the Canal, but the Canal which protected the Army. The approach of the Ottoman columns had however been continually reported by the English Army pilots and by the sea-planes of the French Lieutenant de Vaisseau de l'Escaille, and the defenders were on the alert. Meanwhile the detachments of Hindus left on the east bank were swept aside, and the Turks having reached the Canal, put their pontoons into the water and a few elements managed to reach the west bank, where they came up against vigorous opposition and lost a number of men. The Hindu troops, making a strong counter-attack, recrossed to the east bank and even attempted an enveloping movement to the north of the Ottoman column; artillery pounded the attackers; two French ships moored in the Canal, the *Requin* and the *d'Entrecasteaux*, did considerable damage to the Turkish lines with the fire of their heavy guns. The position of Jemal's army became desperate, separated as it was from its base by two hundred miles of desert. To the north and the south the diversionary attacks had had no more success than the principal assault. In agreement with Kress, the Turkish general decided to break off the engagement without committing his Anatolian regiments: on the evening of the 3rd of February he gave the order to retreat.

The English High Command now had an unexpected opportunity to crush an adversary that was placed in so dangerous a situation. At its disposal was the excellent Australian cavalry, but it was not used for the pursuit of the vanquished Turks, who after their bloody defeat were able to withdraw without being seriously troubled. After a painful march across the solitudes of Sinai, they regained their bases, having lost twelve to fifteen hundred men, and without having inflicted any serious damage on the Canal, since twenty-four hours after the attack, traffic was again flowing between Suez and Port Said. The Allies had only lost one hundred and fifty men.

One of the reasons for Jemal's complete lack of success was probably the too ambitious nature of his objectives. If the intention had been simply to put an important section of the Canal out of action, it could perhaps have been achieved and considerable damage inflicted on the Allies. But the Turks had dreamt of reconquering Egypt; they were convinced that at the mere rumour of their arrival the whole country would rise, and that the British would be caught between two fires. In fact the Egyptians did not budge. They were—in theory—praying for the coming of the Ottomans, but at the idea of being invaded and pillaged by the Bashibazooks all the effendis of Cairo and Alexandria trembled with fear and appealed to God to preserve the English occupation for them.

Jemal brought the body of his troops back into Syria, whence before long they were sent into the slaughter-house of Gallipoli, but he left behind him Kress von Kressenstein, with three battalions of infantry, two batteries of artillery and a camel squadron. With this feeble force the Bavarian colonel began to harass the defenders of the Canal and kept them continually on the alert. This little contingent made life difficult for more than a hundred thousand men who were ceaselessly exposed to intelligently organised raids. Kress was a courageous and skilful soldier and the English, to whom he did a great deal of harm, finished by having for him that sort of affectionate respect which they reserved for Rommel during the second world war.

* * *

The excitement in Egypt caused by these events was intense. Lawrence followed the unfolding of the operations avidly. In a letter of the 20th of April, 1915, he wrote:

"The Canal is still holding out and we are forgetting all about it. Turkey, if she is wise, will raid it from time to time and annoy the garrison there, which is huge and lumbersome and creaks so loudly in the joints that you hear them eight hours before they move. So it's quite easy to run down and chuck a bomb at it and run away again without being caught."

These battles on the Canal and Kress's strategy provoked him to some useful reflections. He could tell how vulnerable was a long line of communication through the desert, and how many men had to be immobilised in order to defend it. The methods of war which he used in the Arabian campaign and his manœuvres around the Hejaz line derive directly from what he observed of the Sinai operations.

Alexandretta

WHEN the excitement of the Turkish offensive had died down in Cairo and Alexandria, when the Egyptians had ceased to fear pillage, rape and massacre at the hands of the Turkish soldier, the anti-English propaganda recommenced with increased vigour. The Arabs of the Ottoman Empire were pro-Ally and at the same time the Egyptians were pro-Turk, a logical consequence of the aspirations to independence of the one as of the other.

The Sultan Hussein, installed by the English in place of the Khedive who had stayed schismatically in Constantinople, navigated as best he could between the autonomist sentiments of his own people, and the interests of the British to whom he owed his throne. He played a double game only in so far as it was indispensable for him to do so. He was a subtle, rather cynical man, with a dislike for violent solutions. On the whole he served the allied cause, whilst organising things so as not to compromise himself. "Storrs, mon ami, j'ai roulé ma bosse un peu partout, mais jamais je n'ai vu un meli-melo pareil" ("Storrs, my friend, I have knocked about the world a good bit, but I have never seen such a mix-up"), said this witty and disillusioned sovereign to the Oriental Secretary one day.

As early as the first months of 1915, conspiracies were hatched against the English, but the conspirators had no taste for martyrdom. In February Lawrence wrote: "The ten principal members of the last conspiracy were sold by their underlings, after which each of them came secretly on his own, by night, to see the general and betray his associates. It was very difficult to prevent them from meeting at the door." In fact, T.E. as a member of the English Intelligence Service, helped eagerly with the hunt for, and discomfiture of the Egyptian nationalists. It was the definite duty of the appointment which he held, but it is surprising that he should have performed it with such pleasure and with so much sarcasm at the expense of the rebels who were applying the principles of which he was to be such an ardent protagonist in Arabia. Impassioned souls have such inconsistencies.

*   *   *

The attack of the 2nd of February, 1915, showed the Allies that as far as Turkey was concerned they could not confine themselves to the defensive. To put the Suez Canal out of danger and if possible to reopen the Dardanelles, it was necessary to mount a counter-attack on Turkey and try and put her quickly out of the war. Despite the difficulty for the Allies of diverting troops from the Western Front, the Headquarters were studying the possibilities of an offensive in the Levant.

As early as the 25th of November, 1914, Winston Churchill, in a memorandum to the British Cabinet, had envisaged an attack on Turkey through southern Asia Minor, in the area of Alexandretta. Since the Turkish railway line between Constantinople and Syria had not yet been finished, as they had not yet been able to cut the tunnels through the Ammanus, the Turks would have some difficulty in sending troops and equipment to this theatre of operations. A landing in the north of Syria if it succeeded would cut the Ottoman Empire in two, the Allies would be able to occupy Syro-Palestine, Arabia and Mesopotamia without much difficulty, and the Canal would be out of danger. Some of the French, and in particular Admiral Dartige du Fournet, were in favour of the scheme. Others in our General Staff were protagonists of a campaign in the Balkans, judging it necessary to cut the line of communications between Germany and her Oriental ally and to go to the help of Serbia. The English Admiralty itself canvassed a naval attack on the Narrows followed by a landing on Constantinople, an operation that was moreover embarked upon as early as February 1915.

The Allied Command asked the Intelligence Service of Cairo to make a study of the possibilities of attacking the Levantine coasts and Lawrence was charged with the task of producing a memorandum on the problems involved in landing troops in the bay of Alexandretta.

We do not know the text of the memorandum, which must be reposing in some file in the War Office and which has not

MAP I

been published, but the long and detailed letters which T.E. wrote to Hogarth on this subject enable us to imagine the spirit in which it was written. In drawing up his plan Lawrence was more preoccupied with striking at the influence of the French in Syria than with the struggle with the Turks. The violence of the anti-French sentiments expressed open strange horizons on this passionate soul. One reads things like these:

(18th of March, 1915) "Alexandretta in the hands of France will provide a sure base for naval attacks on Egypt— and remember with her in Syria and compulsory service there, she will be able any time to fling 100,000 men against the Canal in twelve days from declaration of war.... If France has Alexandretta it is all up with us in the Near East. And in any case in the next war the French will probably be under Russia's finger in Syria. Therefore I think it absolutely necessary we hold Alexandretta.... The High Commissioner is strongly of the same opinion and General Maxwell also. K. has pressed it on us. Winston seems uncertain and someone— not Grey—perhaps Parker in the F.O., is blocking it entirely. I think perhaps you can get a move on."

"Can you get someone to suggest to Winston that there is a petrol spring on the beach ... huge iron deposits ... and coal also? ..."

(22nd of March, 1915) "I sent you a flood of stuff about Alex. Please try and push it through, for I think it is our only chance in face of a French Syria...."

(And the 26th of April) "By all means Cilicia ... and Alex, as the naval base is the crux of the whole show."

Astonishing statements that drew from David Garnett the comment: "Indeed his letters putting forward his plan for seizing Alexandretta and making it an English Naval Base might lead one to think that England and France were on the brink of war."

It is indeed the impression that one received from these curious documents, all the more curious if one thinks of what was happening at the time on the French front: the common struggle, terrible losses, the Germans twenty-five miles from the English coasts and sixty from Paris. One wonders how this intelligent young man could have been so blinded by his personal passions to write absurdities of this sort.

It is difficult to tell what the Alexandretta plan was worth once you have removed from it its anti-French intentions, from the point of view of pure strategy. General Wavell in *Palestine Campaigns* condemns it out of hand:

"The operation would, however, have been hardly as simple as might appear on the map. It was estimated that a force of between a hundred and a hundred and fifty thousand men would have had to be disembarked and the results of Gallipoli did not encourage further experiments in landing operations on a large scale. . . . It was accordingly resolved to proceed no further in the scheme—undoubtedly a wise decision."[1]

There were, besides, political reasons for abandoning the Alexandretta plan: the French distrusted an operation whose underlying aims they could not ignore, and asked to be allowed control of the enterprise. They were besides partisans of a campaign in the Balkans, an idea which for various reasons did not please the British. Despite Kitchener's support the landing was never undertaken, the Allies in the meanwhile being engaged in the attack on the Dardanelles, whose cruel failure has left, in England as in France, the memory of a frightful hecatomb, in which fabulous courage was expended in vain.

When he learnt that the Allied Command had rejected the plan which he had helped to make, Lawrence was cut to the quick, and considered this decision as a personal affront. The idea that France had opposed, for reasons of colonial policy, plans which had attracted him for exactly the same reasons, made him indignant. He had seen himself playing an important rôle in a vast enterprise, and his self-deception filled him with bitterness. His hatred of France was only increased. This hatred colours all his life, and will determine nearly all his actions in the course of the campaign.

This affair later assumed in Lawrence's memory a greater and greater importance, and in the end he convinced himself that he alone, like some young Bonaparte, had produced a plan of strategic brilliance. Nearly twenty years after these events, he told a friend of his that the Alexandretta plan "was

[1] *Palestine Campaigns*, A. P. Wavell, pp. 39–40.

from beginning to end, my invention". This could hardly have been true, for a staff officer of no experience could not have initiated the planning of an operation the size of that of the Dardanelles—calling for the combined action of the army and the fleet, and fraught with complicated problems of transport and supply. Besides we have seen that Winston Churchill had had Alexandretta in mind since the beginning of 1914.

The Direct Line

SINCE his arrival in Egypt Lawrence had worked hard and had become an important cog in Clayton's machine. Great though his qualities were, it is astonishing that an officer of such modest rank should have assumed so much authority. One has the impression of here coming across, as often in Lawrence's life, an element of mystery.

It certainly seems as though from this time T.E. did have facilities for direct communication with certain political and military figures in London, and that he could put up his ideas direct to them without having to pass through the chiefs of staff in Egyptian Headquarters. He was in close correspondence with Hogarth, who was also employed in Government Service, and was a close friend of Sir Edward Grey, then Foreign Minister in the British Cabinet, but T.E. must have had other friends in high places in England, since once Hogarth was posted to the Arab Bureau in Cairo he evidently kept his independent contacts with either the War Office, or the Colonial Office, or the General Staff. We shall probably never know the name of the person or persons with whom he thus had contact, but the existence of this direct line is the only way of explaining many of the obscure aspects of his career in Egypt and elsewhere.

By definition, the biography of an officer employed in an intelligence service will admit of gaps, and Lawrence's activities in Cairo are still little known. We know that in the course of 1915, he went to Greece to make contact with some of his agents operating in enemy territory; a short time afterwards he accomplished a mission in the Libyan desert in which English forces were at grips with the revolted Senussis. Turkish and German agents had managed to stir up the nomads and the inhabitants of the oases of the Eastern Sahara. The rebels were not a serious menace to Egypt, but they created irritating difficulties for the English, and immobilised men and equipment. It is astonishing that a few ragged Bedouins should have given an excellent and well-equipped army such trouble.

So long as the Senussis kept themselves to guerilla warfare, they were a considerable nuisance to the British, but the Turks conceived the idea of sending in an officer called Jaafar Pasha to organise them; he tried to transform the nomad bands into a regular army. When the English found themselves faced with units attempting to manœuvre in the European manner they crushed them easily in a single battle, and Jaafar was taken prisoner.

This adventure which he was able to study at close range gave Lawrence food for thought. He saw clearly that a few rascals armed with indifferent rifles could give more trouble to an occupying army by murdering sentries and ambushing convoys than by fighting a pitched battle. In his future wars in Arabia he was to profit from this experience.

In 1915 the Cairo Intelligence Service, still pursuing its policy, was doing its utmost to separate the peoples of Arabia from Turkey, and to bring the small semi-independent sovereigns of the Red Sea coast into their game. Since the month of March 1915, Lawrence had been ready to leave Cairo and go with Newcombe to the court of Idriss, the Emir of Asir, at Kunfida, between Jidda and Aden, who was being pressed to rebel against the Turks.

It was an important affair, but Lawrence, as in the case of Alexandretta, saw it more from the angle of Anglo-French colonial rivalry, and of his own designs on Syria, than from that of the co-ordinated strategy of the Allies in the Red Sea. "If Idrissi is anything like as good as we hope we can rush right up to Damascus and biff the French out of all hope of Syria. . . . Won't the French be mad if we win through. Don't talk of it yet," he wrote to Hogarth on the 22nd of March, 1915. But it was not to be: the Arab world was not ripe for separation from Turkey, and besides the government of India, on whom all operations in the Red Sea depended, was opposed to such a policy, judging that by encouraging sentiments of independence in Arabia, they might create dan-

7

gerous currents among the Hindu and Moslem nationalists who were impatient of English tutelage.

At the end of 1915 Lawrence played a rôle, of which we know unfortunately very little, in the important operation of the taking of Erzerum by the Russians.[1] In the month of October the troops of the Grand-Duke Nicholas, aided in their advance by the complicity of the Armenian rebels, penetrated as far as this city and invested it. Lawrence, during his time at Carchemish, had been in touch with the Armenian autonomists. Asked by his mysterious friends in London, he was even able to indicate the names of certain officers holding high positions among the besieged Turkish troops and who belonged to secret nationalist Armenian or Arab organisations. The Russians were enabled to get in touch with these people, bought them and thus succeeded in entering Erzeroum without striking a blow.

This negotiation, if it took place in the form that Lawrence relates, must have increased the credit which he had with the Foreign Office and with the English General Staff. At Cairo also it was known or more or less suspected that he had the connections and the means to make his ideas respected in high places. His prestige was high with Clayton, and with the Intrusives, who owed much of their liberty of action and of their influence to this strange colleague, one of the youngest in the team. The little 'pipsqueak' put at their service an inexhaustible and diabolical cunning and all his influential personal contacts. He knew every strand of the Staff intrigues, and he behaved as though he enjoyed himself in the bye-ways of this old seraglio. He was the enemy of military hierarchy, perfectly indifferent to the moral value of the means which he employed to gain his ends, a natural opponent of constituted authority, cunning, underhand and

[1] Lawrence himself mentions it at the beginning of the *Seven Pillars*, as do Graves and Liddell Hart in their biographies. We have not found any other sources. Sir Ronald Storrs, to whom I submitted this page, added in his own hand, "nor are there any", which is not very clear but seems to indicate a certain scepticism. It is difficult to imagine, however, that Lawrence could have attributed quite gratuitously to himself a part in this affair. There must have been some basis for his assertion. It would be very interesting to discover it in the archives of the War Office or of the Intelligence Service.

subtle. He excelled at playing off his superior officers, who were scarcely accustomed to such complex tactics, against each other, and he never hesitated to make use of his 'direct line' with London in order to break the back of those who stood in his way. Thanks to him his friends were often able to influence the High Command and impose their points of view. Without having had the degree of importance which he wished to attribute to them later, it definitely seems that from as early as 1915, his secret activities had, in the final analysis, a significance in the English politics of the Levant.

*   *   *

For all these men engrossed in difficult and enthralling work, the war, the entire war, was happening in the Near East, but at the same time a gigantic struggle was taking place in France to which the Byzantine scheming of the Head-quarters in Cairo could not be compared. Lawrence was to be suddenly and cruelly reminded of the existence of the Western Front: Frank Lawrence, an infantry officer, was killed in France on the 9th of May, 1915. T.E. was never very fond of this brother, who was rather pompous and conventional. He wrote a letter to Will, his younger brother, that was deliberately indifferent and detached: "Frank's death was as you say a shock ... I do not think one can regret it overmuch, because it is a very good way to take, after all."

But Will, an air observer, was killed in his turn in September. Will was Lawrence's favourite brother, and he was overwhelmed by his death. He thought of joining a fighting unit in France, in order to end the life of security he was leading in Cairo while the men of his generation were falling by the thousand. He spoke with horror of what his return to Oxford and a home of mourning would be like.

Once more Hogarth intervened in Lawrence's life at a crucial moment. The young officer was about to leave the Near East in which his career was mapped out, when his old master disembarked at Cairo. His friendly presence restrained him. While in London Hogarth had passed on and supported many of Lawrence's ideas; again and again the latter had

begged him to come out and join him, convinced that his
cool, subtle and socratic mind would alone know how to dis-
entangle the confused threads of Levantine politics. Hogarth
joined up in the Royal Naval Voluntary Reserve, in which he
was given the rank of lieutenant-commander and posted to
Egypt, where Clayton took him into his service.

Kut-el-Amara

FROM the beginning of the war the British had taken the offensive in the Persian Gulf, and on the 22nd of November, 1914, they had occupied Basra. In the same way that France, without knowing how the war would turn out, was pursuing her Syrian dream, England also from this time was anxious to realise her ambitions in Mesopotamia and Persia. In 1915 an army composed of English and Hindu contingents and commanded by General Townsend ascended the Tigris, and putting to flight the indifferent troops which the Turks, stringently pinned down in the Dardanelles, could muster against them, they took Kut-el-Amara, a hundred miles from Baghdad, at the end of September.

Townsend, made confident by this success and convinced of the enemy's weakness, blindly pursued his advantage, but on the 15th of October at Ctesiphon, he came up against some real Anatolian troops, and disaster ensued. The Anglo-Indian army suffered a severe check and flowed back in disorder to Kut, where it entrenched itself. It was immediately surrounded by the Turks under the command of a young general, Kallil Pasha, who was accompanied and advised by old Field-Marshal von der Goltz, the man who had reorganised the Turkish Army.

This defeat, and the investment of Kut with ten thousand British soldiers inside it, produced in England an excitement that can be imagined. During the winter of 1915–1916, the expeditionary corps in Mesopotamia made repeated, vain and bloody efforts to rescue Townsend's army, whose supplies and ammunition were running very low, and which was suffering a slow and frightful agony.

When winter had passed without bringing a solution to the drama of Kut, the affair turned into a nightmare for England. In the War Office they were looking desperately for some way out of this impasse, when somebody thought of

Lawrence, and the way in which he had contributed from a distance to bringing off the surrender of Erzerum. In March 1916, T.E. who was then a captain, received some secret instructions, and accompanied by Aubrey Herbert, who as we know was a Member of Parliament, was sent with special orders from the authorities in London, to Kut, to try and negotiate with the Turks for the liberation of the invested English army. The two Englishmen reached Basra and then proceeded to the front; officially they had come to obtain information on the topography of the country, in fact they had the extended powers of real *missi dominici*.[1]

The British army was stuck on the banks of the Chat-el-Arab; the headquarters were installed in the ships anchored in the river, but the fighting troops were dissolving in the rain, and had bogged down in the mud; the losses from fever, dysentery and even cholera were terrible.

The commanders of the army of Mesopotamia did not welcome Lawrence and Herbert. These plenipotentiaries, of whose rôle and exact instructions they were ignorant, and who were to act without reference to them, were encroaching upon their province. Many of these officers had not given up hope of loosening the Turkish hold on the garrison of Kut by force of arms. They suspected that Lawrence and Herbert had come to negotiate, perhaps to buy the withdrawal of the Turks, and this did not seem to them very chivalrous or in keeping with the ancient and glorious tradition of the British Army.

"The local British had the strongest objection to my coming; and two generals were good enough to explain to me that my mission (which they did not really know) was dishonourable to a soldier (which I was not)," Lawrence said himself. Sir Percy Cox, Chief Political Officer in Mesopotamia, refused to associate himself with these negotiations.

Meanwhile, Lawrence and Herbert had powerful credentials, for despite some opposition they went over to see the Turkish commanders accompanied by Colonel Beach.

[1] Commissioners appointed by the ancient kings of France, and notably by Charlemagne, to tour the provinces, to oversee the administration and to render justice in the name of the king (Translator's note).

Coming out of the front-line trenches, and finding themselves on open ground with only the protection of the white flags which they waved from side to side, they experienced an unpleasant sinking feeling in the stomach. The Turks allowed them to approach and then in the best traditions they bandaged their eyes and led them before Kallil. He was a commander-in-chief of thirty to thirty-two years of age, who had distinguished himself in the massacres of the Armenians of Malasgerd, and whose relationship with Enver, one of the members of the Ottoman Triumvirate, had brought him rank and opulence. He received the envoys with contempt, was distant and derisive, and disdainfully refused the offer of a million and then of two million pounds to allow the English troops to march out freely to their lines. At the very most he would accept the exchange of a thousand wounded against a similar number of prisoners—and he specified that they were to be Anatolian prisoners and not Arabs, deserters for the most part, whom he would be eager to shoot.

The English tried to obtain assurances as to the fate of the civil population of Kut, who had been friendly to them. Kallil laughed heartily at their solicitude for "such carrion" and was unwilling to promise anything, saying only that he had "no intention of being vindictive". In fact, he only hanged nine people on his entry into Kut, which for him was to show a marked moderation.

After these disappointing negotiations, Lawrence and Herbert stayed for several weeks at the headquarters of the army. They were still there when on the 29th of April, 1916, the unhappy garrison laid down its arms and surrendered to the Turks.[1]

* * *

Lawrence made no friends at the headquarters of the Mesopotamian army. He had been superior, insolent, sarcastic, found fault with everything and did not hide from the senior officers that he took them for criminal imbeciles. He was to leave behind him some solid enmities. The officers of the Indian Army were never to forgive him for his attitude

[1] Nearly half the prisoners were to die in Turkish internment camps.

throughout this mission, and henceforth they regarded him with a tenacious hatred.

In May he returned to Egypt. During the long return journey, in the discomfort and heat of the Red Sea, he drew up an incendiary report on what he had seen in Mesopotamia. He criticised the organisation of the army down to the smallest details:

"the quality of the stones used for lithographing, the system of berthing barges alongside the quays, the inefficiency of the cranes handling stores, the lack of system in shunting and entraining at the railways, the want of adequate medical stores, the blunders of the medical authorities and their want of imagination as to their probable requirements. And horror of horrors, he criticised the Higher Command and the conduct of the campaign in general."[1]

On the boat he met General Webb-Gillman who was also returning from the front at Kut, where the War Office had sent him to collect information. After a rather sticky first meeting (Lawrence loved to shock his superiors by his insolence and his outbursts), the two men became extremely cordial towards one another. Lawrence was too quick-witted not to seize this occasion for making his ideas known in high places. He passed his report to Webb-Gillman, who knew how to make use of it.

At Cairo the story caused quite a stir. The report was destined to be sent straight to the War Office, but General Murray, who had just taken over command of the army in Egypt, demanded to have a look at it. Headquarters was horrified at the idea of allowing the great man, who was not easy-tempered, to read so explosive a document. They had to devote a whole night to the expurgation of its more violent parts.

The senior officers in Cairo were very well aware that Lawrence's biting criticisms were not directed solely at the army in Mesopotamia but at the English Army in general, and at the Army of Egypt in particular. Lawrence, who was not very popular at Headquarters, from now on became a *bête-noire*.

[1] Colonel Stirling, *Safety Last,* p. 68.

The Arab Bureau

1916

FROM the beginning of 1916 important changes took place in the High Command in Cairo. In January Sir Archibald Murray, who till then had been Chief of the Imperial General Staff in London, was appointed to the command of the Suez Canal forces. He was a bluff, outspoken man, choleric and jealous of his prerogatives, but apart from this he was extremely intelligent and inured to court intrigues during his time at the War Office, in which he could be sure of solid support. He rapidly came into conflict with the Commander-in-Chief, Sir John Maxwell, and was not long in eliminating his colleague, who in March returned to England, leaving Sir Archibald as the sole boss in Egypt.

Murray was imbued with the strictest traditions of the English Army. A staff man, he was neither interested in the troops nor in the details of their operations and never went out on the ground. As for the complications of native politics, he did not wish to know about them. He was thus hardly suited to appreciate the methods of Clayton and his collaborators. The officers of the old school, who disapproved of the Intrusives' methods of doing things, and who had previously kept quiet on account of Maxwell's regard for these freaks, now openly criticised the Cairo Intelligence Service and those who were employed in it.

Clayton at this time was giving all his attention to Arab affairs. Realising the degree to which Arab nationalism was an element of dissociation in the Turkish Empire, he kept his eye on the attempts at dissent which occurred in the Hejaz; and at the same time sent his agents to stir up discontent against the Turks among the Druzes and people of Syria. Lawrence had revealed to him the negligence of the English Arab policy in Mesopotamia; intelligently prepared, these people would have welcomed the English as liberators and would have helped them; on the contrary they had been alienated by clumsy handling, and the English expeditionary corps had found itself in enemy country, where it should have found help and collaboration.

Clayton formed a special department which he called the Arab Bureau, and in which he put among others, Hogarth and Lawrence. It was "a tiny intelligence and war staff for foreign affairs", working in co-operation with Sir Henry MacMahon, the High Commissioner in Egypt, with the object of following and if possible directing nationalist movements in Arab countries. This service which employed about fifteen officers, had the most diverse activities, among which was the publication of the *Arab Bulletin*, a pamphlet of information and propaganda which the English circulated not only among their own officers, but also among the Egyptian ruling classes.

All the members of the Arab Bureau, placed under the orders of so remarkable a leader, worked without interruption and bubbled over with ideas. In the common effort and celibate life these intellectuals rediscovered their student mentality. The wise Hogarth wrote a doggerel about the department:

> Do you know
> The Arab Bureau:
> Clayton stability,
> Symes versatility,
> Cornwallis is practical,
> Dawnay syntactical,
> Mackintosh havers
> And Fielding palavers,
> Macindoe easy
> And Wordie not breezy,
> Lawrence licentiate to dream and to dare
> And yours very faithfully, bon à tout faire.

In work which suited him so well, among companions who were intelligent, original and lively, and who had an affection for him that was tinctured with admiration, Lawrence's personality found its full flowering.

The Hejaz was among the first of the Arab Bureau's preoccupations. After long tergiversations, the Emir of Mecca, Hussein ben Ali, had in June 1916 broken with Turkey and declared his independence. Sir Henry MacMahon, through the intermediary of his political assistant Ronald Storrs, Wingate, the Sirdar of the Sudan, and Clayton had all collaborated to set the movement going.

This revolt was a happy event, but in fact it was to be a frightful headache to the rulers of Cairo who had been its instigators. The Arabs revealed themselves as allies who were difficult to manage; they made enormous demands for money and material assistance, but they wished to run their war in their own way; after a few successes they met with humiliating reverses, and it appeared as though the whole adventure might end in a shattering fiasco.

Inside the Egyptian Headquarters the undertaking had caused disturbances and conflicts of authority. It had been patronised by the High Commissioner and by the Sirdar, and for this reason had given offence to the commander-in-chief, General Murray, who was hostile to a campaign that rivalled his own operations.

The quarrels among the big men were echoed in the different departments. Up to the middle of 1916, Clayton's service had been common to the civil and military administrations; now General Murray, his chief of staff, Lynden Bell, and their entourage were not fond of this calm, secretive man who lacked almost all formality. They bore him a grudge for having been a supporter of the operations in Arabia, and they could not forgive him for the choice of his assistants. He was brusquely replaced and returned to his civil duties, while his appointment was given to Colonel Holdich. Clayton's service was thus cut in two, some of his officers staying with him, others finding themselves given military appointments outside his control. Holdich decided to keep Lawrence in his department and gave him the impression that he wished to hide his light under a bushel. From now on Lawrence had but one idea: to get out, to return to the Arab Bureau, and to devote himself anew to that which he had so much at heart, the politics of Arabia and Syria.

Somehow or other he had to get out of Holdich's service. Since they were not willing to let him go, he would get him-

self thrown out. He decided (at least, so he claims in his
memoirs) to make himself quite insupportable to his boss and
the whole Headquarters. It was a rôle which he knew well
how to play. He was insolent even when in deference, laid
traps for his senior officers, ridiculed his colleagues every
time they bungled something; he turned his vitriolic wit on
everything and everybody in the Army Headquarters: long
after the war Holdich still spoke with bitterness of T.E.'s
tricks and treachery.

Such a situation could not last for long. Having made
certain that the Army was extremely anxious to be rid of him,
Lawrence brought into play his direct line to London, and,
without consulting anyone at Cairo, asked to be transferred
to the Arab Bureau. Without doubting the issue, he asked for
leave, which was given to him with all the more willingness
since no one in his department wanted to see him again.

Storrs at this time was getting ready to leave for Jidda in
order to renew one of those long discussions with the Emir
Hussein which never led to anything except fresh demands
for money. Lawrence proposed that he should accompany
him.

Ronald Storrs, in his memoirs, tells us that he suspected
neither the activities nor the ambitions of the man whom he
called "the super-cerebral little Lawrence". He willingly
accepted as a travelling companion this youth whose conversation and immense culture he appreciated, and whose company would alleviate the boredom and fatigue of a long
voyage in the Red Sea.

It is difficult to believe him completely, and to imagine
that the subtle Oriental Secretary was really convinced that
T.E. wanted to visit Jidda simply as a tourist. It is anyway
certain that Lawrence's journey had been most carefully
planned by the Arab Bureau and was part of a deeply laid
plot.

Whatever the case, in October 1916 Lawrence, in the
company of Ronald Storrs, set out for Jidda. It was his first
direct contact with the Hejaz revolt to which he was to devote
himself body and soul right up to the end of the war and
beyond.

The Arab Revolt

THE struggle between the Turks and the Arabs was a very old story: the Turks—the Seljoukides and then the Osmanlia—had appeared in the Levant around the eleventh century, at a time when the Arab expansion, which for three centuries had overthrown the Mediterranean and Near Eastern world, was pausing for breath.

Little by little, the men of Touran—less of individualists and gifted with military qualities of a more enduring nature —supplanted the Arabs in the control of Islam. As far as war was concerned it was they who carried on the struggle against Christian Europe: on the religious level they became the leaders of the whole Mahommedan community.

By 1516 the Sultan Selim had conquered Persia, Northern Mesopotamia, Syria, Palestine and finally Egypt; he was ceded the title of Khalif and the protection of Medina and Mecca by the Abbasside sovereign of Cairo.

Thus nearly every country of Arabic race and language found itself under Turkish dominion. At the beginning of the twentieth century, it was estimated that this ethnic bloc represented a third of the population and a half of the Moslems of the Ottoman Empire.

The Arabs found it difficult to support this servitude, which was extremely humiliating for men of a highly developed pride of race with a glorious past as conquerors behind them. Besides, the hand of the Turkish government lay heavily upon them and they had to bear the burdens of taxation and conscription. Militarism was the particular nightmare of these independent-minded people.

Every country of Arabic language and culture was thus in an embryonic state of revolt against their Ottoman masters. It was an obscure but profound sentiment in which were contained all the elements of a separatist movement. The idea of Oriental patriotism has been endlessly discussed, and it has often been said that there was no such thing and that its place was taken by religion, or the profession of allegiance to the person of a sovereign. The evolution of the Arab world in the course of the last half-century seems to have proved the contrary. It is quite probable that the Semitic national ideal is not exactly the same as that of Western nations, but they must have some points in common, for when the principle of nationalism was exported from Europe to Asia less than a century ago, it immediately found corresponding sentiments that were old, powerful and perfectly human, and it had a quick success.

In fact, Arab separatism, which had been in the air for three centuries, was formulated by men who had sought their culture in the West. In 1895 a group of Syrian intellectuals expelled from Turkey had collected in Paris and formed in this city an "Arab National Committee" which organised secret societies designed to stir up feeling in every Turkish province in which Arabic was spoken. The Separatists dreamt of giving independence to these countries, of establishing autonomous governments and finally of restoring to a prince of their race the Khalifate, taken from them by the Turkish Sultan.

Furthermore the movement was not directed solely against the Turks; it also contained opposition to the European colonisation which was extending its hold in Algeria, Tunisia, Egypt and to certain points of the Indian Ocean, to countries who claimed rightly or wrongly to be of Arab nationality.

In 1905 Negib Azoury published in Paris *The Re-awakening of the Arab Nation, the Interests and Rivalries of the Foreign Powers, and of the Roman and Orthodox Churches.*[1] In 1906 the "National Committee" sent a proclamation to the Powers as an exposition of their programme.

For an idea to become a reality more is required than that it should arouse intense feeling, and it must be recognised that the creation of a vast Arab state came up against many practical difficulties: the anarchy of people among whom

---

[1] *Le réveil de la nation arabe dans l'Asie turque en présence des intérêts et des rivalités des puissances étrangères, de la curie romaine et du patriarcat œcumenique.*

there is virtually no public spirit, the ancient and violent hatreds between the nomads and the settled-people, the differences between the religious sects (the Chiites and the Sunnites are as much opposed to each other as the Catholics and the Protestants of Christianity); finally there was keen rivalry between the princely candidates to the sovereignty of the new Empire. It was particularly keen between the Emirs of eastern Saudi Arabia and the Sherifs of Mecca, who both claimed the title of 'Khalifat'. If the movement was to succeed terrible convulsions could be foreseen before victory would be achieved. But such considerations have never prevented a doctrine from having its adherents, its fanatics and even its martyrs.

The appeal of the exiled Syrian intellectuals was heard in the East. The old sentiments, from henceforth clearly formulated, found expression in anti-Turkish agitations. There were revolts in the Yemen, in Syria and in Iraq. The worried Turkish Government had to reinforce its garrisons in the countries which till then it had only occupied very feebly. Abdul Hamid decided to build a railway line linking Anatolia to the Holy Cities, officially with the purely religious object of facilitating pilgrimages, in fact to permit troop movements into the Arabian peninsula. A cunning propaganda induced the pious Moslems to finance the "Hadj Line" with their gifts, but the Bedouins of the Hejaz were not taken in; the railway, they were well aware, would permit the Turkish Government to increase their authority over them, and besides it would very probably interfere in a large degree with their exploitation of the pilgrims, an exploitation from which many of the tribes drew their living. There were insurrections among the nomads, a Turkish governor was attacked near Medina and his escort was three-quarters massacred, the first car to enter Mecca was torn to pieces, and the line which was at first intended to reach Mecca had to stop at Medina.

The Turkish revolution of 1908 gave some hope to the Arab separatists: but in fact it aggravated rather than alleviated their condition. The Young Turks were ardently nationalistic and their pantouranian sentiments led them to a vigorous oppression of every minority with dissenting tendencies. The men of 'Union and Progress' curtailed the

official use of the Arab language whose sacred character and
literary riches had commanded the respect of the Sultans, and
fresh revolts shook the Arab world, revolts which were all the
more dangerous for the Ottoman Government since the
Balkan war was occupying all its armed forces.

The activity of the secret societies became worrying for the
Turks; the two principal of these societies extended their
influence through the richest and most populous parts of
the Arab countries: in Mesopotamia, the Ahad included
more than two-thirds of the officers of Iraqi origin serving in
the Turkish Army; the secret of this fraternity was always
well kept and some of its high dignitaries held important
positions in the Turkish Government and Army throughout
the war: always anti-Turk but very Moslem and anti-
Christian, the Ahad was not during the course of the conflict
to throw itself into the arms of the Allies, and never collaborated with them other than with circumspection. In
Syria, on the other hand, the Fetah, which was very active
and had numbers of adherents, maintained extremely close
relations with the European Powers, and in particular with
France.

England, Russia and France knew all about the existence
of Arab separatism and sought to exploit it for their own
benefit. France saw in it a possibility for the realisation of her
Syrian dream, England thought about the oil of Mosul and
of the land route to India; the two countries intrigued with
the autonomists, encouraged them, subsidised them and
furnished them with arms.

*   *   *

At the beginning of the war, Turkey saw the possibility of
liquidating the ethnic and religious minorities which were
causing trouble for her in Asia similar to what she had known
in her European possessions a century earlier. With cold-
blooded ferocity she undertook the massacre of entire populations. In 1915 two million Armenians were exterminated;
two hundred thousand Greek Christians were deported from
Asia Minor; others were massacred or died miserably in
labour camps: the Kurds were put into the most exposed
units of the army and their youth was decimated; more than

three hundred thousand Chaldean Christians, and as many
Maronites from the Lebanon disappeared from massacre,
famine or disease. The Arab populations were those whom
the Turks dared least to persecute; they represented an ethnic
bloc that was too large and they were necessary for the recruitment of the army; since many of the Arab officers and officials
were indispensable to the functioning of the Turkish Government, they could not deal with this racial group by the simple
method of mass murder. However, the Turks found in the
home of a French consul the whole correspondence between
the National Committee exiled in Paris and certain Syrian
individuals, and attacked those leaders of the Fetah that they
could find; Jemal, the pro-consul in Syria, hanged, imprisoned
and deported a certain number of the best-known men in
Aleppo and Damascus; the Arabs felt that after the Armenians, the Greeks, the Kurds and the Chaldeans, their
turn would come next; the voice that preached revolt was
echoed increasingly among the common people as well as
among the ruling classes.

For the Allies, a general insurrection of the Arab provinces
of the Ottoman Empire would have been an event of far-
reaching importance, as it would probably have put Turkey
out of the war, but it was very difficult to organise: a large
number of soldiers, officials and citizens of the Arab race remained faithful to their Turkish allegiance, and looked upon
the Sultan as their civil and religious leader; others were
hesitant and, convinced of the ultimate victory of the central
empires, were not willing to compromise themselves; at best
they were playing a double game, but they refused to become
completely involved; Syria, Palestine and Northern Mesopotamia were forcefully held down militarily, and the fear of
the Turks deprived the dissidents of any desire to stir.

In these latter countries the Allies were only able to carry
on a clandestine agitation; it was in the regions in which the
Turkish occupation was not so strong, in particular in Arabia
proper, that they openly sought to set going the separatist
movement which was to split the unity of the Ottoman
Empire.

We have seen how as early as February 1915, Clayton's
service had thought of organising the inhabitants of Asir

8

into a combatant force, in their small principality in the south-west of Arabia. Lawrence could dream of going to conquer Damascus at the head of these Bedouins, but Idrissi, Sultan of Asir, was found to be too slight a prince for such an enterprise; it was necessary in order to lead the Arab world into revolt to find a leader of another calibre. Two men only seemed to be able to play this rôle: Abd el-Aziz Ibn Saud, whose influence stretched across the whole of the south-east of Arabia, and Hussein ben Ali, the Grand Sherif of Mecca.

Since before the war England had been in contact with these two notables. Kitchener had opened negotiations with Hussein, while the government of India had made approaches to Ibn Saud. The latter was the Emir of the Nejd and the leader of the Wahabite sect, Moslem pietists who claimed that they wished to impose upon Islam a severe religion re-invigorated by a return to its original sources; Ibn Saud would have made an important contribution to the Arab revolt, but he was a difficult partner; his religious fanaticism made him hostile to anything to do with Europe and Christianity, and his purely Oriental character was elusive; the Allies never succeeded in making him decide definitely against the Turks and he employed the arms and the subsidies which were sent to him much more for fighting the Grand Sherif Hussein, his old enemy, and Ibn Rachid, the Emir of Jebel Shammar, than against the Ottoman troops. Only one man had any influence with him: Shakespeare, the Indian Army officer who had been sent to his court as political officer.

Shakespeare was a remarkable agent, one of the best Arabian specialists which England possessed, and it is possible that he would have finished by deciding Ibn Saud on action, but at the beginning of 1915, while accompanying the Wahabite troops on a raid against the pro-Turk Ibn Rachid, he was killed in a patrol action; England, who no longer had a liaison agent with the lord of Nejd, had to abandon her hope of making him a sure and solid element in allied strategy. There was no alternative but to turn to the Hashemite, Hussein ben Ali, the Grand Sherif of Mecca, in order to stir up Arabia and separate her from Turkey.

The families of the Sherifs of the Hejaz are descended from the Prophet through his daughter Fatima; such an

ancestry confers on this line a great prestige throughout
Islam, and for many centuries has assured it political
power in the vicinity of the Holy Cities. In the Semitic
Orient religion and politics are very closely connected,
and men who through their ancestry can link themselves with a holy man are supposed to possess a virtue, a
divine gift, a luck—the Baraka—which automatically confers
on them the right to sovereignty. These holy families are thus
ripe with pretenders to every vacant throne in the Moslem
world.[1]

As there is no precise law to fix the order of succession in
Oriental dynasties, the Sultan of Constantinople would choose
the Grand Sherif sometimes from the Aoun branch, sometimes from the Hashemite branch of the Sherif's family. Thus
he maintained his own authority and kept up the discord and
rivalry around Mecca which was traditionally corrupt and
full of intrigue (as Mahomet knew when he vituperated
copiously against his fellow citizens in the Koran). Hussein
ben Ali, Chief of the Beni Hachem tribe, was however the
exception to the rule: he was pious and honest, which was
enough to make him suspected by Abdul Hamid, who was
worried over the influence which he was gaining as a private
individual in Mecca. Not liking this kind of rivalry he summoned Hussein to Constantinople and kept him there in
compulsory residence for about twenty years. The Sherif was
treated honourably but his position was very dangerous as
the Sultan, who became angry when he was made jealous,
would make the men who annoyed him disappear quite un-
scrupulously; Hussein never knew whether or not he would
be alive on the following day. However, he survived these
anguished years, and took advantage of his involuntary stay
in the capital to bring up his four sons on modern lines, Ali,
Abdallah and Feisal whom he had by an Arab wife and Zeid
born of a Circassian woman. In 1905 Hussein was nominated
Grand Sherif but was not however authorised to return to

[1] Long before Islam one finds the same phenomenon: the Herods do
not seem to have had any other profession except the candidatures to
the sovereignty of every state in the Levant. This was particularly
the case with Herod Agrippa, the brother of the famous Berenice. The
history of the house of Herod has curious analogies with that of
the Hashemites.

Mecca. It was only after the Young Turks' revolution in 1911 that he was able to go to the Hejaz.

The country, having been left for several years without a ruler, was in a fearful state of anarchy and insecurity. Order had to be restored in the cities, and above all the nomads had to be brought to heel, since they had taken up their millennial habits, were raiding each other, carrying on brigandage on the roads and holding the pilgrims to ransom. Hussein managed to pacify the country: the people of Mecca and Medina were brought to reason and the young emirs had to forget the habits of civilisation, live in the desert, patrol the roads and ensure the safety of the great pilgrim routes. This success at governing gave Hussein and his family great prestige in the Hejaz. Abdullah and Feisal were designated as deputies to the new Turkish Chamber, of which Abdullah was elected Vice President. However, the Sherif's relations with the Young Turks' government were not very good; the Arab deputies formed a bloc with those of the other minorities, Armenian, Kurdish and Maronite; and at Mecca, Hussein quarrelled with the Vali, the Turkish governor, whose authority conflicted with his own.

Profoundly Arab at heart, and having personally suffered from the Turkish tyranny, the Grand Sherif was inevitably separatist in sentiment, and from the beginning of the war he had thought of obtaining the support of the English in order to gain the independence of the Hejaz. Even in April 1914 his son, the Emir Abdullah, on a visit to the Khedive of Egypt, requested a secret interview with Kitchener and his assistant Ronald Storrs, and asked them point-blank whether Great Britain was prepared to furnish the Hejaz with the arms to win her national liberty. The English, a little staggered, replied that they were at peace with Turkey and could not risk taking an attitude that might set the whole of the Near East ablaze, but meanwhile they hedged their refusal with much diplomatic reserve and as the affair seemed to them interesting, taking a more or less long view of it, they avoided giving the lord of Mecca an unqualified 'no'.[1]

In September 1914, a few weeks after Turkey's entry into the war, Kitchener, who had not forgotten the affair, tele-

[1] Sir Ronald Storrs, *Orientations*, p. 142.

graphed from London to Egypt: "Tell Storrs to send secret and carefully chosen messenger from me to Sherif Abdullah to ascertain whether should armed influence in Constantinople coerce Sultan against his will and Sublime Porte to acts of aggression and war against Great Britain, he and his father and Arabs of the Hejaz would be with us or against us." Conforming with these instructions, Storrs sent an emissary to the Hejaz, who met the Sherif and his sons. Hussein was friendly but prudent. He assured England of his friendship but did not dare break officially with the Turks. His attitude was understandable: no one knew how the war would turn out, and the Grand Sherif had no desire to put himself on the losing side.

In December 1914 Storrs' secret agent made another journey to Mecca without any further result.

During the year 1915, England on the one hand, the Grand Sherif on the other pursued their separate and personal policies on the difficult chessboard of the Near East. The British, feeling the need to reduce every cause of disagreement with her principal ally France, decided to abolish the apple of discord which for so long had lain between their two countries, the question of Syria. Mark Sykes, a Member of Parliament, was charged by Kitchener with concluding an agreement with the French Government over the division of the future zones of influence of England and France in the Levant. After a year of discussions, the secret Sykes–Picot treaty was signed in May 1916, by Russia, England and France. It was designed in principle to avoid, when peace came, all friction between the Allies,[1] and among other stipulations it made provision for a French mandate of Syria, whilst England reserved for herself Mesopotamia, both countries with Arab populations.

On his side, the Sherif Hussein was scheming for his own best interests, but he had to face up to two conflicting necessities: the Turkish Government was ordering him to adopt a definite position and proclaim the Jihad, or Holy War, against the Allies, at the same time as the Arab nationalists of Syria and of Mesopotamia were turning towards him and calling on him to lead an open revolt of the Arab

[1] Unfortunately it avoided nothing of the sort.

countries against Turkey. Hussein avoided committing himself to one side or the other. He refused to declare the Jihad, but formulated his refusal with much cunning, emphasising to the Turkish Government that his sterile country could not live without the pilgrims' gold or the provisions which the English allowed to come in through the Hejaz; if he was to take up an official position on the matter, he said, the British would not fail to blockade his coasts and starve his subjects. With regard to the Syrian and Iraqi nationalists he was equally evasive, their country was strongly occupied by the Ottoman divisions, the war was going very badly for the Allies and every attempt at revolt seemed destined to failure.

He sent his son Feisal to Turkey, and in the uniform of a Turkish officer the Emir took part in the Dardanelles campaign, and was able to see with his own eyes the bloody reverses which the Allies were suffering at Gallipoli; he went next to Damascus as a member of Jemal's headquarters, and in doing so showed himself to be a loyal subject of the Ottoman Empire, but it was also with the object of sounding opinion among the people of Syria and of making contact with some of the autonomists. His position was not without danger; Jemal looked on him with distrust and had him watched; in order to prove him, he expanded in front of him in invective against the "Arab traitors", and with a sadistic sense of humour took him to see the hanging of some nationalists.

After her successes in Gallipoli and Mesopotamia, Turkey in fact felt that she was strong enough to crush Arab dissidence in the same way that she had dealt with the dissidence of the Armenians. The Arab units were cut up and divided among the corps that were furthest away from each other, and the repression of autonomism was intensified; arrangements were made for occupying more efficaciously the strategic centres of the Arabian peninsula, and Enver Pasha and Jemal made a tour of inspection in Mecca, taking Feisal with them; the Arabs felt that after the Armenians, the Kurds and the Chaldeans, it would be their turn to suffer exactions and massacres.

Meanwhile the Grand Sherif was still hesitant. He accepted the subsidies and the arms which the Egyptian Government

and the Sirdar of the Sudan sent him, but before he would
decide he meant to obtain exorbitant advantages. In July
1915, when asked by Sir Reginald Wingate on what conditions he would co-operate, he had made it known that he
would come in on the side of the Allies if he was assured of
the creation of an Arab state (of which he fully intended
to be the sovereign) including, apart from the Arabian
peninsula, the whole of Western Asia that was inhabited by
Arabic-speaking peoples.[1] Such a state would have included
Syria, Palestine and Mesopotamia, on which the Allies had
their own particular ideas, which were to be crystallised in
the Sykes–Picot agreement. England, who found that these
claims were rather exaggerated, replied that it was too early
to talk of frontier questions, and thus the matter rested until
the beginning of 1916.

But a new development in the situation was to bring about
a decision: it was learnt in the spring of 1916 that the Turks
were organising an expedition at Constantinople, under the
orders of Khairi Bey, three or four thousand men strong, who
were to go by rail to Medina, and then from there to the
Yemen in order to bring the Arabs to reason by the usual
means. This detachment was accompanied by a German contingent commanded by Major von Stotzingen, whose mission
was to set up a radio station on the coast of the Red Sea, to
make contact with German East Africa, and to organise
anti-English propaganda in the Sudan, in Darfour and in
Abyssinia.

Under this direct threat, the government of the Sudan
intensified its supply of arms, provisions and money to the
Hejaz, and Ronald Storrs, accompanied by Hogarth and
Cornwallis, went on the 5th of June, 1916, to the Arabian
coast, taking Hussein as a final encouragement ten thousand
gold sovereigns, with the promise of fifty thousand more if
war was declared. But this final inducement was unnecessary
since the news of the Turks' arrival had already forced

[1] *Orientations*, p. 177. Storrs, one of the negotiators, said that the
Grand Sherif's demands were ridiculous: "His pretensions bordered
upon the tragi-comic", and besides in his opinion they were un-
realisable for ethnic and religious reasons. It must, however, be noted
that from this time the Sirdar and Sir Henry MacMahon were making
imprudent promises to the Arabs.

the Grand Sherif to action. He had recalled Feisal from Damascus, and at the very moment that Storrs was setting foot on the Arabian coast, he declared himself in open revolt against Turkey.

*　　　*　　　*

The Turks were completely taken by surprise and the Movement almost everywhere met with quick success. The Ottoman troops were spaced between Medina, Jidda and Mecca with small contingents at Lith, Qunfideh, Rabegh and Yambo. The garrison of Mecca had gone into its summer quarters at Taif, in the mountains, and there were no more than a thousand men in the Holy City. Finding himself attacked by the insurgents, the Turkish commander telephoned the Sherif and said, "The Bedouins are in revolt: help me to pacify them." But he was soon to lose his illusions, and crushed by weight of numbers, he surrendered after three days of honourable resistance. A few Turkish sections, however, clung on to the small forts which surround Mecca and made use of their guns to bombard their attackers; a howitzer shell fell on the Kaaba, killed some of the faithful and nearly hit the Black Stone, a talisman sacred above everything, and it took a month to reduce these final defenders.

Jidda was similarly attacked at the outset of the Movement, by the Sheik of the Harb and four thousand Bedouins. They were at first repulsed, but managed to cut off the water conduit which supplied the city. Two English cruisers and some aeroplanes bombarded the Turkish defences and on the 16th of June the garrison of one thousand four hundred men surrendered to the Arabs.

At Taif three thousand Turks, solidly entrenched and armed with field guns, presented a very formidable obstacle to the Bedouins of the Emir Abdullah, who were little suited to siege warfare. Some indecisive engagements took place during the months of July and August. Finally the army of Egypt sent some guns, and a well-directed bombardment brought to an end the resistance of the Vali, Ghalib Pasha, who surrendered with his garrison at the end of September. Yambo and Rabegh had fallen as early as the end of July.

These successes were substantial, but the war of the Hejaz

MAP II

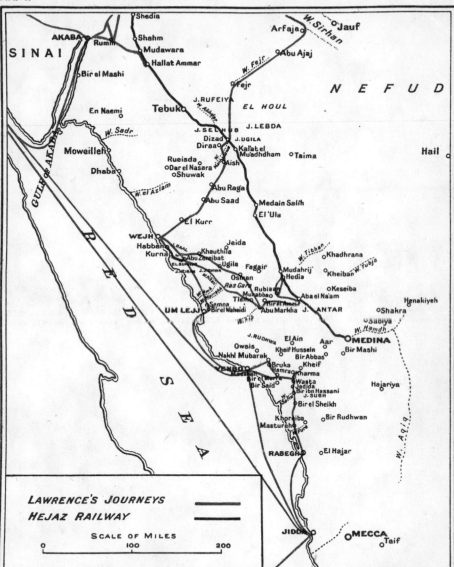

LAWRENCE'S JOURNEYS
HEJAZ RAILWAY

SCALE OF MILES

0   100   200

NOTE _ "J." denotes JEBEL (Mountain)   "W." denotes WADI (Watercourse & Valley.)

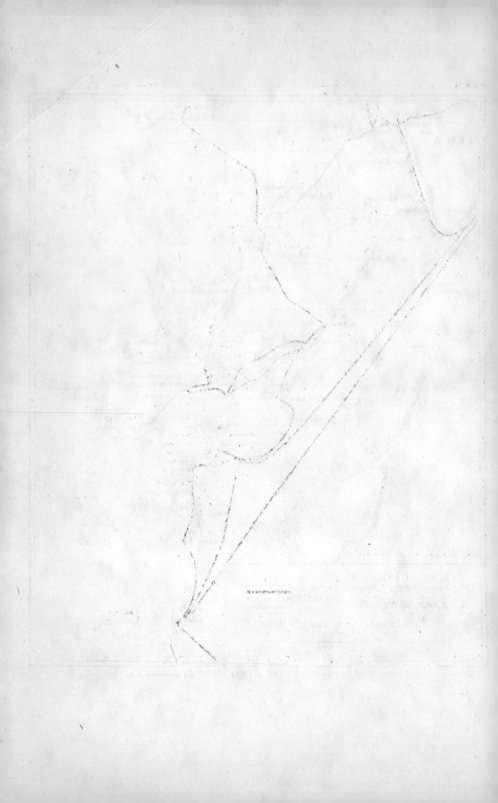

was not however won, as the operations around Medina were going rather badly for the Arabs. The city was held by about twelve thousand men commanded by Fakri Pasha, an old butcher, celebrated for having organised the massacres of Adana in 1909, and whose courage and military qualities were undeniable. On the 5th of June Feisal, at the head of the nomadic warriors attempted to take the city by assault, but they came up against some good troops who repulsed the Arabs from the outskirts of the city in which they had gained a footing. Machine-gun and artillery fire scattered the attackers. Feisal had to fall back with some losses and many of his supporters deserted and returned to their tribes; Fakri Pasha pushed his advantage, and overthrowing what remained of the Emir's troops, advanced to within twenty miles of the south of Medina, the nature of the country, which was extremely broken and devoid of water, alone preventing him from going further; Feisal and his partisans took refuge in the mountains, and contented themselves henceforth with preventing the Turks from using the tracks and the passes which lead from Medina to Mecca. The Emir Ali, Hussein's eldest son, had tried to cut the Turkish lines of communication by destroying the Hejaz railway near Medain Salih, but had only caused damage that was easily reparable; he rejoined his brother to the south of Medina, and the two Sherifs waited in hiding and with some anxiety for the way in which things would turn out. They knew Fakri Pasha to be energetic and terribly cruel: if he decided to march on Mecca, Ali and Feisal wondered with anguish if their Bedouins would be capable of stopping him: the Pasha had with him the Sherif Ali Haidar whom the Turkish Government had just nominated official Grand Sherif of Mecca, and if Fakri reached the Holy City there could be no doubt that Hussein, his family and his partisans would all be massacred.

The overall situation was thus worrying for the English: they had encouraged and subsidised the Revolt, had sent into the Hejaz several hundreds of thousands of pounds and fifty thousand rifles; they could not abandon the Movement to its fate, or allow it to fall into jeopardy. The Sirdar had installed Colonel Wilson at Jidda, as the British representative, but this excellent officer had a thankless and difficult task: the

Sherif, old, touchy, and at once dictatorial and indecisive,
feared the interference of the Christians, knew nothing of
Europe and of the realities of the war, and convinced that the
Hejaz was the hub of the world, would do nothing unless he
had his own way. He oscillated between frantic discouragement and a sulky intransigence, and no one knew how to deal
with him. Installed in Mecca, and inaccessible to Christians,
it was not possible to contact him except by telephone, and
though they had interminable discussions with him they produced no definite results. Wingate felt as if he had been
thrown into a wasps' nest. "His army is practically a rabble
and run on Dervish lines," he said, raising his hands to the
sky. The arrival of a French mission at Jidda in September
did not settle very much. The prudent Clayton, foreseeing
that the Arabian business could create friction between the
Allies, had asked that our country should be represented in
Arabia, and our government had hastily appointed, under
the command of Colonel Brémond, a mission which reached
Jidda in September 1916. Colonel Brémond was a valuable
officer who had had a long and brilliant military career in
Morocco. On the French front he had been Deputy Chief of
Staff to an army corps, but this cultivated man of integrity,
who knew Arabic perfectly, was abrupt, jealous of his reputation, and towards the English full of the traditional distrust
of French colonials, a distrust which the British returned in
full measure. He intended to conduct a policy which was
purely French without weakness or concession, and on ground
as treacherous as that of Arabia this was to risk creating
trouble between the Allies. His presence was to complicate
a situation which was already insoluble.

*   *   *

To the objurgations and advice of the English, Hussein
and his sons only replied by greater and always greater demands for money. Periodically Storrs and Hogarth went to
Jidda anxiously to lean over the cradle of the young revolutionary Arab state, a poor stunted infant; they gave the
Sherif's supporters sacks of sovereigns which they knew would
be squandered on ends other than that of victory; the country
was gorged with money and the nomads were experiencing

a prosperity such as they had never dreamt of; some of the supplies and the arms furnished by the English were sold again to the Turks; Hussein's officials in the ancient Oriental tradition vied with each other in theft, and stuffed their pockets; the Emirs Ali and Zeid, discouraged by the turn of events, left the front and set themselves up at Rabegh in order to live handsomely on the English provisions.

In this state of disorder and corruption, the Turks of Medina, who had been forgotten, suddenly made their presence felt. On the 19th of October, 1916, they sent out a camel reconnaissance which fell unexpectedly on Feisal's Bedouins, then based at Bir Abbas, sixty odd miles to the southwest of Medina. This small detachment threw the Emir's troops into panic; without fighting they fled to the south and did not stop until they reached Hamra, a day's march further on. Hussein and his sons cried feverishly for help. This then was the situation when Storrs accompained by Lawrence landed at Jidda in the middle of October 1916.

First Contact

THE Red Sea is usually compared to a furnace; but in winter teeth often chatter with cold, and in the spring and the autumn a light breeze makes it delightful to sail there.

Storrs and Lawrence left Cairo on the 12th of October, 1916, and reached Jidda in the little steamboat *Lama*, chock-full of men and equipment. It was a mixed company: English officers and troopers rubbed shoulders with Hindus and Sudanese and with Arab deserters from the Turkish Army on their way to join the Hejaz forces; Lawrence boiled over with inaction, went ferreting about the boat, and with some other young officers shot with a pistol at bottles thrown into the sea. Storrs was amazed at his companion's continual tenseness, at his desire to see everything and learn everything, at what he called his 'supercerebrality': "I continue to wonder whether for all his amazing knowledge, his sum total of pleasure is, given of course circumstances favourable to each, any greater than mine," wrote in his diary this man who was imbued with the philosophy of Montaigne and Anatole France.

The friendship of the two men was not without its thorns. Lawrence was resentful of all rank and talent, especially when it appeared in domains that he believed to be reserved for himself, those of art, scholarship or knowledge of the Levant; now Ronald Storrs had read everything and very little in the Near East ever escaped him. Neither of this high-spirited pair could prevent himself from exercising his sense of humour at the expense of the other, but a mutual respect, a common subtlety of mind, their culture and their need for a companionship of a certain quality, prevented them from quarrelling.

After the freshness of the sea, the heat of Jidda beneath a leaden sky seemed overwhelming. It was in those days a small primitive town which only came to life at the time of the pilgrimages; the rest of the year it relapsed into lethargy, and the inhabitants, of mixed race, counted their piastres behind the teak-latticed balconies which have made their city famous, while waiting for the next pilgrims to fleece; the desert penetrated the town, filling the narrow streets with sand; the strong stench of the Orient, still almost inviolate, filled the nostrils of the travellers.

When they landed on the 15th of October, they went to find Colonel Wilson, the Sirdar's representative in Jidda. Wilson received Lawrence rather abruptly: the two officers had been in conflict not long before in Cairo, and were not very fond of each other; Wilson, a strict man, probably disapproved to the depths of his being of the slovenliness of his visitors, whose crumpled white clothes were stained with large scarlet rosettes which the red chairs of the *Lama* had left on their sweat-soaked tunics. Storrs and Lawrence, who had little time for sartorial taboos, were greatly amused by this misfortune.

The same day Storrs, accompanied by Wilson, went to pay his respects to Abdullah, Hussein's second son, who was in camp just outside the town, near the famous tomb of Eve which has given its name to Jidda.[1] The Emir was a man of over thirty, friendly, subtle and sleek. Behind his cynical frankness, he hid a considerable astuteness; the favourite son of the Sherif, he played a preponderant rôle in the politics of the Hejaz; a sensualist and lover of luxury, he received the English in a magnificent damascene tent; he wore the clothes of the Bedouin, the agal, the double cord which surrounds the heads of the nomads of Arabia and keeps the headcloth in place, and patent-leather boots.

The discussion, which was tense, bore on the assistance which Abdullah was demanding for the Revolt: he wanted artillery, machine-guns, men and above all money. Storrs answered obliquely, refused to commit himself, and invited the Sherif to come on the following day to the British Consulate.

[1] Jidda means 'grand mother'. At that time the tomb of Eve could still be seen there, a strange monument which doubtless recalled religions more ancient than Islam. The historian E. F. Gauthier, who in 1917 went to Jidda to visit his friend Colonel Brémond, has described it in detail and made a sketch of it in his book *Mœurs et coutumes des Musulmans*. When the Wahabites took possession of the Hejaz in 1923, they destroyed the tomb of Eve because it had been seen and touched by Christians.

Lawrence was present at the second interview; the negotiations continued, but this time T.E., who understood Arabic
much better than Wilson, was able to give his support to the
Oriental Secretary. It was necessary to explain to Abdullah
that England could not at that time send to Rabegh the
brigade which the Grand Sherif was demanding in order to
block the road to Mecca to the Ottoman troops; the conversation was interrupted by telephone calls from old Hussein, in
Mecca, who indulged in interminable and confused diatribes
against the English; to complete the tragi-comic aspect of this
conference, Abdullah treated his visitors to a morning concert
given by a Turkish military band captured at Taif, which
played the *Hymn of Hate* and *Deutschland uber Alles*, with
German instruments and with atrociously false notes.

Lawrence took an intimate part in the negotiations, and
when Abdullah talked of the hordes of Turks who were
threatening the Sherif's armies he brought things back into
perspective, cited the Ottoman units that were engaged, their
fighting strengths, and the names of the officers who commanded them. Disconcerted, the Sherif turned towards
Storrs and asked "Is this man God to know everything?"
Lawrence, profiting from Abdullah's astonishment and admiration, asked him point-blank to give him a free pass to go
to Rabegh and Hamra, to visit the Sherif's front and make
contact with the Emirs Ali, Feisal and Zeid who were commanding the troops. Abdullah hesitated, held back by the
instinctive xenophobia of the Arab: Storrs supported his
companion's request with all his persuasive eloquence. In the
end Abdullah telephoned his father, who after much evasion
gave the required authority.

The two Englishmen left Jidda for Rabegh on the 18th of
October, and whilst Storrs returned to Egypt, Lawrence left
on a visit to the camp of the Emirs.

*   *   *

At the moment that he embarks on the adventure of his
life, Lawrence is perfectly equipped intellectually, morally
and physically for the mission which he is about to be given.

He is twenty-eight—almost the age of maturity for a mind
of his quality.

He has studied—as an amateur, it is true, but very deeply—the history of ancient and modern warfare, and the problems of strategy and tactics.

To theory he has added practice, as he has been involved in the life of a headquarters and in that of a colonial government, and he is broken to the intrigues of civil and military staffs. Besides, he has been able to follow closely the campaigns in Sinai and Mesopotamia and the war with the Senussis. In London he is known, and individuals in high places follow his career and support him.

He speaks Arabic, if not very well, at least with fluency, and has a knowledge that is almost unique of the Arabs' customs and ways of thought. Since 1911 he has been around the countries in which the Sherifs' army is about to operate and from donkey-boy to sheik he has made friends among the inhabitants: during his time with the Intelligence Service in Cairo, he has created (assuming that he had not done so earlier) a network of agents and spies in Turkish territory.

Despite his small height, he is extremely vigorous and strong and has trained himself from childhood to be contemptuous of his body, of fatigue and of suffering; he has disciplined his will-power and his mind in the same way; perpetually highly strung, he has a capacity for work that is equal to his power of concentration.

His intelligence is sparkling, his quick grasp, his coolness, his mastery of himself are those of a leader. And like a born leader, he is secretive, egocentric and tough, with a love for taking risks and assuming responsibility. He has no scruples on the choice of the means which will lead him to the ends on which he has decided, and since these ends are never interested or base, he is never tormented with remorse. Everything, in short, that is required for a Caesar or a Bonaparte. Certainly too much for the rôle which fate has reserved for him. And in this is contained the whole drama: the disproportion between his personal ideal and his mission. He is to lead rapacious, indisciplined and hesitant nomads to mediocre attainments, with an ambition that befits a young Alexander. The adventure over, he will see in it only its limitations and his success will appear to himself to be the worst of failures.

Feisal

LAWRENCE went immediately to see the Emir Ali who, after the failure of the attack on Medina, had installed himself at Rabegh, and was feebly attempting to create, with deserters, liberated Arab prisoners and a few men recruited on the spot, an army of a more solid nature than that constituted by the Bedouin bands.

Ali was a man of thirty-seven, of poor physical strength, whose narrow Muslim piety and caste prejudices suited him ill for collaboration with Europeans. While Colonel Parker, the English liaison agent with him, was trying to build up a base for operations at Rabegh, he allowed himself to be tossed about by events; his repugnance to seeing the Infidels intervening in the Hejaz was, however, counter-balanced by his need for military support and financial assistance. The Emir Zeid, his half-brother, a boy of nineteen, acted as his deputy; he was a slight, vain young man with little enthusiasm for the Revolt; the son of a Turkish mother, and brought up at Constantinople, he could never be a fanatic for Arab independence.

The order which Ali received from his father through the intermediary of Abdullah shocked him severely: to allow a Christian to penetrate sacred territory seemed to him impious, and he feared repercussions among his partisans if it became known. But Lawrence had his antennae everywhere: close to Ali there were individuals with whom he had had contact either in Cairo or during his stay in Syria: Nuri Said, an ex-officer of the Baghdad staff, and Fais el-Ghusein, a Sheif of the Hauran, pledged themselves as a surety for him and after some hesitation Ali decided to have this English officer escorted as far as Hamra, halfway between Rabegh and Medina, where he would find Feisal's contingents.

The littoral plain, a few leagues broad, which runs the length of the Red Sea coast is divided from the enormous,

almost flat, extent of the Arabian desert by a chain of lunar
mountains, a formidable obstacle for those who wish to penetrate the interior from the coast. This country with its tormented relief is one of the most forbidding of the globe. It
is a chaos of granite, basalt and lava, whose rugged peaks are
higher than six thousand feet, waterless, scorched by the heat
in summer, and in winter frozen by blizzards; it is almost uninhabited, except in the depressions of the wadis, where here
and there are found rather miserable oases and the encamp-
ments of nomads. Their inhuman life has not endowed the
few natives of these desolate regions with a tenderness of soul.

This steep mountain barrier, crossed by stony flint tracks
through passes that were two thousand five hundred feet
high, and in which no significant body of troops could find
sufficient water to subsist, defended Mecca and the armies of
the coast far more efficaciously than the Sherifs' troops. The
Emir Feisal was to be found to the west of Medina, in the
foothills of this chain. It was here that Lawrence was to meet
him.

The expedition was full of risks: around Rabegh, the tribes
had not declared for the Revolt, and remained in allegiance
to the Turks; the roads were infested with looters of no good
intent; the travellers ran the risk of being held up and
murdered en route. Ali lent Lawrence his own camel, and
entrusted him to two warriors of the Hawazim tribe who
promised to take good care of him; to avoid any indiscretions
or scandal the journey was kept a secret and the three men
left at night, Lawrence wrapped in a caftan, and wearing the
Bedouin headcloth.

The ride took nearly three days. For a European who had
just spent two years in an office and who had never been
trained to ride a racing camel it was an extremely tough
ordeal. Lawrence had to go at the pace of a raiding party, ride
without stopping across terribly broken country beneath an
inhuman sun, eat the sordid food of the nomads, and sleep on
the ground. He was overcome by the heat, broken by the
speed of the ride, starved and parched. It was exactly what he
wanted, to suffer and to overcome himself: and he also knew
the effect of astonishment and admiration which he would

9

provoke among the Arabs when they saw him appear calm
and in control of himself after this trip.

Feisal, having been routed by the Turkish reconnaissance
on the 19th of October, had fallen back on Hamra. With him
were a thousand Bedouins, and the few Egyptian units, foot
and artillery, which the English had sent him as reinforce-
ment, and he had installed these troops in the group of oases
watered by Wadi Safra. He was a hundred miles from
Medina, and his men, demoralised by the rather bloody repulse of their attempt on the town, and by two weak counter-
attacks by the Turks, had lost all their warlike spirit and
were deserting en masse. They had been terrified by the
Turkish artillery, and the old Krupps guns used by the
Egyptians and which had a range of no more than three
thousand yards had been shown to be quite ridiculously in-
effective against the Turkish field pieces; the Arabs were
crying aloud for guns, and it was obvious that they would
do nothing so long as the Allies did not supply them with
ammunition and equipment.

Amidst this confusion Feisal was endeavouring to cut a
good figure. Lawrence has related in a very fine passage and
with perhaps a touch of romance, his first meeting with the
man of his destiny:

"Framed between the uprights of a black doorway, stood a
white figure waiting tensely for me. I felt at first glance that
this was the man I had come to Arabia to seek—the leader
who would bring the Arab Revolt to full glory. Feisal looked
very tall and pillar-like, very slender in his long white silk
robes and his brown headcloth bound with a brilliant scarlet
and gold cord. His eyelids were dropped; and his black beard
and colourless face were like a mask against the strange, still
watchfulness of his body. His hands were crossed in front of
him on his dagger. . . .
'And do you like our place here in Wadi Safra?'
'Well; but it is far from Damascus.'
The word had fallen like a sword in their midst."

Lawrence spent several days in Feisal's camp, noting and
classifying everything in his prodigious memory. He talked
with the members of the Sherif's entourage, Bedouin sheiks,
notables from Mecca, officers who had come over from the

Turkish Army. He spoke to the Egyptians who without much
enthusiasm and compelled by the English found themselves
engaged in this disorderly war, of which they did not approve;
finally and especially, he mixed with the crowd of warrior
nomads, who constituted the bulk of Feisal's forces.

Hatred of the Turks and the love of pay and of booty
enabled the Emir to raise partisans among the Bedouin tribes
of the countries in which he operated. These picturesque
ruffians were trained to desert warfare by millenniums of
wandering and raiding; Lawrence knew these camel riders
and ragged footsloggers well, whose eternal type is found
from the Upper Euphrates to the South of Arabia; many of
them are semi-negroes, born of concubinage with African
slaves, but the old Semitic blood with its asperity and harsh-
ness is always dominant in them. They are wild beasts,
rapacious, cunning and of incredible hardihood, as different
as possible in their methods of fighting to the chivalrous
warriors that the romantic authors wished to make of them,
but formidable in surprise or in ambush.

Lawrence was filled with enthusiasm by these barbarous
troops. He knew better than anyone their real qualities, and
the terrible defects that would make them difficult to use in
an organised war. The Bedouin bands were as anarchic and
elusive as the feudal contingents of the eleventh century, but
he worked out in his mind what he, with his tactical sense
and his ability to handle simple and primitive people, would
be able to make of these savages. It was among these men that
he had to live.

At the end of three or four days spent in the camp at
Hamra, having seen what he wanted to see, and having produced the effect that he wished to produce, Lawrence asked
Feisal to be sent back to Yambo. Two long marches by camel
brought him to this port, whence he came by sea to Jidda,
where he arrived about the 1st of November.

*   *   *

Lawrence, accompanying Admiral Wemyss, the commander
of the Red Sea fleet, went to Khartoum, where he took part
in a military conference presided over by Reginald Wingate,
the Sirdar of the Sudan, recently appointed High Com-

missioner in Egypt, and he laid before the great men the
ideas which he had brought back from his journey.[1]

The Arabs, he said, should be able to defend the route
from Medina to Mecca. The relief of the country and the lack
of water points made its passage almost impossible for a force
of any significance; with a few machine-guns and snipers
hidden in the defiles, Feisal and his partisans would be able
to hold the mountains indefinitely.

At all cost European troops must not be sent into Arabia.
The Bedouins would in fact desert immediately and return
to their camps if they saw foreigners and especially non-
Moslems landing in their country. On the contrary it was
necessary to furnish the Sherifs' forces with arms, with money,
with food supplies and a few English officers to give them
advice.

Colonel Brémond was conducting in Jidda and by means
of a contact in Mecca a French policy which rivalled that of
the English; if he counselled sending in Allied forces, it was
with the object of seeing French regiments occupying the
Hejaz and later Syria, and these suggestions therefore ought
to be energetically opposed.

The man who should be the great leader of the Revolt was
the Emir Feisal. Here was the Hero and the Prophet who
would galvanise the patriotism of the peoples from Mecca to
Aleppo. England should support him, and brush aside as far
as was possible the niggardly and capricious old Hussein,
Abdullah who was too tortuous and cynical, Ali, sickly, without ambition and a narrow Muslim fanatic, and Zeid, too
young and slight. Feisal alone "was the leader with the necessary fire and yet with reason to give effect to our science".

Wingate and Wemyss listened to Lawrence's ideas, but
were far from agreeing with his views. Wingate, in particular,
was in favour of a large-scale landing of European troops in
the Hejaz. He was sceptical as to the military efficiency of the
'Dervishes'. Perhaps also the idea of commanding an Anglo-
French campaign of all arms in Arabia was not a disagreeable

[1] By a curious chance Wingate was a cousin of Lawrence, since one
of his forebears had been a Chapman. Colonel Newcombe, who informed me of this fact, believes that the Sirdar, like Lawrence, was
ignorant of their relationship when they met in Egypt and in the
Sudan, and only discovered it later.

one. As for Admiral Wemyss, he knew the Arab business very
well, for it was he who had with his marines taken Yambo,
and he was personally concerned with the defence of Rabegh.
He shared the Sirdar's ideas as to the little confidence that
could be placed in the Arabs. The two commanders did not
therefore agree with Lawrence's suggestions, and the conference of Khartoum broke up after deciding to intensify
European intervention, and to proceed, if they could dispose
of sufficient troops, with landing Allied contingents on the
coast of Arabia.

This conclusion was contrary to all Lawrence's wishes, as
for reasons which seemed to him logical, and for those which
were sentimental and personal, he had envisaged English
action in the Hejaz entirely differently. To gain the triumph
of his own ideas, he had therefore to intrigue. A few days
later, on his return to Cairo, he went back to his place in the
Arab Bureau, to which in the meanwhile the War Office had
reassigned him, and started to make some extremely cunning
moves.

He handed in his report on the situation in Arabia to his
chief Clayton, asking him to see that this document reached
General Murray's staff. This report, which strongly advised
against sending Allied units into Arabia, could not but please
the Egyptian High Command, who were preparing an offensive, and asserted that they had not a single man or boat to
spare for this campaign of which they disapproved. Murray
telegraphed to London the terms of the report to prove that
"the Arab experts asking this sacrifice of valuable troops from
him were divided about its wisdom and honesty, even in their
own camp", and the English General Staff, which was having
to face up to gigantic difficulties at the end of 1916, were
happy not to have to set apart troops for this secondary
theatre of operations, and agreed with Murray's views.

Lawrence, who had been very little appreciated by the
senior officers of Cairo, now became popular there, and the
Chief of Staff Lynden Bell told him that he accepted his programme in entirety, and promised to furnish the Arabs with
the necessary specialists, arms and subsidies. A few days later
Lawrence was ordered to return to Arabia as liaison officer
with Feisal. He raised some objections to this appointment:

he was not, he said, cut out for such a mission: he lacked the military knowledge, detested the soldier's profession, loved study and reflection more than action. It would seem to have been a purely formal protest. We can believe that the decision of his superiors fulfilled his most secret wishes. He left Cairo, reached the Hejaz and arrived at Yambo on the 9th of November, 1916.

We know of the events that preceded Lawrence's posting to the Arabian Army from Storrs's book *Orientations*, from certain passages in Brémond's work, and above all from the hero himself. We can see him putting into operation a very definite plan that does not carry, as Lawrence would suggest, the marks of improvisation.

It is not possible that T.E. could have gone to Jidda on his own initiative; this leave of ten days that lasted thirty has the distinct appearance of a mission. "I had believed these misfortunes of the Revolt to be due mainly to faulty leadership. . . . So I went down to Arabia to see and consider its great men." Lawrence is certainly here abusing the use of the first person: as a simple staff captain he did not go without orders, he was sent.

Further, he knew in advance what he would find and what advice he would give. Storrs's memoirs, which have the advantage over the *Seven Pillars* of giving some idea of dates, allow us to see behind the façade, for they tell us that before even having seen Feisal on the 17th of October, at the end of his stay in Jidda, Lawrence sent Clayton a dispatch which contained the broad lines of the whole policy which he was to preach in the months to come.[1]

It would be reasonable to think that Lawrence only went to Feisal's camp in order to give more authority to his thesis as a whole, while the choice of the Emir as the principal leader of the Revolt had already been decided on by the Arab Bureau. This choice was the outcome of some rather tortuous but maturely reflected considerations: Feisal was known to be of a malleable character; he was a dreamer, a hesitant, he loved neither decision nor action and he had a physical horror of danger; he had no desire to fight and to expose himself at the head of his troops, and he would leave the way open to his

[1] See the text of the telegram in Storrs's *Orientations*, p. 221.

English advisers and allow them to command in his place—in short an ideal façade, but a façade only. Besides, the Emir spoke English well, which would make relations with the British officers much easier.

Such a plan could only please Lawrence, since he had a few ideas of his own to add to those of his leaders. To play with Feisal the rôle of *eminence grise*, of the occult leader, would enable him to pursue that Syrian policy which he had had at heart for so long.

But the thesis had still to be accepted by the High Command. We have seen with what ability he made it prevail. Sir Reginald Wingate being opposed to it, he astutely played off Murray (whom he detested) against the Sirdar (for whom he had a high regard) in the course of an intrigue of which he gives a cynical account in his memoirs.

All this, which one can only guess at, as the documents are missing, is in any case fairly far from the version which Lawrence gives us in his book. One thing is almost certain, that his hesitation to accept his new appointment was scarcely sincere, even supposing that he displayed it to the degree which he would have us believe.

Lawrence in the Hejaz

Whilst Lawrence was in Cairo, things went as badly as possible in the Hejaz.

Disorder reigned among the Arabs. Hussein, frightened out of his wits by the Turkish threat, lost his head and wavered between extreme solutions. He thought of treating with the Turks, and then plunged suddenly into a wild Arab nationalism. At the beginning of November he had had himself proclaimed King of the Arabs, and this had caused acid exchanges, diplomatic notes and cavilling between himself and the Allies.

The Emirs were jealous of each other and hotly discussed how the Allied subsidies should be divided among themselves; they had quickly perceived the friction between the British and the French, and had made use of the one to counter the other. "We will show the French as little as possible of our country, so as not to arouse their covetousness," confided Abdullah to Storrs while he was on his way through Jidda. A few days afterwards the same Abdullah said to Brémond: "If the English do not land European troops in the Hejaz, it is not because they fear Moslem opinion, but because they are afraid of bringing you in after them."[1]

It is a fact that the English and the French regarded each other with much distrust. They were divided between two conflicting preoccupations: the desire to allow their associates to make the expenditure of troops and equipment, and the fear of allowing a colonial rival to gain too much influence in Arabia. These incompatible objectives made collaboration difficult. It had required two weeks of palavering before Brémond could bring the two sections of machine-guns which he had at Cairo to Rabegh. "I am waiting," he said, "for the English to land infantry to give them support", which did not indicate the most cordial co-operation.

[1] Brémond, p. 71.

The recruitment of the Sherifs' regular army, which was being organised at Rabegh, was difficult; there were only a few hundred men under training, while the British Government like the General Staff in Cairo was less and less inclined to commit men in the Hejaz. The Asquith Cabinet had just fallen and was about to be replaced by that of Lloyd George, and the Government was entirely preoccupied either with its own internal political intrigues or with the slaughter and failures of the war in France. General Murray was absorbed with the preparations for the attacks on Rafa and Maghdeba and refused to deprive himself of troops for the benefit of Arabia. Meanwhile they had managed to send a few slender reinforcements to Rabegh; two companies and two batteries of Egyptians, and a squadron of four aeroplanes. The advance guard of the French contingents, commanded by Lieutenant-Colonel Cadi with eight officers, had arrived in this port, and they were expecting a little artillery. Admiral Wemyss assembled his whole fleet in the roadstead, ready if need be to send in landing parties for the protection of the town whose defence he had organised himself. The *d'Entrecasteaux* and the *Pothuau* were co-operating with the British fleet.

It is easy to imagine the state of mind among this small band of English and French, who were struggling desperately without means and without support from their governments for the half-lost cause of distrustful and unreliable Orientals, who refused all advice and showed themselves quite incapable of helping themselves.

The Turks could not completely ignore the situation in the Hejaz. They knew that the rains would come and facilitate the crossing of the mountain. At the beginning of December they came out of their apathy and once more took to the offensive.

After Lawrence's visit, Feisal had fallen back from Hamra to Wadi Yambo; the Turks mounted a column of three battalions with the support of a few guns, some machine-guns and a camel detachment six hundred strong, and attacked his camp. In the battle the nomads gave way and a body of them deserted; the fugitives scattered towards the west; the Emir Zeid was almost taken in his tent and fled to the coast.

At about the same time, Ali, who had advanced towards

Bir Hassan, forty miles to the north-east of Rabegh, in order to make contact with his brother Feisal's troops, was also attacked by a Turkish detachment. As the first shells exploded, his troops fell into disorder, although they had suffered no losses. One tribe went over to the enemy, and what remained of the three or four thousand of the Emir's partisans took flight. Ali returned embittered to Rabegh, and his bitterness was understandable, since he had poured out two months' pay in advance and distributed two thousand rifles among the Bedouins who had just abandoned him: he attributed his defeat to jealousy and to Feisal's intrigues. Ali besides was very ill, and it was thought that, eaten away with tuberculosis, he would leave the front.

This was the situation when on the 9th of November, 1916, Lawrence landed at Yambo to take up his appointment as liaison officer with Feisal.

*   *   *

On his arrival at Yambo, he knew nothing of the recent rout of the Sherifs' forces. He left with a small escort and, a day's march from Yambo, at Nakhl-Mubarak, he came across Feisal's column violently shaken by its defeat and in the full disorder of retreat. The Emir's morale, now that he was within reach of the English base and eventual refuge, was not, however, too low. Lawrence entered into the life of the camp, and strove to restore confidence among the Arabs; he sought above all to be accepted as an ally and companion by these men who were quick to take offence and whose nerves were on edge from the defeat. He only stayed two days with Feisal, and then returned to Yambo in order to see Zeid who had arrived there. He had hardly left Mubarak, when the Turks again attacked the Emir's force. The three battalions that had already routed the Arabs had continued their advance along the Wadi Yambo; they were commanded by Ghalib Bey, and Fakri Pasha, the governor of Medina, accompanied them. The Bedouins, already demoralised by their recent lack of success, scattered into the desert, and Feisal with what remained of his troops marched towards Yambo.

All things considered, it seemed that Lawrence's predic-

tions would not be borne out, and that the Arabs would not
be able to defend the route from Medina to the sea. It was a
hard blow for the officer whose part in the adventure seemed
to be ending before it had begun. He accepted the disappointment with a certain philosophic humour.

"Our war seemed entering its last act—I took my camera
and, from the parapet of the Medina gate, got a fine photograph of the brothers coming in."

He deserves some credit for being cheerful in the circumstances. It was known that the Turks were on the heels of the
fugitives, that if they entered the town massacres would follow
and throats would be cut, and that the Ottoman bayonets
would make no distinction between English throats and Arab
throats.

*   *   *

The Arabs were in complete panic. Feisal and the notables
of the town took refuge in one of the British ships that was in
the port, but the English were made of other stuff. Lawrence,
with the assistance of Garland, an old Sapper officer, a vaga-
bond brawling type, who was looking after the supplies of the
port, a few Egyptian officers and a few marines, feverishly
went about putting the town in a state of defence.

The position was fairly favourable as Yambo was built on
a coral peninsula. What remained of the Arab partisans were
installed behind the ancient town wall, and in front of this
rampart were placed a few barbed-wire entanglements; the
Egyptian machine-guns and artillery were placed on the
flank; for his part, Boyle, a lieutenant of Admiral Wemyss,
had made some rapid dispositions, and sent from Rabegh five
ships which included a monitor and the *Dufferin*; the sailors
asked no more than to take part in the scrimmage; they had
uncovered their guns which, they said, "were itching". So
much resolution on the part of the Europeans restored some
of the spirit to the resistance of the Arabs.

In the middle of the night there was an alarm: the pickets
were attacked by Turkish patrols. The gunners could not
open fire as they did not know where to shoot, but the
sailors swept the plain with their searchlights; all the ships'

lights were switched on; Yambo, in reality weakly defended, seemed to the attackers to be a formidable place.

Faced with so considerable a deployment of forces, the Turks did not dare attack. They were in a fairly bad condition, exhausted by their advance through this terrible country, their effective strength reduced by thirst, fatigue and sickness, while the nomads swept off the stragglers and cut the tracks on their lines of communication. All things considered Lawrence had made a good appreciation of the difficulties of a country which could defend itself, but his judgment had been put to a stiff test. If their bluff at Yambo had been called and if the three Ottoman battalions had vigorously attacked the place, it is probable that the game would have been up, and that Mecca would have fallen. In fact the Turks' inaction before Yambo marks a turning point in the Hejaz campaign, and the Turks certainly seem to have lost the initiative on that day.

The Will to Power

THE Arab Revolt had been saved from disaster at Rabegh, and it was now necessary to organise it, and turn it into a useful adjunct to Allied strategy. The auguries charged with this task, Wilson, Brémond and a few English and French officers seconded to the Hejaz, did not really know how or in which direction to control a Movement that continued to be chaotic and indecisive.

The simplest idea seemed to be to create a regular Arab army, and achieve the liberation of the country by dislodging the Turks from Medina. But it was doubtful whether the Arabs could succeed in so modest an endeavour by themselves and without the help of European units. It was the thorny problem which had been discussed at Khartoum, and which was always cropping up. While waiting for a decision to be taken on this point, the strategy that was pursued in the Hejaz was somewhat disjointed.

For reasons of diplomacy, the means furnished for the Revolt had to be dispersed. The sons of the Grand Sherif were jealous of each other, and they all wanted to have troops to command, a staff, a court and subsidies. The Allied aid was thus shared among the Emirs and European officers were given to each. Lawrence was posted to Feisal's detachment, which was operating on the north-west of the Arab command, while Ali, accompanied by Zeid, was in the centre and Abdullah to the east, before Medina.

From henceforth, T.E. had but one objective: to give the Revolt a coherent and sustained policy and strategy, make Feisal's contingent the active nucleus of the Movement, secure for the Emir all the Allied support and undertake himself the conduct of all negotiations and operations. In order to achieve such a plan, he had to integrate himself completely with the Arab Movement, to become an Arab in his behaviour, his appearance and even in his thinking. He made

unparalleled efforts to arrive at this end. He resolved from
henceforth to wear the clothes of an Oriental, and to wear
them not only in the Emir's camp, but often also when he
was among European troops and sometimes even in Cairo. For
an Englishman it was something quite unusual, and he claims
to have behaved thus at Feisal's instigation, but in reality he
did it of his own accord.[1]

He had always loved disguises, and it could also be admitted that in so ardent a nature, profoundly romantic beneath
its affected cynicism, this decision had a mystical value; he
gave himself body and soul to the Revolt; from now on he
held a very special position in the eyes of the Sherif's followers
as in those of his fellow countrymen.

He was compelled to divest himself of all the intellectual
attitudes of a European, to think like an Arab, to imitate in
the workings of his mind the complicated meanderings of an
Oriental skull; he copied the posture of the Bedouin or
Meccanese sheiks, and practised the achouma, that detached
dignity which was so foreign to the whimsical nature of this
incorrigible *enfant terrible*. He wished to go to the extreme
limits of the transformation; he learnt to ride a camel, to
walk with bare feet across the overheated ground and sharp
stones, to eat, to sleep, to live like a Bedouin, disciplining
his body to discomfort and pain with the stoicism of a Fakir.

It remains to find out to what degree he really succeeded in
playing the rôle which he has attributed to himself. He will
go down in history as 'the uncrowned King of Arabia', but
was he really accepted completely by the Arabs whom he was
to lead during two years of war? It is difficult to make a definite judgment on this point. Many witnesses of his activities
in the course of the war say that his influence on the Orientals,
and above all with Feisal, was extraordinary; others have
reservations on this point. Lieutenant Bray, who spent several
months with the English mission in the Hejaz, goes so far as
to say that the presence of Lawrence, a foreigner and Christian, weakened the Revolt. It is certain that the great Semitic
movements have always been led by chiefs who were at once
religious and nationalistic warriors. Feisal was nothing of a
warrior and for this reason did not arouse the enthusiasm of

[1] This is what Storrs told me, in a most emphatic way.

the mob; Lawrence, a fighting hero, was not a Moslem, and it
is probable that the Arabs deep down in themselves never
took him for one of themselves. But once we admit Lawrence's policy, it seems that he put it into effect with incredible ability. Of all the Europeans who were to seek
adventure in the East, and who wished to integrate themselves with it, it was probably he who came nearest to
succeeding.

* * *

Lawrence, however, did not limit his activity to his
schemes with the Sherifs, and his diplomacy extended in other
directions. He knew that the greatest obstacle to his plans was
constituted by the French designs on Syria. From this time he
did his best to undermine and sap these ambitions which
were so contrary to his own ideas, and also to those of the
Arab Bureau and of one party of English policy-makers. The
presence of a French officer at Jidda worried and irritated
him. Following the operations around Yambo, Colonels
Wilson and Brémond had come to Rabegh to find out what
was going on. Lawrence went to meet them there. Brémond
and Lawrence had nothing whatever in common. The first
was a professional soldier and a Frenchman, who claimed not
without reason to have an intimate knowledge of the
Moslems; he had travelled incognito in Morocco and he had
had command of native troops, and that sufficed to make
Lawrence's hackles bristle; but above all Brémond never
ceased to think of a future French Syria. He had no faith in
the Revolt, and in agreement with the government of India
and with the army of Mesopotamia he considered this explosion of Arab patriotism as very disturbing for Europe, the
coloniser of Moslem countries.

The discussion turned on the necessity for landing Egyptian troops in the Hejaz and on the opportunity for attacking
Medina. Brémond wished to take Medina with Allied troops
and not with the Sherifs' forces in order to calm the ardour
of the tribesmen and the nationalism of the Emirs; he did not
conceal the fact that France had intentions on Syria, were not
those of England on Iraq just as obvious? Lawrence, himself,
would have liked a free Arab people, that had won for itself

its own liberty, and two such unlike characters, animated by
such different ideas, could only clash violently. "It was a
curious interview, that between an old soldier and a young
man in fancy dress; and it left a bad taste in my mouth," said
Lawrence. And he added curiously:

"The Colonel, like his countrymen, was a realist in love
and war. Even in situations of poetry the French remained
incorrigible prose-writers, seeing by the directly-thrown light
of reason and understanding, not through the half-closed eye,
mistily by things' essential radiance, in the manner of the
imaginative British: so the two races worked ill together on
a great undertaking."

Despite this dubious aphorism (or at any rate, its first part),
Lawrence forgot his sense of poetry to take realistic action in
order to eliminate or at least neutralise a man who was so
dangerous to his projects. He had, as we know, a long arm.
A few days later (December 1916) Brémond received from
France a severe reprimand: a telegram arrived from the
General Headquarters at Chantilly, couched in the following
terms:

"1. France and England have recently signed an agreement
whose basis is the constitution of an Arab federation including Damascus, Homs, Hama, Aleppo and Mosul. Now from
your telegrams it seems that you are opposed to the taking of
Medina by the Arabs, because of the encouragement it would
give them in their intentions on Syria.

"2. This state of mind, already known to the English and
the Sherif, could make it appear that we are trying to go
back on our agreements and could have serious consequences
on the development of our plans in the Levant. It is important that your attitude does not lend itself to such an interpretation.

"3. The French Government, further, judges that the fall
of Medina would have profound repercussions in Arabia,
and could be the signal for the rising of the Bedouin tribes
and of the Druzes. It will thus contribute to the success of
our projects in the East, by hastening the disintegration of
the Ottoman Empire."[1]

It was a severe dressing-down. It was signed 'Joffre', but

[1] Brémond, p. 97.

even down to its smallest detail it could have been signed
T. E. Lawrence. In view of the precision of its terms it does
not seem possible that each word was not inspired by the
latter.

In this first passage of arms with Brémond, Lawrence had
scored a point. He had shown the commander of the French
mission the extent of the power of his underground political
resources, and had caused him to be humiliated by his own
superiors.

The March on Wejh

THE area of the coastal bases and the route to Mecca had not been completely cleared; there were still four or five thousand Turks on the move between Medina and the Red Sea; on Christmas Day 1916, there had been so serious an alert at Rabegh that Wilson, Joyce and Colonel Brémond and the airman Captain Ross had thought that they would have to evacuate the port; Yambo had only just been saved by a well-organised piece of bluff, as we have seen, at the beginning of November; most of the English and French were convinced that the intervention of an Allied brigade was indispensable, and this brigade was in the end granted by the General Staff in Cairo and held in reserve in Egypt under the orders of General Mudge, but General Murray hoped that he would not, in fact, have to send it off. To intensify the activity of the Arabs and to co-ordinate their operations, Colonel Newcombe and a few other officers were set aside, and sent off urgently to the Hejaz. While waiting for their arrival, Wilson and Brémond had to carry on as best they could.

To relieve the Turkish pressure on Mecca, Wilson devised a scheme to throw the enemy into confusion. He decided to reply to their offensive by an offensive of his own, and to push the Arab dispositions to the north in order to threaten the rear of Medina, and the Hejaz railway line, Fakri Pasha's only means of communication with his bases in Syria. While the Emirs Ali and Zeid would continue to contain the Turks between Medina and the sea, Abdullah skirting this town to the east would go and base himself on Wadi Aiss, within striking distance of the track; Feisal, marching along the coast, would attempt in co-operation with the fleet to take the port of Wejh, one hundred and seventy miles to the north of Yambo. The whole month of January was spent in getting ready this flanking march by Feisal's forces.

The organisation of the expedition presented difficulties. Feisal had bitter memories of the rout of his troops at Nakhl-Mubarak and had no particular wish to exchange the security of Yambo for the very risky venture of a long march in the desert ending with an assault on a fortified position. Even when the English had managed to convince him, a number of problems remained to be resolved; the most thorny was the supply of food and water for the ten thousand men and the five thousand camels of his contingent along a desert track that was almost devoid of water points.

Wilson, Boyle and Lawrence decided to split the Emir's forces in two: the body of the partisans would take the track along the coast while the fleet, transporting five hundred Arab regulars and some companies of English marines, would steer a parallel course. Halfway between Yambo and Wejh, the ships would supply the column with food and with twenty tons of water. Once arrived before Wejh, the two groups would make a converging attack on the town by land and sea. This plan involved a minimum of synchronisation between the two detachments and it was hoped to bring it off despite the Orientals' repugnance for schedules. Two of Newcombe's lieutenants, Cox and Vickery, who had preceded their commander to Jidda, were posted one to each of the contingents.

Feisal's force moved off on the 14th of January, in a primitive array with all their banners flying, that was more in keeping with comic opera than with modern warfare. Lawrence admired their shimmering departure, and was later to describe with much talent the sumptuous appearance of the Arab army, but his romanticism never allowed him to forget more serious things; the column duly set in motion, he returned to Yambo to put the finishing touches to the preparations of the fleet and did not rejoin Feisal till the halfway halt between Yambo and Wejh.

The Arabs kept fairly good order; they were in good heart as on the way they had learnt that Abdullah had also commenced his advance and had captured a Turkish convoy carrying twenty thousand pieces of gold and that Ali and Zeid, who were accompanied by the French Lieutenant Lahlouh, had taken Bir Derwich and were patrolling as far as the gates of Medina; they had also heard the first rumours

of the English successes at Rafa and Maghdeba: three
thousand Turks killed or taken prisoner; the road to victory
seemed open, and the hope of future booty uplifted their
hearts. All along the route of the march the mere presence
of Feisal and his partisans constituted a living advertisement for the idea of Arab nationalism; the nomads and the
villagers of the rare habitations, amazed by this cavalcade
and by what they learnt of the generosity of the Emir and
of his English allies, came to join the Movement; this warlike
column became a vast propaganda stunt.

As far as Um Lejj, it was a triumphal march, but they
were soon in difficulty. Before long Vickery and Lawrence
were quarrelling: Lawrence did not like professional soldiers;
he was annoyed by the dispositions which his colleague
wanted to take without consulting him; he was irritated by
Vickery's attitude, as he retained the British officer's aloofness
towards the Arabs; it seems above all that, ever susceptible
to competition, he had scented a rival in this soldier from
the Sudan, who spoke Arabic fluently and who had a long
experience of desert warfare. He immediately sapped
Vickery's influence by ridiculing him in front of the Sherif's
men (the uniform of an Englishman, in fact, did seem rather
incongruous among a band of men in Oriental dress); Vickery
took offence, left Feisal's force, and rejoined Boyle's ships to
take part in the sea attack on Wejh.

Newcombe joined the Arabs a short while after they had
left Um Lejj. He had hardly landed when he borrowed a
horse and, enveloping his uniform in a burnous, rushed off
to find the Sherif's force. Newcombe was more of a diplomat
than Vickery and he had known Lawrence for a long time;
he abstained from interfering in his decisions and followed
the expedition as an observer.

The Arabs were now entering little-known territory, and
their progress was slowing down; on the 24th of January,
with the men already fatigued by an advance of nearly a
hundred and twenty-five miles in ten days, Feisal approached
Habban, fifty miles from Wejh, and he was two days behind
time. On the day when the combined attack should have
taken place, a rabble of exhausted men arrived on the beach
at Habban, desperately hoping to find the water promised

by Boyle. Luckily the *Hardinge* was there, and the whole night a mob of wretched soldiers quenched their thirst in the tanks which the English had brought ashore. In the distance could be heard the bombardment. Boyle, afraid that the Turks would receive reinforcements, had attacked without waiting for Feisal; the Emir had failed to keep the rendezvous.

The last stages of the march were extremely trying. It took them nearly three days to reach Wejh; the men finished the last miles with only a few pints of water to drink, and without any food, and the camels had not eaten for three days; after this strenuous effort, Feisal's troops found the town taken and already sacked by the five hundred of the Sherif's men who had with the marines and the guns of the fleet helped in taking it.

The disappointment was a hard one: Lawrence was learning to his cost the difficulty of managing these allies with whom he had decided to live and to conquer, while the victory went to Vickery, who with a few English officers[1] had led the Arab infantry in the attack in which they had conducted themselves with courage, and had left twenty dead on the ground. T. E. consoled himself with criticising the tactics of his colleague: he had suffered losses, while if he had waited for Feisal, he could have taken the town without losing anyone or causing damage to the poor houses. Feisal telegraphed his father that the Sherifs' troops had taken Wejh, and mentioned neither the English nor their ships.

The whole business was undertaken without Colonel Brémond being warned; his resentment was bitter, as one can imagine, but he concealed his rancour, remarking only that the French marines would have been happy to have taken part in the fight.

*   *   *

At the end of the month of January, Lawrence, full of new experiences and of plans for the future, returned to Cairo to get in touch again with the General Staff and the Arab Bureau. In the entourage of the Commander-in-Chief he had become very popular, and they now smiled on the officer who

[1] Of which one was Bray, who later wrote *Shifting Sands*.

had previously been so strongly criticised and vilified. More and more help was now given to the Hejaz; Sir Archibald Murray, discovering how difficult it was to pierce the Turkish front in Sinai, appreciated the help he was given by an insurrection which immobilised ten thousand enemy soldiers at Medina. He "realised with a sudden shock that more Turkish troops were fighting the Arabs than were fighting him, and began to remember how he had always favoured the Arab Revolt," wrote Lawrence in his memoirs, exaggerating certainly the size of the Ottoman forces which faced the Sherifs' troops, and underestimating those which were on the Palestine front.

Lawrence did not, however, have time to rest for long in Egypt, and had to get back rapidly to Wejh to fulfil the needs of his policy. Colonel Brémond had come to Cairo to propose a new plan of operations; faithful to his original theory, he advised attacking Aqaba with Anglo-French troops, the only port in the north of the Red Sea which remained in enemy hands; it was to go back to the first idea of a large-scale European landing in Arabia; once more Lawrence was opposed to the Colonel's plan, but learning that the latter was going to Wejh to try and persuade Newcombe, Wilson and Feisal, he took the first boat that came and reached the English base in order to undermine the Colonel's proposal in advance: Brémond found himself faced by spokesmen already warned, and could not make his ideas prevail.

The hostility of the two men was spontaneous and incurable. It arose from differences in character as well as in aims. There is something rather pathetic and very sad in the picture of Brémond, an old soldier and in many ways a remarkable one, profoundly attached to the interests of his country, seeing clearly the traps that were accumulated beneath his feet, and powerless to counteract the intrigues of his adversary. Outmanœuvred and humiliated, he could do nothing for lack of support. We have seen that in December 1916 the English had obtained for him a severe reprimand; on the 13th of May, 1917, the offensive was renewed and the British Ambassador in Paris made threatening demands for the immediate recall of Colonel Brémond's mission "as its members had no sympathy with the Arab cause".[1] Meanwhile Brémond was kept on at Jidda, but without material means or the effective support of his government, and it was no longer possible for him seriously to thwart Lawrence's policy.

* * *

At Wejh, the Arab forces were organised in great style. Arms, supplies and money were abundant. A radio station, guns and machine-gun carriers had been landed. A choice recruit had joined Feisal: Jaafar Pasha, a Turkish colonel of Baghdad origin. German trained, and of astonishing physical courage, this Falstaff was a terrible fighter. He had commanded the Ottoman cavalry against the English in the Senussi war; taken prisoner, he had escaped from the citadel in Cairo with the aid of a rope made from his sheets, but it had given way beneath the enormous weight of the fugitive, who was recaptured with a sprained ankle in the drains of the prison. As soon as he learnt of the Arab Revolt, he asked to be allowed to join Feisal; the Emir gave him the task of organising the regular army, which he performed with energy and intelligence, but in the Prussian way, with considerable use of the stick and boot.

Other adherents appeared: the Sheiks of the tribes of Northern Arabia, impressed by the successes, driven by their hereditary hatred of the Turks and drawn also by the English gold which was circulating all round the Sherifs' Movement, came in increasingly large numbers to join in the Revolt. One day a new and picturesque partisan appeared in Feisal's camp: Auda, Sheik of the Abu Tayis clan of the Howeitat tribe, famous for his pillagings and fights in Northern Arabia. Auda represented the real Bedouin tradition, older than Islam, and in which banditry was mingled with the pastoral life. For nearly half a century he had raided the sedentary dwellers on the borders of the Syrian desert and fought the other nomads from Aqaba to the Upper Euphrates, killing men, stealing flocks and murdering Turkish policemen. His life was a saga that was told in the tents like that of Antar.

When the news went round the Emir's camp that Auda Abu Tayi was joining the Movement, it provoked an intense

[1] Brémond, p. 137.

excitement. The Sheik prepared his entry, arrived almost alone, drew aside the flap of Feisal's tent and "boomed salutations to Our Lord the Commander of the Faithful". The Emir, overjoyed at being able to count among his partisans a personality of such prestige among the Bedouins, welcomed him with open arms, and heaped presents upon him; Lawrence applied himself to his conquest; he was to take him for a guide and companion on some of his most hazardous exploits.

In the course of the long negotiations destined to win new adherents to the Movement, Lawrence sat in at the palavers, gave advice and intervened. These tribal politics required much astuteness and a thorough knowledge of the country; to effect a common unity of action among clans who for centuries, divided by vendettas and inexpiable hatreds, had warred against each other, was the most delicate of problems; Lawrence found an infinite pleasure in handling these primitives and in playing with their elemental and contradictory feelings, hatred of the oppressor, distrust of the Christian, the ancient quarrels between the clans and the simple thirst for gold. In these gymnastics he acquired an extraordinary agility. His rôle did nothing but grow, as he had managed to bring his influence to bear not only on the Arabs, but also on the English command, and in particular on Newcombe, in charge of all operations in Arabia. Lawrence, we know, had known this officer before the war, and had met him again on the Sinai reconnaissance of 1913; he had next found himself with him in the Headquarters in Cairo. Newcombe, enthusiastic and adventurous, was a sort of Don Quixote who, unable to support the life of an office in Egypt, had had himself posted to a fighting unit at Gallipoli and then to one in France, where he had been wounded. In the Hejaz, he was keen to get things moving, and he was able to allow initiative to his subordinates; he gave Lawrence a very free hand with Feisal, and little by little the Emir's detachment, ably but inconspicuously directed by T.E., became the king-piece of the English chessboard in Arabia.

On the other hand the position was sometimes difficult for the British. The success of the operation at Wejh had turned the Arabs' heads; drunk with pride, they believed that they were capable of winning the war alone and of taking Medina and Damascus themselves. In their relations with their two advisers they became more and more touchy, xenophobic, anti-European and anti-Christian, while their demand for gold did nothing but increase.

The strange composition of the Sherifs' forces made the task of the English more complicated. The nomads and the tribesmen like the sheiks remained elusive and nourished an eternal distrust of the European, although they could still be won by the lure of gold. The Arabs brought up among the Turkish élite were far more difficult to utilise. Used to meeting with Westerners, they could easily follow their allies' deeper thoughts, and could perfectly well see the interested ambitions that lay behind their assistance. They knew enough history to remember that colonialists from Caesar to Cortes and Lyautey have always conquered the countries which they coveted with the aid of the inhabitants themselves, by astutely setting them against their fellow countrymen; they could not reasonably believe that they were closer to the English or the French than to the Turks, their co-religionaries, and darkly felt that they were being used; they would have liked to have finished their quarrel with the Turks alone, as something between Moslems, without the presence of the infidels; their inability to do so filled them with bitterness.

Every European success—one could say every Christian success—annoyed them: when General Maud took Baghdad, this victory caused general resentment in the Hejaz and old Hussein said in public: "It is the fault of the Touranians. To lose the city that was the cradle of the Khalifs and the Centre of the Luminaries that have lit the world is a great pity",[1] and some members of the Grand Sherif's and the Emirs' entourages spoke of the Turkish soldiers killed in the battles of Sinai and even of Arabia as martyrs of the faith. Between the partisans of the Movement, men who were unalike, susceptible, ambitious and greedy, it was difficult to maintain good relations. The big chiefs were jealous of each other; the nomads and the city dwellers detested each other; the Bedouins joined the Revolt, pocketed the gold, swept off the arms and then disappeared to sell the rifles and food to

[1] Brémond, p. 119.

the nearest Turkish post; the only reliable body in Feisal's army was composed of the Ageyls, a camel corps of six or seven hundred mercenaries, who, recruited in the oases of central Arabia for the Turkish army, had been brought over *en bloc* to the Revolt by a sheik of the Nejd. Far from their homes, and surrounded by strangers, the Ageyls could not desert but they were difficult to lead. One day, when treated with an excess of brutality by their chiefs, they rebelled, took the tent of their commander by assault, knocking out his servants, and then rushed for the Ateiba nomads. When Feisal's guard had succeeded in stopping the brawl, thirty dead and wounded were brought back into camp.

Lawrence, indefatigable, preached tact and patience both to the Arab chief and to his fellow countrymen, and calmed the conflict. No doubt also he gave Feisal assurances which he had no right to give, promising the Emir and his partisans complete independence for all Arab countries, with no foreign colonisation, protectorate or even allegiance, contrary to all the arrangements of Paris and London. Later, these promises were to be kept neither in Syria nor in Mesopotamia, and in consequence Lawrence conceived a profound grievance against his own country and especially against France, but had he the right to make such engagements himself, or to commit his country to them?

The Meeting with the Minotaur

AT the beginning of March, the general situation took a new turn, and urgent messages from Cairo pressed the Arab army for a more effective effort. A signal from Enver Pasha and the German General Staff in Constantinople had been intercepted in Egypt ordering Fakri Pasha to evacuate Medina and to bring his troops back to Syria. At least, this was what an incompletely deciphered despatch seemed to say. Murray, who was pushing his troops painfully on towards Gaza, was afraid that he would find the Turks who faced him reinforced by two divisions, and demanded that an attack be made on Medina to immobilise and if possible capture the Turkish troops defending it. If the town could not be taken, traffic on the Hejaz railway, the only rapid means of evacuation for both troops and equipment, must at least be brought to a stop.

Already the English had started to blow up the line, and Garland had finally achieved the ambitions of his dreams and blown up a train. Newcombe on the 4th of March had attacked the station at Dar el Hamra, taken the place by capturing the Turkish garrison, and destroyed one and a half miles of track and several locomotives, but the Turks had rapidly repaired the breaches thus made and movement between Medina and Syria had not been interrupted for long.

It was decided to spread out the Arab contingents along the line. A detachment of Feisal's troops were sent off towards Fagair, halfway between Medina and Medain Salih, and Lawrence was sent in haste to visit Abdullah in order to shake the Emir out of his apathy; he was based on Abu Markha, on the Wadi Aiss where he was confined in inexplicable inaction, despite the means that had been put at his disposal.

Abu Markha was to the interior of the coastal chain, one hundred and twenty-five miles to the south-east of Wejh and about forty miles from the sea. To reach this place required a ride of five or six days by camel through a chaotic and desolate country. Lawrence left on the 9th of March with an escort composed of Bedouin guides and a few Ageyl mercenaries, in all a dozen men; he was sick, suffering from fever and dysentery, and he was not keen on this mission, as it took him away from Feisal and obliged him to enter into relations with Abdullah whom he did not like.

The camel men set out at night, rested a few hours before dawn, and then marched all day. Their caravan followed an interminable network of dried-up wadis, through gorges so narrow that they had to dismount and drag their camels through by the bridle; the beasts stumbled, groaned and toiled up the slopes, and the countryside had a sinister appearance: screes of black lava alternated with high cliffs of a sombre red; on the heights there fell a freezing rain, and in the valleys they were stifled.

To add to the difficulties of the journey quarrelling broke out in the little band; Bedouins and Ageyls bickered with each other, divided by obscure personal antipathies, and Lawrence, lost in this solitude with this handful of primitives, was unable to restore peace among them. When they halted in the evening, he was at the end of his tether: he lay down in a rocky crevice and tried to sleep while the Arabs unsaddled the camels and prepared a meal. Suddenly he heard a shot; he rose and found one of the Ageyls stretched on the ground with a bullet through his head; a Moor[1] of the escort had just murdered him as the result of a quarrel; intense excitement and disorder reigned, and he felt that all these men were about to kill each other. The Englishman had to pursue the guilty party, and hold a summary council of war. The Arabs demanded immediate death for the murderer, and Lawrence as the leader of the group had to execute the sentence. He took the wretched man behind a rock and shot him with his revolver. He has described these nightmare moments, the supplications, the shots at point-blank range, and the Moor covered in blood writhing at his feet, a sordid and frightful scene.

[1] These Moors are descended from the Algerians, who, after the defeat of Abd-el-Kader, followed the Emir into exile in Syria. They had villages to the south-west of the Jebel-Druze and they had retained their North African customs.

The caravans had still three days to march before reaching Abdullah's camp, and Lawrence moved like an automaton; at Abu Markha he collapsed, so ill that he lost hope of living through the adventure. Passing from insomnia to nightmare, he was haunted by frightful dreams. "The illness, however, had stimulated my ordinarily sluggish fancy, which ran riot this night in dreams, of wandering naked for a dark eternity over interminable lava (like scrambled egg gone iron-blue and very wrong), sharp as insect-bites underfoot; and with some horror, perhaps a dead Moor, always climbing after us."

* * *

In the depths of the slimy pits in which he was floundering, Lawrence retained his lucidity; compelled to physical inaction, he turned over once more the whole Arab business in his mind. He states in his memoirs that it was at Abu Markha, lying on a sordid bed beneath a Bedouin tent, running with sweat and tormented with flies, with fever, dysentery and boils, that he elaborated the whole strategy and policy that was to guide him in the future campaign. But his solitary reflections must have led him well beyond theoretical considerations. In the course of the lugubrious journey he had known war in all its details and horror, real war, with its physical anguish, its slaughter and its corpses. Every front-line soldier one day experiences this shock when he first comes in direct bodily contact with certain realities. It is the meeting of Theseus with the Minotaur: the blood and the skin of the monster have a smell which a civilised man does not forget for the rest of his life.

* * *

Lawrence took ten days to get back on his feet. Almost before he had recovered, he pressed on indefatigably, wishing to end as soon as possible his mission with Abdullah. He hated this cynical but far-seeing Oriental and the evil glint which he saw in his eyes. He feared the influence of the French with the Emir: Prost, Abdullah's former tutor in Constantinople, whom Brémond had discovered as a sergeant in an Oriental unit, was with him. The brave man, who spoke Turkish and Arabic fluently, was treated in the intimate entourage of his old pupil as a member of the Sherif's family, and had perhaps introduced Brémond's dangerous ideas to the camp of Abu Markha. Captain Raho was also there, a French Moslem officer who won the admiration of the Arabs by his courage and with the fine red Spahi tunic which he wore, like Bournazel, in camp as well as in battle. Raho had taken part in the capture of the Turkish convoy near Abu Naam and had charged at the head of the Bedouins (he was to be killed in 1918 in the Arab ranks). His prestige was high in Abdullah's camp, which was not pleasant for Lawrence.

T.E. decided to attempt some sabotage raids on the railway. As early as the 26th of March he left with Raho and a few nomads to attack the station of Aba el Naam, a village one hundred miles to the north of Medina, which was known to be held by a Turkish battalion. Six or eight hundred Ateiba nomads, under the command of Shakir, Abdullah's cousin, were to take part in the expedition and to join up with Lawrence close to the objective.

After three days of hard marches by camel, Lawrence reached this railway, about which he had thought so much, for the first time. The raid was in fact only half successful. Shakir was a fine warrior, but he had only been able to bring with him three hundred nomads, who in any case had little heart for fighting. Lawrence, Raho and their escort did nearly all the work. The shells from the gun which they had brought set fire to the station and to the trucks that were parked in it; the Arabs took about thirty prisoners, but did not have the courage to carry the position. A mine damaged a locomotive and cut the track, interrupting traffic for several days. The raiders suffered no losses.

Two days later Lawrence carried out another raid: a terrible storm almost prevented the exploit; however, he reached the railway, and succeeded in doing considerable damage and in blowing up a train. T.E. had learnt the techniques of demolition from Garland; a born tinkerer, he handled mines, detonators, Bickford fuses and every sort of lethal and complicated machine with skill; he was later to become a virtuoso in this difficult and dangerous art.

In the middle of April, he left Abdullah's camp and went back to Feisal at Wejh.

Strategy

WHILE he was sick in the camp at Abu Markha, and in very poor condition, Lawrence, as has been said, reflected at length over the very particular conditions of the war in Arabia, and had elaborated the principles that were to guide him in the course of future operations.

He has devoted a dozen pages in the *Seven Pillars* to an exposition of the fruit of his meditations. It is full of special pleading, obviously written after the event, and in the light of facts which he could not have known at the time. The following extract is interesting and contains the essence of Lawrence's ideas on partisan warfare; it is a pity that sophisms and a little pathos should have been allowed to creep into theories of great subtlety.

His conclusions were, broadly speaking as follows:

The war in Arabia was not properly speaking a war, but a guerilla campaign, a political and psychological fact to which the theories of a Jomini, a Clausewitz or a Foch could not be applied.

The strength of guerilla actions is that they should remain guerilla actions and not try to develop into a regular war; they must remain an "influence, an idea, a thing intangible, invulnerable without front or back, drifting about like a gas".

With propaganda and money they must win over every Arab country to the Revolt, create a vast 'maquis' and make life impossible for the Turks. The protection of their lines of communication alone, in these vast desert regions, would absorb all their fighting strength; to live surrounded with hostility would undermine their morale more than a defeat on the ground. The Turks despised the lives of their soldiers, but they were short of supplies. It was therefore at the Turkish supplies and not at their men that they must strike. The taking of Medina would serve no useful purpose: on the contrary, to immobilise fifteen thousand Turks invested in

Medina and assigned to guarding the Hejaz railway line would be a strategic success. They must have the moral courage to dispense with a more spectacular victory in order to obtain less flattering but more important results. They must strive to keep Fakri Pasha shut up in the city of the Prophet, harass the line just sufficiently to cut off his retreat and to oblige him to make constant demands on Turkish resources in men and above all in equipment.

When the demoralised Turks evacuated the Arab countries, the Arabs would be free, and the war would be won. And this victory must be gained without loss, for "The Arabs fought for freedom and that was a pleasure to be tasted only by a man alive".

(As if a man who fights for liberty or anything else can do so without endangering his life).

In short, to fight a battle in Arabia would be a mistake, since the ammunition expended by the enemy would be the only benefit to be obtained from it.

*   *   *

There were some very sound ideas in this plan, but others that were extremely questionable. Its principal defect was that it was based solely on the interests of Arab nationalism with which Lawrence was obsessed, and that it neglected those of the Allies.

Even from the point of view of the Arabs, the argument had its weaknesses. To inflate men with a taste for independence has never given them independence, which cannot be won without a struggle. The hypothesis that the Turks would evacuate their country did not guarantee the Arabs their freedom, because if the central empires, of which the Ottomans formed a part, were to win the war in the final event, Turkish troops would before long return to Arabia to reestablish their domination with the customary reprisals; the Arabs were therefore solidly bound to the allied bloc; the day of the hoped-for victory, they would be rewarded in the measure of their sacrifices to the common achievement; to advise them to take a purely personal and egotistical attitude was to risk running counter to their own interests.

It was not even certain that it was such a good thing to

contain the Turks in Medina. From the point of view of
world propaganda and of propaganda in Islam, particularly
in Arabia, it was of extreme importance to the Ottoman
government to be able to say that they still held one of the
Holy Cities and were threatening the other. In hanging on
to Medina, Fakri Pasha was not perhaps quite as stupid as
Lawrence made out. Blindly drawn towards Damascus for
sentimental reasons, T.E. wished to ignore the prestige value
of the Prophet's city in the Moslem world.

Seen from the angle of the Allies, Lawrence's ideas were
even more questionable. Certainly his strategy would immobilise two or three divisions which, were it not for him, would
have gone to reinforce the Sinai front; but was it not possible
to do much better?

An allied force landed at Wejh or at Aqaba, as many
English officers suggested, in agreement with Brémond, could
by operating against the line between Maan and Medain
Salih completely cut off Fakri's retreat (thus obtaining the
desired neutralisation of his fifteen thousand men); and it
could then strike north, and take the Turks that were barring
the route to Gaza and Palestine in the rear. Such a plan
would no doubt have saved the lives of many English soldiers
who fell in the course of this campaign. It is difficult to say
whether this operation would have been possible in view of
the difficulty of the terrain and the fighting strength at the
disposal of the Allies, but it was put forward over and over
again and each time Lawrence opposed it fiercely. It would
have meant the end of the liberation of the Arabs by the
Arabs, of the hope which he cherished of entering Damascus
personally as a conqueror, the end, at all events, of his pre-
ponderating influence in Arabia.

One English officer, Bray, who took part in the first part
of the campaign, has said, with some severity, that throughout this war the chances of allied victory were compromised
by "the queer idiosyncrasies of an individual".[1]

[1] Bray, Shifting Sands, p. 145.

Aqaba

NEWCOMBE was bounding with energy. He wished to gain as much benefit as possible for the allied cause from this Arab Revolt which had already cost England more than half a million pounds, and tons of arms, munitions and supplies. The Emirs' inertia and their prevarications exasperated him: unable to keep a promise or to stick to a schedule, these Orientals infuriated the soldier. He knew that Medina was being besieged with more than indolence by the Arabs, who, when they were not organising them themselves, permitted supply caravans to enter the town. It was necessary to neutralise Fakri Pasha completely, and if possible to seize the Holy City, a severe blow to the prestige of the Ottomans.

He decided to carry out a large-scale operation and to bring up the whole Sherifs' army, supported by as many of the Egyptians as the High Command might be willing to furnish him with, against Medain Salih, two hundred miles to the north of Medina; once this little town and its station were taken, Fakri would be cut off from his bases and would have to surrender quickly.

This project was contrary to Lawrence's ideas which we have just outlined, and he energetically opposed it. But Newcombe like his colleagues did not find his subtleties easy to follow. They had orders to act and they had at all costs to 'do something'.

Lawrence seethed with bitterness and irritation: he was back in the rank and file, his advice on strategy and policy was being ignored; these plans had to be thwarted. He decided to do it by bringing off a spectacular success by himself and in his own way. Since Newcombe wished to mount a grand attack on Medain Salih whose success was in doubt and whose object was, in his opinion, debatable, he would attempt, alone, with a handful of nomads, to seize the fortified port of Aqaba, thus demonstrating in a striking fashion the value of his methods compared with those of his orthodox colleagues who were professional officers. He obtained agreement from his superior officers, wrote to Clayton to explain the project, and set off on the adventure.

*   *   *

Lawrence's plan was as follows: to swoop across the desert with a few partisans, penetrate to the north-west as far as Wadi Sirhan, a long succession of oases and pasture lands which link the Arabian Peninsula with Southern Syria, and preach rebellion among the tribes; then striking west with the warriors which he had raised in the locality, take Aqaba in rear and so seize the last port that remained in Turkish hands in the north of the Red Sea. If the operation was successful the Arabian army would be in contact with the army of Egypt, and the Turkish flank would be turned more and more effectively: the cumbersome operation planned by Newcombe would take second place, and in the direction of the Movement Lawrence would take the first, thrusting aside all opposition and all rivalry.

It is surprising to find a subaltern taking such initiative and launching himself on an independent expedition on the eve of the operations which his superiors were preparing. However, all the witnesses are agreed on this point, and they prove that things did happen as they have just been related. Colonel Newcombe who had Lawrence under his command at the time has said so himself.[1] During this period, he said, the leaders of the English mission were still groping in the dark, each one of them doing his best in his own sphere. Everyone had noticed the extraordinary ascendancy which T. E. had gained over Feisal, and they were pleased to see him decide the Sherifs' men on effective action; they allowed their comrade to operate on his own so long as he only used native units and did not draw on the still limited resources of the allied base. Colonel Newcombe has confirmed that the Aqaba exploit was entirely conceived by Lawrence who was its real leader and animating spirit, although for reasons of diplomacy that are understandable the official command was left in the hands of the Arab chieftains.

[1] In a personal conversation in 1954.

Lawrence always prepared his enterprises with particular care. He was assured of the collaboration of two men, the bravest and the most intelligent of the Arab army, Auda and Sherif Nasir. Auda had an almost unique knowledge of the desert acquired in long years of brigandage and freebooting, a part of the present journey lay across the territory of the Howeitat tribes of which he was the sheik, and he had a reputation for courage and loyalty which meant that he could be counted on in a hazardous raid of this sort. As for Sherif Nasir, he was one of the most ardent partisans of the Revolt, for which he had fought since its inception. A man of twenty-eight, he was a grand seigneur of Medina, rich, cultivated, endowed with the good things of this world and slightly decadent; his faith in Arab nationalism had thrown him into the adventure, to which he gave himself body and soul; a cousin of Feisal's, the latter delegated all his powers to him when it came to fighting; Nasir would probably have made the warrior chief that the Movement required, if Feisal and Lawrence had not, each in his own domain, stifled him. The rare portraits which we have of him show us a face immersed in an unkempt beard, with heavy lips and burning eyes that dominate a rather short body. Throughout the war he succeeded in everything that he undertook.

Lawrence and Nasir were close friends. The two men were of the same age and the Englishman perceived some strange parallels between his own destiny and the Sherif's, more civilised than his Bedouins and compelled by the exigencies of war to live rough among nomads and share their sordid and wretched life. Thrown into a primitive world and submitting to the miseries and the absurd violences of war, the Medina aristocrat and the Oxford graduate knew that they alone saw the same side of things, and secretly shared amidst the soldiers their moods of sardonic humour and of depression.

The detachment, apart from Lawrence, Auda and Nasir, included Nezib el-Bekri and Zeki, two Syrians whom Feisal sent to the Druze country and central Syria to preach the Revolt, and thirty camel-men armed only with rifles. For provisions on the route each man carried no more than forty-five pounds of flour, as they reckoned on living off the country; in his saddle-bags, Lawrence carried twenty thousand sovereigns (three hundred pounds of gold), to help spread propaganda among the tribes. This sum, he stated, had been given to him by Feisal and was drawn from the allocation which the Emir received personally from the English.

The expedition left Wejh on the 9th of May, 1917, and headed north; it took ten days to reach the railway line at Dizad, two hundred miles to the north of Medina, and the first trial showed Lawrence the effort he would have to make and how difficult would be his rôle as the occult leader of the expedition. Still unfit after the illness from which he had suffered in Abdullah's camp, he had without weakening to do the same day's march as the Bedouins; he was dressed only in Arab clothes, was shod with sandals, slept on the ground in the promiscuity, the dirt, the immodesty and the fleas of a handful of semi-savages; on the trip he had to keep the peace between men who were jealous of their prestige, and secretly keep the fickle Orientals to the route on which he had decided.

The followers of Nasir, Auda and Nezib formed distinct and captious groups and Auda was particularly difficult to control. The old warhorse, whose assistance was indispensable to the success of the operation, had faults and odd characteristics that made life around him complicated; he was eager for gain, sensitive, immensely vain of his reputation as a raider, garrulous and a scandal-monger; his slanders never ceased to make him enemies; Lawrence had great difficulty in maintaining good relations between this battle-scarred warrior and Nasir, the disdainful aristocrat, the official head of the expedition.

However, this tough life, this perpetual tension, the obligation for incessant scheming and intrigue, delighted Lawrence; he became an Arab warrior, a guerilla leader, and experienced such elemental sensations and sentiments as might have the heroes of legend, Jason or Ulysses, thrown into far-off adventures in unknown countries. The danger, the uncertainty of the morrow, had as counterpart an independence and possibilities until then undreamt of: one day during a halt close to a tribal camp, two young men came to look for him and begged him to take them into his service; they were called Daud and Farraj and "they were an instance of the Eastern boy and boy affection which the segregation of women made inevitable". Lawrence was captivated by this couple: Daud was vigorous and virile, "Farraj: a beautiful, soft-framed girlish creature, with innocent, smooth face and swimming eyes". Since he was an Arab chieftain why should he not have slaves like Auda and Nasir, beings who belonged body and soul to their master, who could be ordered to any service, whipped, and put to death in accordance with the laws of a brutal and primitive society? He attached the two ephebes to himself and they became the first nucleus of that guard which he was to constitute later. Both were to die in his service.

On the 19th of May the little band reached the railway line; between Turkish patrols they crossed it, after having blown up some rails and knocked down some telegraph poles; the most dangerous part of the route remained to be covered, nearly two hundred miles across the Nefudh, the great desert of the north. Henceforward they were entirely in Auda's hands, a specialist in marches through these solitudes. The old nomad growled that "Their business was to reach Arfaja alive", as he took his caravan across this frightful desolation.

The men and the camels dragged themselves along the interminable days' marches, exhausted, thirsty, burnt-up by the sun, crossing in summer one of the hottest and most arid spots in the world. At the end of the trip they had to live for two and a half days without water before they found a well and in a storm of dry burning wind. On the penultimate day's march, Lawrence noticed the absence of one of his servants; his camel was in the caravan, but the man must have fallen behind. "Gassim . . . a gap-toothed, grumbling fellow, skrimshank in all our marches, bad-tempered, suspicious, brutal . . . ", but he was part of Lawrence's retinue, and in accordance with the imperious law of the desert was his responsibility; the Englishman went back down the track along which they had just come, found Gassim half mad with thirst and fear, and brought him into camp.

And on this route nature was not alone in being hostile: at the end of a day's march, whilst Lawrence and his companions were resting round the camp fire, a volley of bullets struck the band and an Ageyl, killed by a ball through his head, fell face down in the dust. "Mohammed with his massive foot thrust a wave of sand over the fire and in the quick blinding darkness we rolled behind banks of tamarisk and scattered to get rifles. . . . " But the marauders, having struck their blow, disappeared into the darkness.

The 27th of May, the expedition came upon the first tents of Auda's tribes, near Arfaja, on the edge of the Sirhan. The few days' rest which Lawrence and his Arabs took among the Bedouins only brought them a relative relaxation. The Sirhan, after the dried-up air of the desert, seemed unhealthy and stifling, a sort of curse seemed to hang over the country, the snakes, vipers, cobras and black serpents infested their encampments, the men suffered from fever and were tormented by flies. The hospitality of the Abu Tayis was as painful to bear as the abstinence of the march. Auda's contributives, seeing the rain of gold, of which the whole desert now dreamt, at last falling on them, believed that they had to entertain their guests with perpetual and pantagruelic carousings. Every day, Nasir, the two Syrians and the Englishman went to take an enormous meal in some Bedouin tent. Sickened by the terrible squalor, they had for reasons of diplomacy and to the extent of nausea to mingle with the throng of captious and half-starved nomads, and to take their share of the greasy piles of rice and meat.

Politics were not in abeyance. Lawrence had, through the intermediary of Auda, made contact with Nuri Shaalan, the prudent sheik of the Sirhan, who refused to take sides between the Turks and the Revolt. It was at least necessary to buy his inaction and six thousand pounds in gold were sent to him. He could, it was discreetly made known to him, remain officially on the side of the Ottomans and even advise them of the passage of the Sherif's men, but they counted on his benevolent neutrality.

The whole Sirhan was in a fever, the warriors were rushing in to join the Movement, and from this success was born a new difficulty: the Sirhan is halfway between Damascus and Aqaba, and the two Syrians, Nezib and Zeki, filled with enthusiasm, asked Lawrence to make an attempt on Damascus, since the whole country welcomed them so freely.

From all the evidence, the idea of striking with ill-armed nomads at the principal concentration point of the Turkish
armies was absurd, but "Nezib was towering above geography
and beyond tactics and only sordid means would bring him
down. So I went to Auda and said that with the new objective
cash and credit would go to Nuri Shaalan and not to him. I
went to Nasir . . . fanning high the too easily-lit jealousy between a Sherif and a Damascene. . . . " Once more Lawrence
imposed his will by oblique methods. The two Syrians left the
column and went off to stir up political agitation around
Damascus, while the expedition continued on its way.

* * *

Auda and Nasir pitched their tents to the south-west of
the Sirhan and engaged in an active propaganda among the
tribes: for the expedition there was a moment's respite, and
Lawrence decided to profit from it by going with but one or
two companions to see what was happening in Syria, to sound
the state of mind of the peoples, and get into touch again
with the agents which he had in this country (5th of June to
19th of June, 1917).

Lawrence has only spoken with the utmost reticence of this
solitary trip; in the *Seven Pillars* he does no more than mention it and leaves in the narration of facts and movements
a hiatus of fifteen days. He says briefly: "I undertook this
long dangerous ride, in which to see the more important of
Feisal's secret friends and to study key-positions of our future
campaigns: but the results were incommensurate with the
risks. . . ." In his correspondence with his biographers, fifteen
years later, he remains equally mysterious, merely indicating
that he went as far as Baalbeck, stayed in the suburbs of
Damascus and saw a certain number of important individuals associated with the Arab Revolt, talked even with the
military commandant of Damascus, Ali Reza Pasha, who had
been won over to the Movement, and that on the way he blew
up several structures well to the north of the Dead Sea. He
has also told how in the course of this tour, while sleeping
in the tent of a chieftain of the Beni-Sakhr, close to Ziza, he
was betrayed by one of the sheiks whom he believed he could
trust, and only escaped from the affair by a miracle. But on

the whole he has said quite distinctly that what he did was
only his concern, and that he did not hold with spoiling the
cherished memories of adventures, of politics and perhaps
of love, in revealing them to the public gaze. Thus one can
only guess at the objects of an expedition which was probably
one of the most hazardous and most romantic that Lawrence
made, and imagine, although there is nothing to prove it,
that he undertook it, at least in part, in order to see again
after long months of separation an unknown and mysterious
friend, a loved one or a political agent, whom he had left in
Syria, and of whom he has spoken on several occasions, as
much in the *Seven Pillars* as in his personal letters.

*　　*　　*

Towards the 19th of June, Lawrence and the Arabs started
on the second part of their enterprise, the march to Aqaba.
From now on the column represented an imposing force:
more than five hundred men mounted on fleet camels had
joined the expedition and they dreamed of fights and sumptuous lootings.

For several weeks the Arab detachment had created havoc
behind the Turkish lines. Lawrence reckoned that his calculations were correct and that a swift and mobile Bedouin
camel force, accustomed to the desert, could operate on the
flank of the Ottoman army, like ships in the days of sail,
attacking an enemy coast where and when they liked, and
having struck their blow, disappear into the blue.

The whole country was on the alert: the Turks were
unable to strike at an enemy who seemed endowed with
diabolical ubiquity; they panicked, blindly sent out patrols
to comb the country, reinforced the guard on the railway line
and went to the extent of destroying the wells on the great
trunk routes to prevent the movements of these elusive
adversaries.

Now completely adapted to the Bedouin life, Lawrence, in
order to complete the discountenancing of the Turks, organised with Zaal, Auda's nephew, a raiding party several hundred miles to the north, between Amman and Deraa, blew up
a train, and harassed the enemy posts; this demonstration in
the north-east distracted the Turks' attention from the Aqaba

sector. At the end of the expedition, as they returned towards
Bair, the Arabs passed within easy distance of the station
at Atwi. The unsuspecting Turks were cooking around their
trenches: "Zaal ... crept along, ... he took slow aim at the
coffee-sipping officers and officials in shaded chairs outside the
ticket office. As he pressed the trigger the report overtook
the crash of the bullet against the stone wall, while the fattest
man bowed slowly in his chair and sank to the ground under
the frozen stare of his fellows", and the shrieking Arabs threw
themselves into the assault.

The Turks managed to barricade themselves in and held
out in one of the buildings of the station, but the Arabs took
the other, pillaged it and set it on fire. Lawrence and Zaal
came back to Bair without having been worried; above their
rags the Bedouins wore Turkish uniforms, and their saddle
bags were full to bursting with the spoils of the enemy.

*   *   *

On the 28th of June the column marched westwards. Between the desert plain through which winds the railway line,
and the Gulf of Aqaba, there rises a range of arid mountains,
the Jebel Shtar. This incoherent chaos of sombre rocks is
crossed by a few rare defiles; they are narrow, steep and easy
to defend, the easiest way through being the old Roman road
from the Red Sea to Antioch which slips north and south
from Maan to Guweira, between two folds of the mountain,
and then goes from Guweira to the sea by way of Wadi
Itm. At Aba el Lissan, at the entrance to the canyon, the
Turks had installed a fortified post which commanded the
route. To march on Aqaba they had to force a way through
here.

The column had great difficulty in crossing the desert
which separated it from the railway line. The Turks had
mined and blown up the wells of Jefer and men and beasts
were in danger of dying of thirst; however, they crossed the
line a few miles to the south of Maan on the 1st of July, but
they had still to cross the mountains.

Auda had sent ahead a camel party to surprise the post
which commanded the water point at Aba el Lissan. The
operation had succeeded and the Arabs had massacred the

few defenders of the blockhouse, but on the advance they learnt that the Turks had been alerted, had sent reinforcements, and that a battalion and a section of artillery were holding the entrance to the defile; without fighting the Arabs could not take the route to the sea.

Auda put himself at the head of the column, singing war songs, "and the men joined in from time to time, with the greatness, the catch at heart of an army moving into battle". Perched on his saddle, Lawrence was delighted to be with this savage band.

At dawn on the following day the Arabs were within sight of the enemy; the Turks had halted in the gorge of Aba el Lissan. Exhausted by the July heat, and demoralised by the sight of the corpses which they had found around the post of Fuweilah, they had neglected to post sentries. Silently the Bedouins lined the circle of mountains around the water point, and then from the shelter of the rocks started to shoot down on the Turks.

This lasted the whole morning. The men were fighting in the heat of a furnace, burnt by the rocks against which they were leaning, without water, without rest, throughout the long hours of battle. The enemy, caught in this infernal ring, turned vainly to find a way out, spraying the crests ineffectively with shrapnel from their two guns. At the beginning of the afternoon, Lawrence and Nasir, exhausted, lay down in the shade of a small gulley in which oozed a little muddy water; Auda joined the two men and seeing them sprawling on the ground, asked with an aggressive, sneering laugh:

"Well, how is it with the Howeitat?"

"By God indeed", Lawrence replied, "they shoot a lot and hit a little."

Auda, furious, snatched off his headcloth, tore it up and threw it to the ground; then climbing back up the hill, he rallied his men and shouted over his shoulder to his two companions: "Get your camel if you want to see the old man's work".

Nasir and Lawrence ran to get into the saddle, and grouped their warriors behind the rocks a few hundred yards from the Turks. "Yells and shots poured up in a sudden torrent from beyond the crest". Auda at the head of fifty men was charging

the exhausted Turks. Nasir in his turn precipitated his four
hundred camels at the head of the breaking enemy column.
Lawrence drove his camel wildly towards the enemy, yelling
and "shooting, with a pistol of course, for only an expert
could use a rifle from such plunging beasts". Suddenly he
felt his camel collapse beneath him, and fell to the ground
knocked senseless by the shock. He had just blown out the
brains of his mount with his own pistol.

When he recovered consciousness, the battle was over.
Three hundred Turks were dead, and Nasir had snatched a
hundred and sixty prisoners, who were nearly all wounded,
from the fury of the Bedouins. Very few of the enemy had
been able to flee; only a few gunners, some mounted men
and some officers had forced their way through the circle of
Arabs. Two Bedouins, only, had fallen in the fight.

* * *

Aba el Lissan was taken, the road to Aqaba was clear. The
Arabs entrusted most of the prisoners to the nomads with
orders to bring them to Aqaba, and then hastened through
the defile to the gorges of the Wadi Itm that were to take
them to the Red Sea. The fighting strength of the column
had more than doubled; two thousand Bedouins had come
in from all over the desert.

The adventure ended in triumph. Only three hundred
Turks held Aqaba, and all their defence works faced towards
the sea; they were cut off from their base and had only a few
days' food-supply. An assault was easy enough against an
enemy so completely demoralised, but Lawrence wished to
end the operation with the smallest possible loss and avoid
a general massacre of the defenders; after a few hours of
parley, the Turks surrendered. Aqaba was taken on the 6th
of July, two months from the day that Lawrence left Wejh.

* * *

Hardly had he achieved his goal than Lawrence put the
position which he had just conquered in a state of defence.
He had some very definite views about Aqaba, and wished
to make it the new base for Feisal's army. Auda and his
Bedouin partisans were immediately sent off to the east to

hold the mouths of the steep, easily defended gorges at
Delagha, Batra and Guweira, and in the almost impregnable
ruins of ancient Petra and an enemy counter-attack became
improbable.[1]

But there were other problems to be faced: the most press-
ing were those of food and money. The twenty thousand
pounds had vanished in paying for the assistance of the
nomads; two thousand Bedouins would devour the meagre
rations of the Turks at Aqaba in no time, and if there was
a shortage of food they would return to their desert; so they
had to be fed to retain them on the side of the Revolt.

Cairo could not be reached except by the camel track, and
Lawrence alone was in a position to go there; he collected
eight men and the best beasts he could find, and driving
across Sinai along the pilgrims' route, he crossed in forty-
nine hours the hundred and fifty miles of a desert which at
this time of the year is practically waterless. On the 9th of
July he arrived in Cairo.

The General Staff of the army of Egypt, dumbfounded at
seeing this little man arrive with such tremendous news,
granted everything he asked for, and a few days afterwards
the *Euryalus*, loaded with flour and rice, supplied Aqaba
with fresh provisions and brought Nasir all the gold—sixteen
thousand sovereigns—that he needed.

[1] Aqaba (an Arabic word meaning 'the climb') was then less a port
than an anchorage on an inhospitable coast. A circle of mountains
surrounds this village, which was constituted by a few dilapidated administrative buildings, some dried mud huts and a small oasis, the
whole dominated by a ruined Kasbah.

At the Gates of Syria

IN Cairo the effect had been overwhelming. Not only was Lawrence promoted to major and recommended for the Order of the Bath, but his credit became considerable. The success which he had just achieved on his own initiative, against the opinion of his immediate superiors, without exposing any other English life but his own, had an effective and wide bearing. The long line of Turkish communications was menaced for six hundred miles, the Arab partisans were nearing the right wing of the English with whom they were going to be able to link up; the whole of the north of the Red Sea was cleared of the Ottomans, who could no longer lay mines or slip in their spies.

In his book, Colonel Brémond has tried to minimise Lawrence's victory. There is a little malice and much injustice in his criticisms. Aqaba, he said, had already been taken twice, the first time in 1915 by a landing party from the *Desaix,* the second by an English warship. But these raids cannot be compared with the occupation effected by Lawrence: the Turks had never been driven out of the ridges that command the port; a frontal attack, followed by the crossing of jagged mountains, would have required a strenuous effort on the part of the assailants and imposed on them severe losses; Lawrence's solution was an exceptionally skilful one.

His success, besides, bore fruit which he held higher than honours and braid. All attention was now turned on him, he was the man of the moment, while his superiors and his colleagues who remained in Arabia were eclipsed. Newcombe's efforts in particular now seemed rather vain and second-rate: his plan of an occupation of the Hejaz line by Feisal's forces and by Colonel Joyce's Egyptian camel corps had proved almost entirely abortive; the Emir, perhaps instructed by Lawrence before his departure, vacillated for a long time before he would agree to leave the security of

Wejh; with great difficulty they had pushed him as far as Jidda,[1] three days' march from the interior, but there he had stopped, refusing to attack El Ala, its important station and reservoirs; Ali was stagnating in the area of Medina; Abdullah, despite the efforts of his adviser, Captain Raho, carried on a feeble war against the Shammar Bedouins who had remained faithful to the Turks; Newcombe wore himself out in trying to shake this inertia; he performed prodigies, ran from the camp of one Emir to the camp of another and without sparing himself, went off to blow up the railway line. "Arabs said Newcombe would not sleep except head on rails". They watched him working without showing much enthusiasm for helping him. But all this was rather indecisive, and above all the Hejaz campaign seemed far off and useless now that Lawrence had directed attention, with his lightning blow at Aqaba, towards Northern Arabia.

Lawrence immediately exploited his success. He went to find Clayton, and put his proposals to him point-blank.

The base at Wejh must be suppressed, and Feisal's contingents transported to Aqaba.

Much more, the operations around Medina having no further interest, all English assistance in officers, equipment and money must be transferred to Aqaba.

Feisal must be detached from the forces of the Grand Sherif Hussein, and become the commander of the army under the orders of the General Staff in Egypt.

Above all Lawrence should from now on have a free hand in the Arabian affair, a large sum should be put at his disposal, two hundred thousand sovereigns, he would suggest, which would be dispensed according as he wished for the purposes of propaganda; finally he would be directly answerable to the High Command in Cairo.

Such demands raised delicate problems of diplomacy and hierarchy, and to resolve them was beyond Clayton's competence. "I am unable to decide", he said; "you must see the General". Murray in fact had just been recalled to London, and a new commander, Allenby, had arrived from France.

* * *

[1] Another Jidda, between Wejh and the railway line.

Allenby, the Bull, was a powerful and original personality. This sporting and rubicund Colossus had, in appearance at least, nothing of the intellectual, but despite his footballing and fox-hunting country squire physique, he was very shrewd, cultured and unusually intelligent. A cavalry officer, he had fought brilliantly in the Boer War. In France his career had been less fortunate: the stagnation of trench warfare and the administrative task imposed by the use of vast quantities of equipment did not suit his nature. To escape from this despairing immobility he had attempted a few thrusts against the enemy which had ended in bloody holocausts. After these rebuffs, his stock on the Western Front had fallen fairly low, but the qualities which he had shown in South Africa were not forgotten; he was more a tactician than an administrator, perhaps he would be a greater success on the Egyptian front than Murray, who had proved to be more of a bureaucrat than a soldier.

Allenby sent for Lawrence, who came dressed in his Bedouin finery:

"It was a comic interview, for Allenby was physically large and confident. . . . He sat in his chair looking at me, not straight as his custom was, but sideways, puzzled . . . he was hardly prepared for anything so odd as myself—a little bare-footed silk-skirted man, offering to hobble the enemy by his preaching if given stores and arms and a fund of two hundred thousand sovereigns to convince and control his converts.

"Allenby could not make out how much was genuine performer and how much charlatan. The problem was working behind his eyes and I left him unhelped to solve it. He did not ask many questions nor talk much but studied the map and listened. . . . At the end he put up his chin and said quite directly, 'Well, I will do for you what I can.' . . . We learned gradually that he meant exactly what he said, and that what General Allenby could do was enough for his very greediest servant."

Such was, if one is to believe the account in the *Seven Pillars,* the interview between two profoundly different men. Lawrence would have liked to have made of this meeting a sort of pact between two big chiefs, certainly a rather romanticised view of it, since the Bedouin bands and the Syrian maquis could never be more than a secondary element in the vast and complex organisation of the Palestine campaign.

Whatever the case Allenby gave Lawrence almost entire satisfaction. He was granted the considerable sums he asked for; Feisal and his troops were directly attached to the army of Egypt; Newcombe was left in the south to try vainly to stir Ali and Abdullah out of their apathy, and to negotiate with the sour, suspicious and ill-tempered Grand Sherif; the greater part of the English effort was directed on Feisal. The new base at Aqaba was put under the nominal control of Colonel Joyce, an energetic and direct soldier, but 'limited', as Lawrence said, and who did not excite his subaltern's jealousy; Lawrence, officially no more than liaison officer with Feisal, in fact had his hands free from now on.

It is not known what the reactions of the allied officers who remained in the Hejaz, Newcombe, Davenport, Wilson and Colonel Brémond, were to these new dispositions. It was a sharp blow for them; almost all aid was withdrawn from them, and in an operational theatre already forgotten and remote, they had to carry on a dangerous and difficult war with the most uncertain of allies; Brémond, sent to Arabia to defend the French interests in Syria, saw an officer whose francophobia he knew, and to whose ideas he had been incessantly opposed, free to act as he wished and to carry his policy to the gates of this country. But the Colonel's opinion did not carry much weight even with the French command, who scarcely gave him any support; besides he was to leave the Hejaz a few months later and play no further part in the Arab imbroglio.

* * *

The desire to maintain themselves at Medina and to keep control of a part of Arabia had imposed on the Turks military dispositions that were rather disjointed. In Southern Palestine their front barred the coastal plain from Gaza to Beersheba, it then bent round to the south to the end of the Dead Sea to defend the ridge of the hills of Judaea, and then stretched to Maan and Tebuk. Beyond this town there was no real Ottoman front but a string of fortified points designed

12

to guard the railway line which ran across six hundred miles
of desert as far as Medina.

Such dispositions implied a dangerous dispersal of forces
that was very vulnerable, and Lawrence wished to make of
Aqaba the base from which he could harass the track and
the Turks' eastern flank. He counted on only employing
Bedouins in these actions, the march on Aqaba having seemed
to demonstrate that the nomads could carry out operations of
a far-reaching nature. As to the regulars, he did not intend
to entrust them with more than a defensive task: it was they
who would guard the defiles leading to Aqaba and who
would protect the base. Above all they would have a political
rôle: a young state needs an army in order to feel sure of
itself and, besides, national troops would later on assure
Feisal's position in Syria.

There only remained to put Feisal's contingent on a working footing. The Emir's troops reached Aqaba in several detachments. At the end of the month of August Feisal's staff,
Joyce, Jaafar and three thousand of the Sherif's regular
troops had reached their new camp.

The base was a hive of activity: an English warship, the
Humber, was stationed in the port, and two Egyptian companies, five machine-gun carriers and a wireless set were sent
there; a fairly large number of English officers were occupied
with the administrative and supply arrangements, while
Joyce supervised the base as a whole, and Jaafar trained the
regulars.

A landing ground was laid out at Kuntilla, forty miles to
the north-west; the Egyptian labour force, with the help of
the English machine-gunners, started to build a road to
enable vehicles to debouch from the circle of mountains
which surrounded the port, and to operate in the desert. A
fairly large French contingent was posted to Aqaba: a section
of two machine-guns, under the command of Sergeant Metery
of the home army, went to reinforce the 'road-block' at
Guweira, and Captain Pisani brought a section of 80 mm.
mountain guns, operated by Muslims from North Africa, a
medical major and services; in all there were two French
officers and a hundred and fifty men at the new base.

*　　　*　　　*

All these dispositions were logical but they did not take account of certain imponderables, and when Lawrence wished to put his programme into effect, he came up against a number of difficulties which he had not foreseen.

The most serious was a sudden change in the Bedouins on whom he had founded so much hope for his future operations. At the end of the summer of 1916 he learnt from the Arab Bureau that the ally who seemed the most sure was beginning to betray him. Auda, the romantic warrior, gorged with English gold and with booty, was negotiating with the Turks, offering to sell his neutrality and eventually his effective assistance against the British. Through the intermediary of his cousin, Mohammed el Dheilan, a brother in arms at Aqaba, he had written to Maan to initiate discussions with the Ottomans, and the spies in Clayton's pay had sent copies of the culpable correspondence to Cairo.

Lawrence was dumbfounded by this news, but he was always able to act quickly; he jumped on a camel, reached Guweira in one march, and greatly surprised the Bedouin sheiks who believed that he was in Jidda in conference with Hussein. He affected complete casualness, joked and exchanged presents, and incidentally talked of negotiations with the Ottomans. The dumbfounded Arabs replied with embarrassed explanations. They had tried, they said, to extract some money from the Turks, without of course thinking for a moment of abandoning the English cause. It was a good farce, no more. Lawrence pretended to be taken in, and laughed with them. He talked of the enormous influx of money, provisions and arms which the installation of the base would bring to the area, promised Auda a large sum and left for Aqaba relatively reassured. That the men who for two months had fought at his side were beginning to betray him gave him food for thought. Meanwhile he telegraphed Cairo that "the situation at Guweira was thoroughly good and no treachery abroad. This may have been hardly true, but . . . we must reduce impolitic truth to keep Egypt confident and ourselves a legend".

On the side of the regular army also, he had disappointments to confront. They had not been able to create an Arab Legion in Egypt as had been hoped; in the Hejaz the pro-Turk anti-allied propaganda which insinuated itself even into the entourage of the Grand Sherif was making headway with the Arab soldiers. Feisal was depicted as completely under the sway of the Christians, some of the units which they wished to embark for Aqaba mutinied and refused to leave the Hejaz, and among the officers there was also some irresolution; the important chieftains like Jaafar, Nuri Said or Maulud required all their energy to maintain discipline in the young army.

The promises made to Allenby in the enthusiasm of first success were slow in being effected, and the base at Aqaba, set up at great expense and with great éclat, seemed a rather hollow organisation, a 'balloon', said Brémond. Lawrence therefore had to act as fast as he could, justify the dispositions which he had taken by some operation, and make use of the considerable resources that had been placed at his disposal.

* * *

The Turks, faced with the menace presented to them by the installation of this base for the Sherif's forces, had not been inactive. They had brought to Maan six thousand foot, a regiment of cavalry and some guns, strongly reoccupied Aba el Lissan and reinforced the posts on the railway; above all the Allies must avoid having Feisal's base swept away by a vigorously led Ottoman attack.

Lawrence appealed for aircraft and Allenby, always generous, put at the disposal of the Arabs a bomber squadron, which from El Arish where it was stationed took over the strip at Kuntilla. The commander of this unit, Captain Trent, and his pilots were terrible daredevils, who carried out their orders with enthusiasm. They drove the Turks into a panic, dropped bombs in the middle of Maan and on the troops' billets, spotted the Turkish cavalry encamped near Aba el Lissan and inflicted heavy losses on them.

Thus harassed the enemy decided to attack. Lawrence meanwhile had had the defiles strongly occupied, and in particular he had posted Maulud at Petra with two hundred regulars; the Turks came up against soldiers that were well commanded, determined to fight and in an extremely strong position; they lost an entire company and had to withdraw. It was a tangible success but insufficient to justify the creation of the base. Returning to his idea of maritime strategy and nomadic warfare, Lawrence launched two raids to disrupt the traffic on the railway and demoralise the Turks.

In his memoirs, T.E. has employed all his sparkling talent to describe expeditions that were full of romantic adventure, but he was doing no more than skilfully disguising his semi-failures. The military results of these raids were relatively slender, greatly inferior to what he had hoped for, since against his expectations he was unable to raise vast nomad hordes and carry out camel-borne operations. In fact he was acting alone, or nearly alone, with two or three European companions, and the Bedouins gave him no more than an insufficient and fleeting support at the time of his attacks. It was impossible to repeat the imposing march behind the Turkish lines of the Howeitat tribe on Aqaba.

But in these sorties, whatever their military significance, Lawrence reveals himself completely. People have made of him a strategist without seeing that he was much more a born guerilla leader, a raider, a corsair: a Drake or Jean Bart who devised his blows with a mixture of prudence, astuteness and recklessness, and fought at the head of his boarding parties followed by his ruffian band. Apart from his striking courage, he had like them an imperturbable sangfroid in moments of danger, a magnetic ascendancy over his men, the ability for constant planning of schemes, ruses, surprises, the lightning grasp of a situation and the tactical flair for battle which cannot be learnt; it was what Rommel, that other pirate of the desert, called his *Fingerspitze,* the tips of his fingers, his antennae.

It was in the middle of September that Lawrence mounted his first raid. His counter-attack should obviously have taken place to the north of Maan to cut off from its bases the force which menaced him, but he could not do it, as Feisal's propaganda was not making progress and the tribesmen of the north refused to join in the Revolt.

It was then to the south, on the station of Mudowwara,

a water point fifty miles south of Maan, that he had to direct the expedition.

He counted on enlisting for the raid some Bedouins from around Guweira where Auda was encamped, and only took with him a very small escort: Aid, a sherif of Feisal's entourage, two or three of the Emir's soldiers and some camel-men to carry the explosives; he had besides some unexpected help: two British N.C.O.s who were teaching the Arabs to use the machine-guns and trench mortars came to enlist as volunteers from the moment that they got wind of the raid. Lawrence accepted their assistance after having reminded them of the dangers of the enterprise, and of the poverty and the sordid filth in which they would have to live. "They were warned that their experiment might not at the moment seem altogether joyful. . . . If they went they would lose their British Army comfort and privilege to share, and share with the Arabs (except in booty!) and suffer exactly their hap in food and discipline". But the two sergeants, one a typically English John Bull type, silent and tenacious, the other an adventurous Australian with a Don Quixote nose, persisted in their decision.

The little caravan left for Guweira on the 7th of September, in terrible heat. Lawrence watched pensively one of Feisal's soldiers whom later he could not prevent himself from describing:

"The youngest interested me most. He, Rahail, was quite a lad: a free-built, sturdy fellow, too fleshy for the life we were to lead. . . . The mouth was budded and small, the chin very pointed. This added to the high strong brows and anti-mony-enlarged eyes gave him a mixed air of artifice and petulance, with weary patience imposed upon a base of pride. . . . When exhausted or cross he broke into miserable tears easily chased away by any interference. . . . "

Lawrence found Auda's camp effervescing. The old sheik was in conflict with his contributives; intoxicated by success and by the gold that was flowing into his coffers, he made himself insupportable to the other clan chieftains. All involved in their quarrels, the Howeitats refused to follow the English, who had to leave the camp of these "intractable, wrangling, voracious" Bedouins. The most he could obtain was that Zaal, Auda's nephew, should come on the raid, which he promised to join a few days later.

Always alone or almost so, Lawrence went on to the south-east, through the defiles of Rumm, grandiose canyons above which towered cliffs of red rock more than a thousand feet high. They camped near a spring. The heat was terrible, nearly 120 degrees in the shade, and this shade "was a surge of flies".

In the night Lawrence was woken up by the little Sherif Aid, who crept up to him and said in a cold voice, "Lord, I am gone blind". All that he could say was that "there had been no sight, only pain in his eyes. The sun blink had burnt them out". Taking the unfortunate man, who did not wish to leave the caravan, Lawrence marched towards the encamp-ments of the Bedouins who were pasturing their beasts to the south of Rumm. They were the enemy of Auda's Abu Tayis, and very inclined to join the Turks; seated round the fire, alone with the two sergeants, a few servants and the poor blind Sherif, Lawrence wondered which way the primitives who surrounded him would lean. In the morning Zaal arrived in camp, but the Arabs continued to quarrel so violently that no solution seemed possible. T.E. had to entrust the two N.C.O.s to Zaal, and after a furious ride by camel reached Feisal's camp, whence he brought the Sherif Abdullah el-Fair, who with difficulty put matters right. After long palavers the expedition finally managed to get under way; it was only supported by a hundred and fifty partisans, but amongst this band discord reigned, and no one group would march or talk with any other; it was in such conditions that the column made its way towards Mudowwara.

In the proximity of the railway and to defend themselves from the Bedouins, the Turks had poisoned the water points by throwing dead camels down the wells. On the last day's march before the line they had to drink from one of these wells. "Over its face lay a thick mantle of green slime, from which swelled curious bladder islands of floating fatty pink". They had however to drink this water or die of thirst, and the English did as the others.

The station of Mudowwara seemed a very large objective

for a force of a hundred and fifty men, disunited by quarrels and distrust, and Lawrence had to renounce the idea of attacking it. He went back along the line and decided, in default of having been able to carry out the planned operation, to try and blow up a train. After several long days of waiting, of marches and counter-marches along the line which the Turks were patrolling, he laid a powerful mine whilst a very long train drawn by two locomotives was approaching. On the coaches they could see a crowd of soldiers; the convoy seemed to be bristling with guns.

The mine went off under the second engine.

"There followed a terrific roar and the line vanished from sight behind a spouting column of black dust and smoke a hundred feet high and wide. Out of the darkness came shattering crashes and long loud metallic clangings of ripped steel, with many lumps of iron and plate; while one entire wheel of a locomotive whirled up suddenly black out of the cloud against the sky, and sailed musically over our heads to fall slowly and heavily into the desert behind."

The Bedouins rushed towards the train; one of the sergeants cut down with his machine-gun the Turks who were caught on the coaches, in bunches. Others were flattened by the missiles from the field mortar which the second sergeant was operating. In the shouting, the confusion and the slaughter the train was taken by storm.

There was everything in the convoy: officers, soldiers, refugees, women and even a coach full of sick being evacuated from Medina. "The smash had killed all but three or four and had rolled dead and dying into a bleeding heap against the splintered end. One of those yet alive deliriously cried out the word Typhus. So I wedged shut the door and left them there, alone. . . ."

Further on, a few Austrians, officers and N.C.O.s, who had remained calm amidst the pandemonium of the combat, came to ask Lawrence for quarter, but it was impossible to save their lives, for a dispute broke out between them and Rahail, the man with the fine eyes heavy with kohl; they drew a pistol, and the furious Arabs tore them to pieces before the Englishman could intervene.

The Bedouins, in feverish excitement, pillaged the train and savagely stripped the passengers. Three times Lawrence had to defend himself against Arabs who pretended not to recognise him and wished to seize his arms and clothes; he was afraid that his two sergeants would be attacked by these unchained savages, and hastily collected his ninety prisoners and took them to the rear. The Bedouins, gorged with booty, disappeared towards the mountains, driving before them camels laden with booty. The Sherifs' men of Lawrence's personal retinue, maddened by the joys of pillage, had scattered with the nomads, and he found himself alone on the field of battle with his two sergeants; in the end Zaal came back, and accompanied the English a distance from the line, since Turkish patrols were approaching.

* * *

The adventure such as Lawrence describes it for us, with undoubted fidelity, leaves an impression of outrageous cruelty and brutality. One is carried back several centuries, one stumbles over corpses, slips in the hot blood, and one can imagine the violent sentiments of the thirty-year-old English-man who, alone amongst these primitives, had unleashed these atrocities and this carnage.

Lawrence brought back to Aqaba an incredible caravan of prisoners, of Arab women who had entrusted themselves to him, prize camels, captured guns and the spoils of the Turks; it was the barbarous cortège of a victorious pirate. As for the Bedouins they had evaporated into the desert. "Victory always undid an Arab force", he said philosophically.

The expedition reverberated among the Arabs. The stories of plunder, amplified by Oriental imaginations, inflamed the desert and were of much more service to the propaganda of the Movement than the felt-lined palavers conducted by Feisal in his tent. At the beginning of October Lawrence decided to carry out a further raid, again to the south of Maan. He took with him a single European, Captain Pisani, "an active soldier who burned for distinction—and distinctions", he said a little treacherously.

The story unfolded exactly as in the first attack: quarrels among the Bedouins during the approach march, a charge exploded under a train, pillage and massacre of the Turks. Lawrence and Pisani, screaming Moroccan war cries, led the assault and a Turkish officer with a revolver shot and wounded the Englishman in the thigh. Once again, after the fight, the two Europeans found themselves alone, abandoned by the Bedouins on the field of battle with Turkish reinforcements no more than four hundred yards away.

For this action Pisani received the Military Cross. He had himself presented Lawrence with the French Croix de Guerre which Brémond had awarded him after the Aqaba raid.[1]

In the passing of October and November, other raids were with various fortunes attempted on the railway by detachments of the English or of the Sherifs' men. A track had been built which allowed the carriers to reach the relatively negotiable surface of the desert and the Rolls-Royces which had previously fought in the Senussi war were brought into the business and became a rapid means of reaching the railway and carrying out demolitions. More than seventeen locomotives were thus destroyed. Traffic on the line became a problem for the enemy; the shortage of equipment was making itself felt not only on the Hejaz line, but also in Syria and Palestine.

Among the Arabs, Lawrence's prestige grew unceasingly. Certainly he was the purveyor of subsidies, the great distributor of gold to the nomadic sheiks, who arrived hesitating between hatred and fear of the Turks, distrust of the Christians, between prudence and rapacity, to join the Revolt. But he was also 'the Hero', the Warrior Chief, capable of riding sixty miles a day on a camel at the speed of a raiding party,

[1] The citation, dated the 23rd of November, had been drawn up by Brémond himself. The text ran as follows:

Le Président du Conseil, Ministre de la Guerre, cite à l'ordre de l'Armée:

LAWRENCE, Thomas Edouard, Major à l'Etat-Major du Haut-Commissaire du Gouvernement Britannique en Egypte, pour le motif suivant:

"Officier supérieur de la plus haute valeur. Par son action personnelle a su grouper autour de lui des contingents bédouins à la tête desquels il a accompli des opérations de la plus grande audace, avec le succès le plus complet, sans eau et sans ravitaillement, compromettant les communications des troupes turques du Hedjaz."

Paris, le 23 Novembre 1917.
Signé: L. MORDACQ.

of fighting hand to hand and of leading his band to glory and plunder.

Some of the English who followed him in the desert have described the explosion of enthusiasm with which he was greeted when he appeared in an Arab camp, the fantasias, the shouts, the greetings and the cry of "Aurens! Aurens!" repeated a thousand times. That was genuine popularity, the love of the partisans for the good raiding-party leader, which cupidity alone does not explain.

*   *   *

Meanwhile this expenditure of activity, imagination and individual courage was achieving fairly slender results from the general point of view of the war in the Orient. All these operations were directed against the garrison of Medina, which was a secondary objective. The traffic was never interrupted for any length of time, and the Turks always managed to rebuild the structures that were destroyed. Incapable of attacking any strongly defended point. Lawrence and the Arabs could only deal with the line itself or culverts that were easily repaired; their exploits were spectacular but they had no great strategic interest. Now Allenby was not the man to invest his capital without expecting dividends. At that moment he had no resources to squander, for he was preparing for a vast offensive in December, which he hoped would take him to Jerusalem. What contribution could he expect from Feisal and the Sherif's men, who should have been, it was said, the right wing of his army?

In the middle of October, Lawrence was sent for by Allenby, who asked him bluntly "what his railway efforts meant; or rather if they meant anything beyond the melodramatic advertisement they gave to Feisal's cause".[1]

It was a direct and hard blow to T.E.'s pride, and there was not much that he could reply to the General's criticisms. The fear that Allenby would withdraw from him his support, send European troops to Aqaba and take over the direction of Arab affairs gnawed at his heart, and he was obliged to propose to his chief a concrete plan for an operation designed to assist the English offensive.

[1] *Seven Pillars*, p. 475.

A Chapter of Accidents

DURING his conferences with Allenby, Lawrence had often mentioned his hope of soon being in a position, thanks to his propaganda and also to the astutely distributed English gold, of raising the desert Bedouins and the settled people of Southern Syria against the Turks. It is certain (although we do not know what actually passed during conversations conducted between the two officers at this time) that Allenby asked Lawrence to provoke a general insurrection at the moment of the British offensive, in order that the Ottomans, caught between the enemy attack and the menace from the interior, should thus be paralysed.

T.E. must have admitted that the results which he was achieving were well below what he had expected, and that it was premature to demand such an effort from the hesitant nomads and the still unorganised Syrian maquis. Much more modest operations only could be envisaged, and in place of a vast movement comprising all the forces of the Revolt, which was still impracticable, Lawrence proposed to organise a raid which, directed by himself and employing limited numbers of men, would however, if successful, have a considerable effect on the enemy dispositions. He would go with a light detachment of Europeans and Hindus, supported by Bedouins recruited in the locality, to destroy the Yarmuk viaducts inside the Turkish lines, thus cutting the only means of communication between the north and the Palestine front. These viaducts were considerable works of art, spanning deep gorges; it would require months to rebuild them, and their destruction would paralyse the enemy.

Faute de mieux, Allenby accepted this proposition and asked that the demolition should be made during the first days of November, a little after the opening of his offensive, and at the moment when the Turks would need to be deploying their units and bringing up reinforcements and munitions from the north.

The account of these conferences in the *Seven Pillars* cannot really be taken seriously. Lawrence says: "I wondered whether we should raise all the partisans of the Revolt. . . . We were certain, with any management, of twelve thousand men, enough to rush Deraa, to smash all the railway lines, even to take Damascus by surprise. . . ." But in case of failure such a rising would have implied the destruction of the rebels. . . . "I weighed the English army in my mind and could not honestly assure myself of them. . . . Allenby was quite untried, sent to us with a not blameless record from France. . . . So I decided to postpone the hazard for the Arabs' sake".

For an officer to have made such calculations on the eve of a general offensive, and to have weighed the degree of assistance which he was prepared to give to the thousands of combatants, his own fellow-countrymen who would be engaged in the battle, would have been a heinous action. Lawrence's only excuse was that he could not possibly have asked himself the question. He would have been quite incapable at that time of raising twelve thousand Arabs: besides, as we shall see, neither the Bedouins nor the Syrian maquis were ever in the condition to attack the Turks in an organised formation, and at the end of 1918 they only decided on a total rising when the Ottomans, their front smashed by the English, had been completely routed. Until then they neither could nor would do anything.

*   *   *

Lawrence had only a few days in which to organise his expedition, and immediately went to work. Feisal gave him, as assistant and guide, a young sherif, Ali Ibn el-Hussein, a youth of twenty-seven, "impertinent, headstrong, vain, but as brave in deeds as he was in words", and he took with him Wood, a Sapper officer and a specialist in the handling of explosives, who had recently joined them from the French front where he had been wounded, four sections of Hindu machine-gunners whose courage could be completely relied upon, and a few of the men of the personal guard which he was beginning to form; as for the Bedouins who were to support him, he would raise them en route.

T.E. never forgot the propaganda element. George Lloyd, his old comrade of the Arab Bureau, a Member of Parliament and at this time the English delegate to Versailles, was passing through Egypt, and he asked him to accompany him for a few days of the march. If the raid was successful, Lloyd would be able to give every possible publicity in London to Lawrence and the Revolt.

The general plan was to cross the track to the south of Maan, to strike out into the desert, and to reach Azrak, by way of the wells of Bair, an oasis situated beyond the north end of the Dead Sea, eighty miles to the east of the Hejaz railway; and from this point to swoop down on the objective with fifty men in one or two long marches and blow up the viaduct.

The little column set out on the 24th of October, but from the beginning everything went wrong. Crossing the line to the south of Maan was difficult; Auda and Zaal, installed in their camps at Jefer, refused to join the expedition. The two men were no longer the hungry wolves of the beginning of the year; fattened and softened by success and riches, a desperate raid no longer appealed to them. Lawrence had taken with him a sheik of Algerian origin, Abd el-Kader. He was one of the descendants of the Emir who once fought against France in Algeria; his tribe, which had taken refuge in Syria on the banks of the Yarmuk, was, he asserted, completely won over to the Revolt, and his presence ought to have been a contribution to the expedition, but vain, excitable and half mad, the man was most unreliable; Brémond had warned Lawrence that Abd el-Kader was a Turkish agent who would certainly give information to the enemy, but Brémond's advice was sufficient to put Lawrence in favour of the Sheik; in actual fact, during the march Abd el-Kader did disappear and, it seems, went to warn the Turks.

Close to Bair the column was surrounded by a cloud of camel-men. They had to form a square, put the machine-guns in position, and then parley; it was a raiding party of Beni-Sakhr, in theory in sympathy with the Movement, but who with one foot in each camp had risked a treacherous attack

MAP III

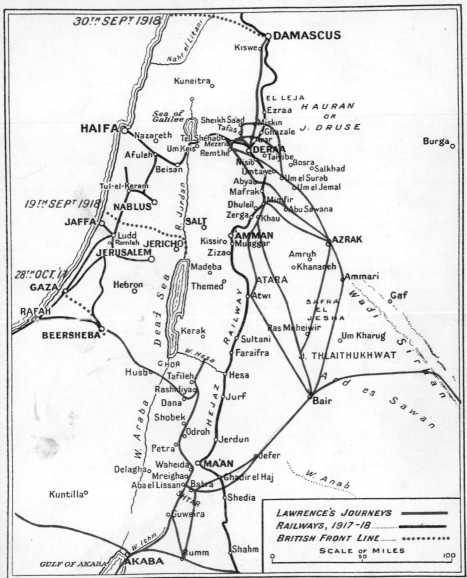

30TH SEPT 1918

DAMASCUS

Kiswe

Kuneitra

EL LEJA
Ezraa
HAURAN
OR
J. DRUSE

Nahr el Litani

Sea of
Galilee
Sheikh Sa'ad
Tafas
Miskin
Ghazale
Anar

HAIFA
Nazareth
Tell Shehab
Mezerib
Remthe
DERAA
Tajibe

Afuleh
Um Keis
Nisib
Bosra
Salkhad

Beisan
Umtaiye
Um el Surab

Abyad
Um el Jemal

Tul-el-Keram
Mafrak
Mismir

19TH SEPT 1918
NABLUS
SALT
Dhuleil
Zerga
Khau
Abu Sawana

JAFFA
Ludd
Ramleh
JERICHO
Kissiro
AMMAN
Muaggar
AZRAK

JERUSALEM
Zizao
Amruh
Khananeh

28TH OCT. 17
GAZA
Hebron
Madeba
ATARA
Ammari

Themed
Atwi
Gaf

RAFAH

Dead Sea
SAFRA
EL
JESHA

BEERSHEBA
Kerak
Ras Meheiwir
Um Kharug

W. Hesa
Sultani
Faraifra
J. THLAITHUKHWAT

Husb
GHOR
Tafileh
Hesa

Rashidiya
Jurf
Bair

Dana

Shobek
Odroh
Jerdun

Petra
Jefer

W. Anab

Delagha
Waheida
MA'AN

Kuntilla
Mreigha
Aba el Lissan
Batra
Ghadir el Haj
Shedia

W. Araba
SITAR
Guweira

RAILWAY
HEJAN
Wadi Sirhan
A d es Sawan
R. Jordan
Burga

W. Ichm
Rumm
Shahm

GULF OF AKABA
AKABA

LAWRENCE'S JOURNEYS ————
RAILWAYS, 1917-18 ....
BRITISH FRONT LINE ....••••••
SCALE OF MILES
50   100

NOTE - "J." denotes JEBEL (Mountain).   "W." denotes WADI (Watercourse & Valley)

from which they would have derived some booty and gained credit with the Turks. All this smelt of treason and of ill luck. In the end the Beni-Sakhr accepted the column around the wells of Bair, and even furnished the expedition with twenty soldiers.

Finally, after a ten days' march they came to Azrak, domain of the Serahin Bedouins. It was among these that Lawrence and Ali thought that they would find the warriors to assist them in accomplishing the last phase of the operation, the mad dash to Yarmuk, but like Auda's Howeitats, the Serahins refused to march. In despair, Lawrence made a long, confused and breathless speech to persuade them to fight for the Revolt. A few camel-men reluctantly agreed to follow him. It was a far cry from that general rising of the desert nomads and of the peasants of Syria who were to sweep away the Turkish army, take Deraa and perhaps Damascus!

The column finally set out to the north-west; already they could hear in the distance the dull, uninterrupted sound of Allenby's cannonade in preparation for his offensive and they had to make haste. The Bedouins, reluctant allies of the Christians, thought of the Turks, their brothers in religion, submitting to this inferno of artillery fire, and murmured among themselves: "They are nearer, the English are advancing, God deliver the men under that rain!"

To the west of the railway the column hid in a depression of the desert amid the enemy lines. Besides his personal followers and those of the Sherif, Lawrence chose six Hindu machine-gunners, twenty Beni-Sakhr, forty of the Serahins, who as not very reliable were put in charge of carrying the equipment and explosives, and the raiding party set out. They had to skirt Deraa, cover eighty miles by camel at night in thirteen hours, and carry out whilst on the march a complicated piece of sabotage. They had chosen as their objective the viaduct of Tel el Sahb, to the east of the Lake of Tiberias.

During the night of the 6th of November, they reached the bridge; it bestrode a deep gorge, in the depths of which roared the torrent. In the darkness Lawrence placed the Hindu machine-gunners under Wood's command, and then with Ali and the Bedouins who were carrying the explosives, he crept towards the bridge. In the light of the moon he could see the Turkish sentry striding along the sleepers. Lawrence was a few yards from the enormous still girders when the clatter of a falling rifle rang out: a soldier had dropped his weapon and it rolled noisily down the slope, alerting the Turkish post.

From every side the fusillade broke out; the Turks ran to their trenches and sprayed their assailants with bullets, and the Serahins dropped their explosives, which fell into the ravine. Lawrence, Ali and their companions had great difficulty in climbing back under fire up the goat track which wound up the side of the gorge. The raid had failed.

The column returned with difficulty to Azrak through country that was on the alert. On the way home and to console himself for his lack of success, Lawrence blew up a train on the Hejaz line, but it was crammed with troops and the affair nearly ended in disaster. Lawrence was too close to the explosion, was wounded by the debris and remained stunned, within range of the Turkish rifles. Ali and a few Arabs came back to look for him, losing seven of their number to save him, and they brought him back with five bullet wounds in his body. Although a few Turks were slaughtered, it was impossible to take the train in which Jemal Kouchkouk, the commander of the VIII Ottoman Army Corps, was travelling. Having failed in his attempt on the viaduct, and not having even been able to give the Serahins and the Beni-Sakhrs the booty which they had promised themselves, Lawrence plunged into the desert and returned to Azrak (November 1917).

* * *

If this operation is analysed, one is struck both by the strength and the weakness of the tactics which Lawrence employed, a weakness which came for the most part from the nomads' lack of enthusiasm for fighting for the Christians. The Bedouins were indispensable to the English as guides, porters and providers of mounts and provisions. Feisal's propaganda and the Allies' gold made them more or less tolerate the passage of the Sherif's troops in their territory, and from time to time won their temporary adhesion for a rapid raid, but they could never be counted on for certain. At the time of the expedition to the Yarmuk viaducts Lawrence had not been able to raise a force in the desert capable of taking the Turkish post of sixty soldiers which guarded the bridge. His courage, his skill, the enormous risks which he did not hesitate to take were of no avail against the inertia and the ill-will of the Bedouins.

In the end one realises that he was carrying on a war single-handed or almost so, and besides with an extraordinary skill, for at Yarmuk he was within a hair's-breadth of success. With a little luck he might have blown up that enormous structure, and the consequences for Allenby's operations of this destruction would have been considerable. But the inspired and hazardous actions of a single man are no substitute for the efforts of an entire nation.

*   *   *

The failure of the attempt on Yarmuk was a bitter pill for Lawrence's pride and threatened to ruin his influence with the Commander-in-Chief. Allenby's army was engaged in a risky operation, and he needed to hold all the trumps if he was to succeed. The general's dispositions had been very subtle and comprised a whole series of manœuvres and ruses. He had made a demonstration to the west against Gaza, which was very strongly defended, and had then made his principal thrust to the east against Beersheba, concentrating his troops with great secrecy. Thanks to this feint he had completely shattered the enemy position. The English cavalry was hurled through the breach made by the infantry and had taken Gaza from the rear; the Turkish army in the south would probably have been destroyed if the cavalry had not been held up on the march by the lack of water and the difficulties of the terrain. The advance continued, but more slowly and more painfully, and the British pushed on towards Jerusalem, strewing the hills of Judaea with dead.

Feisal's army had in no way helped the English effort; on the other hand, at the moment when Lawrence was disappointing Allenby, Newcombe was covering himself with glory. At the time of the English offensive, he was in Cairo and he decided to create a diversion, similar to that for which

13

Lawrence had been asked, on Allenby's right. With sixty-six English camel troops he made a circuit through the desert and set up a road block between Beersheba and Hebron. The Turkish reinforcements, rushing up to the front, ran into this unexpected obstacle, and a handful of resolute men held the Hebron route for two days, throwing the Turks' rear into disorder and leading them to believe that their left wing had been turned by a large English formation. Newcombe held out against infinitely superior forces till he had lost half his men and exhausted his ammunition. His heroism had contributed to slowing down the arrival of Turkish reinforcements at the precise moment that Allenby was making his principal thrust.[1]

* * *

Lawrence decided to stay at Azrak instead of returning to Aqaba. This savage spot, which the Arabs said was haunted, soothed his bitterness. Situated on a rocky spur, it was a town that had long ago guarded the Roman *Limes* before becoming a Byzantine fortress, then Frankish and finally Arab. Renault de Chatillon, the Crusader brigand, had used it as one of his hide-outs.

Wood was sent back to Aqaba, but Lawrence, Ali, their few followers and the Hindu machine-gunners installed themselves in the towers and ruined halls of the castle. From there T.E. hoped to spread his propaganda towards Syria, and perhaps he wished to remain within reach of Deraa, meditating some swift blow; perhaps also he did not wish to return to Aqaba and admit to his defeat.

Life went on at Azrak. Lawrence liked the company of Ali Ibn el-Hussein and with him he rediscovered the intimacy that had bound him to Nasir. The young Sherif was not, however, a saint. He was quarrelsome and ill-humoured; an ephebe whom he loved passionately lived always at his side, but he had an astonishing courage, he was on fire for the Revolt, and had saved Lawrence's life in action. The Englishman and the Sherif took up again the slow and often dis-

---

[1] Newcombe spent nearly a year in Turkish internment camps; in October 1918 he succeeded in escaping, and in being picked up by an English ship close to Smyrna.

appointing work of propaganda, using the rest of the gold that they had brought in their baggage. Soon Azrak saw the appearance of the nomad sheiks, the Syrian revolutionaries and the village chieftains of the Druze mountains and of the region of Deraa. Now Lawrence could not get this city out of his mind, which, within reach of Azrak, fascinated him. It was there, he felt, at this vital nub of the Turks' communications, that he should have struck at the time of Allenby's offensive. Dogged by this idea, he decided to explore the place on foot, and for this purpose made contact with the sheiks of the country, in particular with a certain Talal el-Hareidhin, chief of the village of Tafas, to the north-west of Deraa. This was a famous outlaw, who lived a proscribed life in the Druze mountains, but who had, however, kept the friendship and support of his tribe. He had, it was said, killed twenty-three Turks with his own hand. An independent spirit of this sort was to T.E.'s liking; guided by him he visited the outskirts of Deraa, making plans for the day when "with men, money and guns we should start the general rising to win inevitable victory".

To complete his knowledge of Deraa Lawrence decided to enter the town and study its lay-out and its defences; dressed in Oriental rags, he wandered sauntering through the streets of the town, examining the aeroplane hangars, the ammunition depots, the barracks and the Palestine railway line that he had not been able to cut, when he was arrested by a patrol. Because of his fair complexion he had been taken for someone from Northern Turkey, a deserter from the army. He was led before the commandant. "He was a bulky man and sat on the bed in a night gown, trembling and sweating as though with fever. . . . I gazed at the top of his great head, on which the bristling hair stood up, no longer than the dark stubble on his cheeks and chin. . . ."

The fat man drew the Englishman to him, pawed him and tried to possess him, and as the other struggled, he called to his men to undress the so-called deserter; this disgusting scene continued until the moment when Lawrence brought up his knee into the Turk's groin. Furious, groaning and doubled up with pain, the officer had his victim held, bit him on the neck and lacerated his skin all down his sides with a bayonet. Blood spurted. "He looked pleased and dabbled it over my stomach with his finger tips". Lawrence thought at this moment that his tormentor had recognised him, but this was not true: the Turk was only thinking, seeing the marks of his old wounds, that T.E. belonged to some fighting regiment. In the end he abandoned Lawrence to his men, with orders "to take me out and teach me everything".

The Englishman, stretched out on the ground and held down by four soldiers, was whipped till he fainted. He could do no more than shout and groan in Arabic and not in English; if they had discovered his identity, he would have had to expect worse tortures yet.

"I remembered the corporal kicking me with his nailed boot to get me up. . . . I remembered smiling idly at him, for a delicious warmth, probably sexual, was swelling through me: and then that he flung up his arm and hacked with the full length of his whip into my groin. This doubled me half over, screaming, or, rather, trying impotently to scream, only shuddering through my open mouth. One giggled with amusement. A voice cried 'Shame! you have killed him!'"

But he was still sufficiently alive for the others to amuse themselves with him in the Oriental manner.

When he was taken back before the Bey, "He rejected me in haste, as a thing too torn and bloody for his bed, blaming their excess of zeal which had spoilt me. . . . So the crestfallen corporal, as the youngest and best looking of the guard, had to stay behind. . . ." Lawrence was thrown into a planked lumber room, from which at dawn he was able to escape. He found some shabby clothes in a sick room, slipped out, managed to rejoin his companions who had stayed in the suburbs of the town, and returned to Azrak.

Lawrence has related this Gestapo scene in detail, this slice of black romance. It is a frightful page, almost unique in literature if it is remembered that his hallucinating talent was applied to a personal experience.

The nervous equilibrium of a highly intelligent, highly sensitive man could not stand up to such a trial. Azrak, the constant contact with the Arabs, the eternal routine of propaganda suddenly aroused his disgust. He had to escape, see other faces and other places, try other actions, get away in any case from the memories of Deraa. He took with him a single companion, and struck off in full winter along the track which through Bair, Jefer, the south of Maan and Rumm, leads to Aqaba, two hundred and fifty miles from there. To try to do this trip in three or four days was madness, but the fatigues of such a journey seemed to him the only remedy for his disorder, he marched like a somnambulist, eaten with fever, and haunted during the rare hours of sleep by frightful nightmares; his companion wept with fatigue but he took a troubled pleasure in sensing the moment of the final collapse of his body and mind gradually approach.

At Aqaba, where he arrived on the 26th of November, he received orders to report to Allenby's Headquarters, north of Gaza. The great commander listened without comment to the story of the Yarmuk failure. Events that were infinitely more important occupied his mind. On the 9th of December the fall of Jerusalem was reported to him. Magnanimously Allenby took Lawrence with him on the solemn entry of the British into the captured city. T.E. removed his Bedouin robes, borrowed the uniform of a staff major and joined the triumphal cortège, close to Clayton, recently promoted to general by Allenby.

1918

WHEN Lawrence came back to Aqaba at the beginning of 1918, the war took on a new aspect for Feisal's troops; equipment was plentiful; a certain number of Rolls-Royce and Ford cars equipped for the desert and six Talbot armoured cars fitted with mountain guns had arrived at the base; ten aeroplanes were based at Guweira.

Vigorously commanded by Jaafar and Nuri Said, the three thousand regular Sherifs' troops had become a disciplined and useful body; they were armed with modern rifles, with a few machine-guns and French sub-machine-guns. A hundred Hindus, two hundred Egyptians and Captain Pisani's one hundred and fifty men, with machine-guns and artillery, supported the Arab contingents; two French 65s and a few modern German guns taken from the enemy, but for which ammunition was lacking, constituted the artillery of what was pompously called the Arab Army of the North.

Lawrence finally managed to rid himself of Brémond. The Colonel, discouraged, had at the beginning of 1918 abandoned the command of the mission at Jidda and had returned to France, where as chief of staff to an army corps, he was to finish the war brilliantly.[1]

Of French interference in the Levant there only remained Pisani at Aqaba, with his gunners and infantry. The Captain took no part in politics and his guns were indispensable; he was used for all the tough work, but Lawrence was careful to dispose the Sherifs' men against him and prevent him from gaining any influence whatever.

---

[1] Colonel Brémond has left us a history of the Arab Revolt, a book full of rancour, in places inaccurate, and which he is sometimes led astray by passion, but which is indispensable for the understanding of the campaign of the Sherifs' troops. It is curious that he takes up point by point, and often with more restraint, the criticisms which the English observers of Lawrence's activities, Young or Bray for example, do not spare him.

Meanwhile Allenby, who had created this strange army out
of his own resources, intended to make use of it. The assistance which he had asked for at the time of his offensive in
November 1917 had not been efficacious; to obtain better
results, he sent early in 1918 one of the best officers on his
staff, Alan Dawnay, to stir up the running of the Sherif's
army. Lawrence was not, however, replaced in command by
this move: although the official situation was badly defined,
and although in principle he was subordinate to Joyce and
Dawnay, he had an almost exclusive influence in tribal
politics and in the guerilla operations; in constant contact
with Allenby's staff, with Feisal completely under his thumb,
he retained that personal liberty of action which the great
commander had promised him. All the evidence agrees about
this, whether it is from Brémond, Wavell or Young, and it
seems that there can be no doubt in this respect. In his book
Lawrence has not appreciably exaggerated the powers of
which he disposed.

Whatever these powers were, he had to take account of
Allenby's directives and of the state of mind of the Arabs;
now, on two sides, the turn which things were taking did
not please him. There was a tendency to put an end to the
Bedouin period of the war and to start regular European-
style operations, which was exactly what Lawrence did not
want, for he claimed to be able to inflict much more harm on
the enemy by using his original formula of harassing him
with the guerilla tactics of the partisans. To gain his ends he
needed only money, light automatic weapons and a small
number of trusty companions, something that was much
more economical and more efficacious than the scientific war
that was envisaged.

Unable to oppose the generals, or to restrain the Sherif's
officers who wished to embark on a trench warfare similar to
that of the Western Front, he very skilfully placed himself
outside the general movement in order to conserve his own
liberty. With this object he created a personal troop of which
he retained the effective command. This was what he called
his guard, eighty or ninety mercenary camel-men, plunderers
and scoundrels but of proven courage and fidelity, who were
led and trained in the Bedouin fashion, with a liberal use of

the whip if need be, by Abdullah el-Nahabi, surnamed the
Robber, and Zaagi, the two chiefs whom he had chosen.
These picturesque cut-throats, "dressed like a bed of tulips",
who were not affected by the anarchy and the inertia of the
East thanks to a strict discipline and good pay, were always
at his orders, ready to leave at a few hours' notice for a six-
week expedition, and they served him at once as warriors
and information agents. More than half of them, so he said,
were to die in his service.

Thanks to these men, he was able to keep the initiative
with extremely daring operations, mysteriously undertaken
and of which much probably has remained obscure. He was
also able to protect himself. His reputation was not unknown
to the Turks, who had put a price on his head: twenty
thousand pounds living and ten thousand dead. It was an
enormous sum for the Bedouins whether they supported the
Revolt or not. Henceforward Lawrence travelled with a
strong escort during the lightning expeditions which he
made behind the Turkish lines.

He equipped these camel-men with modern light machine-
guns, which they carried attached to their saddles, so that a
light detachment could dispose of a heavy fire power; it was
the application to camel raids of modern tactics greatly in
advance of those used on the European front. In Lawrence's
methods these two tendencies are always to be found: a love
of the past and a respect for the picturesque aspect of primitive peoples, allied to a rapid understanding of every novelty,
and the ability to make use of it, embarrassed neither by
rules nor regulations: the men of his guard, mounted on
swift camels and dressed in shining robes, carried the same
equipment as the commandos of 1944.

The Arabs admired the leader who could treat himself to
a personal escort of this kind, and his prestige increased. At
Aqaba the English officers were rather shocked. It was not
usual in the British Army to raise mercenaries like this and
it implied a scandalous liberty of action on Lawrence's part,
but he did not find it disagreeable to show that he was apart
from and above the others.

*   *   *

In the course of the winter Allenby asked the Arabs to keep the enemy occupied on his extreme right by attacking Maan and by holding up the traffic in the south of the Dead Sea which brought the grain to Syria and Palestine from the corn belt known as 'the Fertile Crescent' which runs from Kerak to the mountains of Judaea.

At the beginning of January, Joyce, accompanied by Lawrence, struck a blow fifty miles south of Maan, by cutting the railway line at Tell Shahm. It was at once a diversion and a test. For the first time in their operations in Arabia the English employed armoured cars. The raid was a success; once they were through the mountains by the road which had been built with such difficulty, the cars could roll across the soft firm surface. The railway line was henceforward a few hours by car from Aqaba.

It was during this raid that Lawrence made friends with the good-natured stalwarts who drove the Rolls and the Talbots. The English troopers were delighted at finding an officer who was at once as brave as he was friendly and with whom there was not that deep gulf which in the British Army separates the officers from the men. From then on they were entirely devoted to him and he was to carry out some memorable exploits with them.[1]

Mysterious, superior and reserved with his equals, the other English officers, Lawrence was familiar and relaxed with the soldiers, joked with them and even confided in them his disappointments and his rebuffs in dealing with the deceitful Sherifs' men. Already he was exhibiting one of the most curious sides of his character: this man who was cultivated to the extent of Byzantinism, this Oxford graduate, was always attracted by simple people, whether Arab or English, and he felt more at ease with men who were scarcely educated than with his intellectual and social equals, a propensity that was later to shape his life.

[1] One of them, S. C. Rolls, wrote *Steel Chariots in the Desert*, in which he describes his experiences during the campaign with Lawrence in Arabia.

The Battle of Tafileh

THE Arab army after long months of footslogging and disappointments, appeared to be on the verge of success. At the
same time as the English were attacking Tell Shahm, Nasir
was raiding Jurf el Derwish (the Valley of the Dervish) thirty
miles north of Maan, with the regulars, one gun and some
Bedouins and had taken the station, capturing two hundred
Turks. Maan, thus isolated to the north and south, was neu-
tralised; the Sherifs' troops could push on towards the Fertile
Crescent to the south of the Dead Sea.

An Arab detachment took Shobek to the west of the line,
halfway between Maan and the Dead Sea.[1] Nasir, accompanied by Auda, made a long march by camel and presented
himself in front of Tafileh. The village was only defended by
a hundred and eighty Turks and by the armed peasants of
the area under the command of the Ottoman governor. The
Bedouins wished to take Tafileh by assault in order to be
able to hold it to ransom more at their leisure, but Auda,
furious that the villagers should have the audacity to resist
the Abu Tayis, their secular masters, advanced alone up to
the first houses and shouted in his prodigious voice: "Dogs,
do you not know Auda?" As at Jericho in other times, the
roar of the old lion was sufficient to bring the defence of the
place to an end.

At the end of January, Zeid, accompanied by Lawrence
and Jaafar, came to take over the direction of operations, and
installed himself in Tafileh. The weather had turned, and
cold reigned in the mountains of Moab; snow blocked the
passes, and the infantry and the guns were left behind; to
defend Tafileh the Sherif's men had no more than the hundred camel-men of Zeid's retinue, Lawrence's guard, a few
Egyptian machine-gunners, a French detachment under

[1] Right up in the mountains, Shobek is the Montréal of the
Crusades.

the Moroccan Sergeant-Major Trabelsi with his machine-guns, and finally some Motalga nomads. The cold was terrible.

This was the situation when on the 25th of January the Turks counter-attacked Tafileh with three battalions of infantry, some cavalry, two mortars and thirty machine-guns. The Arabs were taken entirely by surprise, and within the instant the whole village was thrown into complete confusion. The inhabitants who had made so poor a show in defending the place and who had fraternised with the Sherif's men were in a panic at the thought of the reprisals which the Turks would take, and fled in every direction; Zeid's troops began to waver even before the battle was joined.

Zeid and Jaafar tried in vain to stop the panic; they had decided to abandon Tafileh and to defend themselves in the ravine to the south of the village, but it was unlikely that their composite force could hold out against a large, regular and well-disciplined formation.

Lawrence allowed the Arab chiefs to lose their heads, and then offered to take command. The situation was not so bad, he said, let him handle it, and the Turks would not get through. Zeid and Jaafar were only too happy to let him have the responsibility of a compromised operation, and willingly handed over command.

He pushed out the few troops of which he disposed in front of Tafileh and supported them with the villagers, who were ready to fight for fear of the Turks' return. Several small crests broke the enemy's advance, and he had them occupied with light detachments which fell back successively, breaking the *élan* of the Turks' advance till the moment that the enemy ran into the fire of the Egyptian and Moroccan machine-guns. Lawrence then sent a hundred men armed with light machine-guns to turn the enemy's flank on the right and to cut them to pieces with well-sustained fire.

The manœuvre succeeded perfectly; the three Turkish battalions fought courageously, but were shattered, and four hundred men were left on the ground; the Sherifs' men took two hundred and fifty prisoners, twenty-seven machine-guns, and two hundred pack animals, and the few survivors of the Turkish units fled down the snow-bound roads, pursued by the nomads; on the field of battle the slaughter had been frightful, and the wounded Turks, left on the frozen ground and stripped naked by the Bedouins, all died of cold in the night.

The fight at Tafileh is Lawrence's great battle. It is precisely of his genre. He won it with a minute force, and with his sure judgment, tactical flair and personal magnetism, that alone enabled him to hold troops, demoralised by a surprise attack, in the firing line. In his book he deprecates his success, speaking with derision of this "orthodox" victory, carried off according to the principles of tactical manuals; in fact this episode, with the march on Aqaba, remains one of the highlights of his career.

*   *   *

From Tafileh, the Dead Sea and the Fertile Crescent were within striking distance for the Arabs. As soon as he could, Lawrence launched some raids against this source of food supplies for the Turks. Three days after the battle of Tafileh, a party of sixty-six Bedouins surprised the little port in which were anchored the motor launches and sailing lighters which transported the corn destined for the armies of Jordan. The nomads pillaged the provisions and sank the boats. Thus, in the way in which Allenby had asked, the enemy's rear was disorganised and the traffic on the Dead Sea was brought to a standstill for some time.

There remained, to complete the mission given to him by the Commander-in-Chief, to attempt a raid on the mouth of the Jordan, to the east of Jericho. The operation was found to be impossible for the moment, as he would have had to send his camel troops out through the snow and the defiles of the mountains of Moab, and Lawrence decided to wait at Tafileh for the weather to allow him to operate; with his guard he installed himself in the village, close to Zeid and the Sherifs' men.

Living conditions in this wretched country, at an altitude of four thousand five hundred feet, at the height of winter were appalling. Lawrence lived with his men. "We were penned in verminous houses of cold stone; lacking fuel, lacking food, storm bound in streets like sewers, amid blizzards of sleet and an icy wind . . . we were filthy and miserable; stringy like shaven cats. . . ." Philosophically he tried to read *Le Morte d'Arthur,* one of his favourite books, but after a few days of this sordid life, he could stand it no more and decided to go down to the south.

A long ride through the snow and the cold brought him to Guweira, where he found Joyce and Alan Dawnay. Bad news was waiting for him: Feisal had wanted to fight a battle himself, and having attacked the station of Mudowwara with four companies of regulars, several thousand nomads and Pisani's guns (22nd and 23rd of January, 1918), he had suffered a humiliating repulse, and Pisani, abandoned on the field by the Sherif's men, had had great difficulty in saving his pieces; Lawrence, who knew the fighting value of the Emir better than anyone, would never have allowed him to undertake such an operation alone.

Meanwhile money to the tune of thirty thousand sovereigns had arrived at Guweira, three hundred pounds of gold; Lawrence loaded it on to camels and left for Tafileh, where he entrusted his treasure to Zeid, enjoining him to let the soldiers have their pay and to keep the bulk of what remained to finance future operations; then, without pausing for breath, he left again with a few men of his guard to reconnoitre, sixty miles to the north of Tafileh, the approaches of the Jordan that were to be the theatre of his final actions.

He took six or seven days to accomplish this rapid patrol, which took him as far as Ain Hesban, fifteen miles from the north end of the Dead Sea, and on the 19th of February, 1918, he returned to Tafileh, full of ideas and plans. A bold advance, he said to Zeid, would carry the Arab contingents to the levels of Jericho, where they would be able to link up with Allenby.

Zeid listened coldly to the Englishman. With what money, he asked, could they make this expedition?

"With what remains of the thirty thousand pounds which I gave you."

"But," replied Zeid, "it is all spent".

Lawrence was utterly crushed. All his projects, all his hopes were foundering, and he could not keep faith with Allenby; with the Commander-in-Chief who for months had trusted and supported him so generously, he would lose face; they were going to be able to judge what these Arabs, whose champion he had made himself, were worth, the apathetic, uncertain, unreliable Feisal, and the disdainful, vain, grand seigneur Zeid, who were furious that the English should call the tune, and all these Syrian or Iraqi officers who with but very few exceptions thought of nothing but of betraying their allies.

Lawrence went to see Nasir, who sick with fever had been unable to intervene. Everything was going badly, said the Sherif: Zeid had allowed himself to be influenced by his entourage of imbeciles and cowards, dissipating now to one, now to others the manna which had fallen into his hands. What could Lawrence do? For months he had been in the breach, driving himself unsparingly for the Sherifs' cause, he had undergone incredible fatigues, he had been wounded and tortured, and his nerves were at breaking point; under this final blow which struck at his pride, he cracked. He paid up his guard, dismissed them, warned Joyce and Dawnay, and intent on leaving the Arabs for ever, he reached Allenby's headquarters north of Beersheba on the 22nd of February.

* * *

At G.H.Q. Lawrence did not find Allenby, but by chance he met Clayton and Hogarth, who were acting in liaison with the General; Clayton believed in Lawrence and had always supported him; Hogarth was his old master, his best friend, the only one in whom T.E. had blind confidence. With these two men he could pour out all the bitterness that he felt:

" I had made a mess of things . . . I had put all myself into the Arab business and had come to wreck . . . I had no tricks left worth a meal in the Arab market-place and wanted the security of custom; to be conveyed, to pillow myself on duty and obedience: irresponsibly.

"I complained . . . I was tired to death of free-will. . . . In my last five actions I had been hit . . . generally I had been hungry, lately always cold. . . . I feared to be alone lest the winds of circumstance, or power, or lust, blow my empty soul away".

Clayton and Hogarth let him talk, understanding his disappointments and his nervous collapse, and then they cheered him up again: there could be no question of quitting: the English had just taken Jericho, Allenby was about to be given fresh means, the General had great plans, and Lawrence was indispensable; besides he was to be sent an assistant: Young, an Indian Army officer, who knew the Arab business well, was going to Feisal's army to give him help.

Lawrence allowed himself to be lectured, feeling his discouragement evaporate at the idea of future operations and at the rôle which he was going to play in them; in order to complete his recovery they took him to Allenby, who explained to him his plans and told him the part which he intended to assign to the Sherifs' men. Lawrence again took the road south. On the 4th of March he was at Aqaba.

Operations around Maan

March-August 1918

AT the beginning of 1918 the Grand Interallied War Council, at the instigation of Lloyd George and General Smuts, had decided to put Turkey definitely out of the war. The Army of Egypt was to unleash a vast offensive which would take them, so they hoped, right into Asia Minor.

The Turkish forces opposed to the British army were composed of the 7th and the 8th Armies, defending the coastal plain between Jaffa and the north of the Dead Sea, and of the 4th Army, occupying the front to the east of Jordan. Allenby's plan was to launch a preliminary attack in a north-eastern direction at the level of Jericho, in order to separate the two enemy groups, and then proceed with an offensive on the west of the front against the Palestine lines.

In these projects the Sherifs' forces were to play their part. They were to immobilise the Turkish troops that held Medina by making a definitive cutting of the Hejaz line, neutralise and if possible take Maan, and finally effect a junction with the bulk of the British troops to the north of the Dead Sea. To achieve this programme the Commander-in-Chief put at Feisal's disposal artillery, machine-guns, seven hundred pack camels and three hundred thousand pounds in gold with which to buy the support of the Bedouins.

In preparation for these operations the leaders of the Arab army divided the work amongst themselves. Joyce and the Sherifs' staff, Jaafar, Maulud and Nuri Said, were to attack Maan with the regulars, Dawnay was to cut the railway line in order to isolate Medina, and Lawrence took charge of the raising of the Bedouin tribesmen in the vicinity of Amman, who were to attack the Turks, hard pressed by the British attack, in the rear.

On the 2nd of April Lawrence left Aba el Lissan, taking

with him two thousand pack camels loaded with enough provisions, rifles, cartridges and gold to rally the Beni-Sakhr clans
to the Revolt, as he wished to hurl them against the Ottomans.
He was accompanied by Sheik Mirzuk and by some of the
men of his guard which he had reformed. Four days' marching brought him to Atara, south-east of Amman, the centre
of the Beni-Sakhr: he made camp there and prepared to act
as soon as he should hear news of the English offensive.

Once more Lawrence was alone amongst the Bedouins, exposed to every form of treachery, without any contact with
Feisal or with the British army. The oppressive period of
waiting lasted several days; no message reached him from
Allenby, but alarming rumours were beginning to circulate.
The English, it was said, had been repulsed, were flying in
disorder, had gone back over Jordan, the victorious Turks
were going to crush them and retake Jerusalem; the Beni-
Sakhr sheiks congratulated themselves on not having come
out openly against the Ottomans, exaggerated the stories of
the British rout and described the reprisals which the Turks
were taking on the Arabs of Es Salt who were accused of
having collaborated with the enemy. Lawrence had to strike
camp and return through the desert to the Sherif's base near
Maan.

Unfortunately the information which the Bedouins were
spreading was partly correct and Allenby had recently
suffered, to the east of Jordan, a severe repulse. Everything
had held up the British advance, the bad weather, the river
swollen by the rains, and a terrain that was particularly difficult. Having started the attack on the 21st of March, the
Anzacs and the English had not reached Es Salt till the 26th.
The cavalry, followed by the infantry, had not arrived in the
vicinity of Amman, on the railway line, till the 27th, had
come up against well-entrenched defences, and had been
unable to take the town. The weather was terrible, the natives
were hostile, and the British, after having lost fifteen hundred
men, had to beat a retreat towards Jordan. But apart from
this, the retreat ordered by Allenby was in no way a disaster;
the English brought back three thousand prisoners and fell
back in good order, with their wounded, but the effect on the
already hesitant Bedouins was deplorable and the tribesmen

14

of the north who had been so evasive about joining the Sherifs' cause now went *en masse* to renew their tokens of obedience to the Turks.

Full of anxiety, Lawrence returned to Feisal's camp. There further bad news awaited him. Zeid had lost Tafileh. Attacked by several Turkish battalions he had lost his head, set fire to his ammunition and his provisions and retreated towards Maan, abandoning behind him the Moroccan machine-gunners of Sergeant-Major Trabelsi, who only extricated themselves from the adventure with great difficulty, thanks to the sangfroid of their leader. Around Maan things were going no better. Lawrence, Joyce and Jaafar had originally intended to attack the place from the rear, after having cut it off from all communications with the north, but the officers of the Sherif had insisted on carrying out a frontal offensive; launching their troops on the well-organised barbed-wire entrenchments, they had been repulsed with heavy losses.

Only Dawnay had been able to carry out the part of the operation which had been assigned to him. On the 19th of April, with the armoured cars, some of the Egyptian camels and supported by Bedouin partisans, he took and destroyed the station of Tell Shahm, to the south-east of Maan and definitely interrupted traffic between Medina and Maan. Dawnay was a professional soldier, precise and strict, for whom Lawrence had great praise, but his 'orthodox' success did not please T.E., who made some sarcastic comments on the way in which he had conducted the business. "Desert warfare is not the same as a training scheme", he said. He resented every incursion into his domain, the raiding of the line and the guerilla war.

* * *

In fact, despite the support which he received from Allenby and Clayton, Lawrence had to carry on an unceasing struggle to make his ideas prevail with the High Command, and gain support for his methods, the alliances which he had advocated, and that which he considered his personal work; often he was constrained to take himself away from the operations in progress on the Sherifs' front, in order to go hastily to Cairo to defend his points of view.

Indeed there were many on the General Staff of the army of Egypt who criticised his policy and his passionate obstinacy in supporting the Sherifs' forces and in particular Feisal. It was remarked that the Hejaz Revolt was far from bringing together all the Arab peoples; the nomads of the north remained obedient to the Ottomans, supplied them with combatants, guides and caravaneers; Ibn Saud, the Emir of the Nejd, the chief of the Wahabite sect who ruled over more than half of Arabia, not only refused to join the Movement, but also made war on the Grand Sherif, his hereditary enemy, thus diminishing the help that the Sherifian forces were able to give to the Allies.

In June 1918 the Wahabites attacked the oasis of Turaba, to the east of Mecca, and massacred a detachment of Abdullah's troops. St. John Philby, the political officer attached by the Indian government to Ibn Saud, came to Cairo and stated that England had made a terrible mistake in supporting the Sherif of Mecca and not Ibn Saud. Feisal, who in the words of Lawrence and of the Arab Bureau was to "bring the Arab Revolt to full glory", was an incompetent, a coward and the most false of men; they should rather have assured themselves of the assistance of the Wahabites who represented a more warlike and sounder element in Arabia. Lawrence blew St. John Philby's theories to pieces; he considered him (like all those who did not share his ideas) as an anti-Christ, and these attacks against a policy which he had so profoundly at heart hurt his pride and obliged him to constant intrigues with the English rulers of Egypt.

* * *

For several months the Arabs tried unsuccessfully, but with much courage and many bloody losses, to penetrate the Turkish defences around Maan. Their units were used up in attacks that imitated the vain holocausts of the Western Front. Lawrence disapproved of these useless and murderous operations but he could not prevent them; he was unable to make the Sherifs' staff, composed of officers trained in the Turko-Germanic school, understand that in this broken

country and against a brave and disciplined enemy who knew
how to use the ground but whose forces were dispersed and
whose communications were difficult, the only hope of victory
lay in manœuvre and mobility.[1]

The only satisfaction in these depressing months was to
have trained a pupil who applied his methods to perfection.
Nasir was succeeding better than anyone in the guerilla
operations; sixty miles to the north of Maan, with a few
partisans, one or two guns, and enough English gold to buy
the co-operation of the Bedouins, he was harassing the Ottomans' communications. Two British officers accompanied him
on his exploits inside the Turkish lines: Hornby with his
Sappers was in charge of demolitions, and Peake with his
Egyptian camels; but no other chieftain imitated Nasir's
methods and the Sherif's army spent most of its resources on
a trench warfare which produced no tangible results and
terrible slaughter.

At the beginning of the summer, the assistant whom Headquarters had promised Lawrence arrived at Aqaba. It was
Captain Young, the Indian Army officer whom T.E. had met
in the far-off days of Carchemish, and again in Mesopotamia
during his mission of 1915, and later at Jidda when the
captain had for a certain time taken Wilson's place. Young
was a direct man, very much a soldier, and little inclined to
follow the Alexandrine subtleties of Lawrence's mind. The
latter greeted him with caustic reserve. "They wanted to
give me a deputy for dealing with the Bedouins in case I
disappeared. I suggested Gertrude Bell, but since women are
not wanted in war, I said that you would do". Then he left,
leaving his colleague to sort himself out without any further
information or orders in the midst of the Sherif's men. Young
allowed his beard to grow, learnt to ride a camel, and then

---

[1] See *Les Armées française dans la Grande Guerre*, t. IX, annexe 617,
Djeddah, le 10 mai 1918. In his report Captain Lapadu-Hargues gives
us very complete information about the attacks on Maan and details
of the part played by the French contingents, in particular that played
by Lieutenant de Rivoyre. Another report by Commandant Cousse,
dated from Cairo the 16th of June 1918, contains some interesting
appreciations of the Sherif's army; he praises the courage of the soldiers
but stresses the bad spirit among some of the officers and the imper-
fections in the organisation of Feisal's troops.

tried to play his part with the Arabs and to combat their anarchy. Their disorder, their contempt for any definite time-table and for all pre-arranged plans made him despair; he was to be seen running from one end of the base at Aqaba to the other and in Feisal's camp before Maan, trying to organise transport, supplies and co-ordinated plans of attack. The Arabs laughed at him, called him the 'shuttle' and continued to do exactly as they wished. With a perverse pleasure Law-rence watched as the understudy whom they had imposed on him foundered.

The opportunity soon presented itself for T.E. to show how much a chimera it was to think of replacing him in the man-agement of tribal politics. The affair is not very clear and it can only be read between the lines in the memoirs of Law-rence, Young and Brémond and in the accounts of the official history.

Visiting the General Headquarters in Palestine, at the beginning of May, Lawrence was called in by the Chief of Staff, Bols, whom he did not much like, and who said to him with a triumphant air: "Well, we're in Salt all right".

"What?" said Lawrence.

"The Beni-Sakhr Bedouins who live in the hinterland have sent us delegates; on account of the subsidies which we have poured out on them, they wish to assist us to the extent of twenty thousand warriors: we are going to sweep out the Turks". Lawrence knew that the Beni-Sakhr had no such fighting strength, quite apart from the fact that they had left for their summer pastures in the mountains, but above all he was furious at this encroachment on his exclusive domain of nomadic politics. He remarked that they were heading for a disaster and that the Beni-Sakhrs, who were in any case not very reliable, did not have four hundred warriors in the area. Bols would listen to nothing, delighted with having "put one across" Lawrence; besides, he said, Allenby had accepted his suggestions and the attack, led by General Chauvel, was already in progress.

In fact the English and the Anzacs crossed the Jordan, and using the roads that they had followed during their first unfortunate operation, plunged at the beginning of May into the mountains of Moab, north-east of the Dead Sea. But they

ran into the artillery and machine-gun fire of the Turks, who,
warned very probably by the Beni-Sakhrs themselves, had
sent reinforcements to Es Salt. An enemy counter-attack
along the eastern bank of the Jordan threatened the British
rear; the Australian cavalry found its retreat nearly cut off,
and was only saved by Allenby's quick decision, for with the
flair of a great general he grasped the situation and ordered
the engagement to be broken off at the crucial moment. The
English left fifteen hundred men behind in this unfortunate
affair. Lawrence seems to have confined himself to doing
nothing and not to have been very much moved by this
bloody failure. He declared philosophically that the staff
would from now on be less severe about his difficulties with
the nomads.

As his only contribution to the offensive he had sent Young
north with orders to get as many of the Beni-Sakhrs as he
could persuade on the move. Young was not prepared for
such a mission; he was up against the inertia of the Sherif's
men as of the Bedouins and could do nothing. Auda, whose
assistance he tried to obtain, turned a deaf ear. This officer
learnt that he could never understudy Lawrence to whom he
was of such little assistance, and returned to Aqaba, where
with patience, orderliness and energy he organised the transport of the Arab army.

                    *   *   *

A few miles away, on the other side of the barrier, the
officers of the German mission in Turkey were having experiences with the Orientals analogous to those which Lawrence,
Young and Joyce were having at the camp in Aqaba. Their
commander, Liman von Sanders, in his book *Five Years in
Turkey,* has told of his efforts to control the Ottomans, who
like the Sherif's men were suspicious, xenophobic incapable
of keeping to a schedule, and who always wanted to have their
own way and never ceased to complain of the Germans.

His memoirs to a certain extent corroborate the facts related and the theories put forward by Lawrence in the *Seven
Pillars.* The German general speaks frequently of the Arab
rising which gave him much worry, immobilised his forces,
killed his men and created a constant state of insecurity on

his flank. On one point of strategy he is entirely in agreement
with Lawrence. He says that he disapproved of the defence of
Medina, which he held to be costly and pointless, and that on
several occasions he earnestly pleaded with the Turkish command that they evacuate this city and align their front east
and west on a level with Amman, but that Enver and Jemal
for political and religious reasons, refused to abandon it.

The Solitary Warrior

THUS after several successful operations, the war in Arabia dragged on, confused and disappointing. This stagnation, the mistakes, these repulses made Lawrence depair; it seemed to him, rightly or wrongly, that if all initiative had been left to him he would have been able to produce very different results with the Arab and British resources. During all this period he isolated himself in a personal activity which he surrounded in mystery, embarking on solitary exploits each a little crazier than the last.

In the first world conflict a long positional war reduced the military art to a concise form; officers and men had to face the most extreme of dangers but the most ridiculously simple of situations. The essence was to defend or attack under withering fire with the smallest chances of survival. The platoon commander had but to show authority and stoicism. It was only in the course of the second world war with lightning armoured attacks, commandos and parachute raids that intelligence and invention regained their place in the military art.

Lawrence hated all routine, and he was as imaginative as he was brave; all his operations carry the marks of intelligence and careful forethought, even when most adventurous; but they also show an almost morbid need to run terrible risks. To carry out a demolition, to spy out the enemy position, or to make contact with the Bedouin clans, he set off alone with a band of scoundrels, who were kept in obedience by his personal prestige as much as with gold and the use of the whip, on raids on which the slightest error of direction could have caused his death from hunger or thirst, and on which he was at the constant mercy of a bandit's shot or an act of treason. He seemed to take a perverse pleasure in increasingly exposing himself.

This need to do things himself, to be everywhere, to act

now as if he was the inspiration of a complicated diplomacy and of military manœuvres on a wide field, now like a subaltern in command of a patrol, was one of Lawrence's limitations. A great general cannot also be an executive, and if he had known how to refuse the secondary tasks in order to organise and direct from a higher level, he would probably have achieved more complete results in Arabia. But it must also be remarked that his active participation in the fighting and his courage which was known to all the followers of the Sherif enabled him to keep a brittle and hesitant Movement going, and gave him a powerful hold over the Orientals. Whether it was justified or not this attitude involved him in senseless dangers.

When he returned from Atara, at the time of Allenby's unsuccessful offensive on Es Salt, he did not hesitate to enter Amman in disguise. The frightful memory of his tortures in Deraa should have stopped him, but probably only spurred him on to make this audacious attempt. Disguised as a gipsy woman and accompanied by Farraj, also dressed as a woman, he walked through the streets of the town which were full of Turkish soldiers, exchanging coquettish jokes with them and delighting in thus flirting with captivity and death.

This love of danger was immensely satisfying to his pride, but it also gave him some terrible moments. He always took with him the little Farraj, one of the two ephebes whom he had engaged as personal servants during the Aqaba expedition. Daud, Farraj's friend and kindred spirit, had died from exposure and the despairing survivor was only the more attached to his master, whom he never left. During the summer of 1918, returning with some camel-men from a trip to the east of the Dead Sea, Lawrence attacked a small Turkish post on the Hejaz line. This affray had no military purpose; it was simply a matter of satisfying the lust for blood and plunder of the wild beasts who composed his guard, and of allowing them to take a few arms and items of equipment from the bodies. During the fight Farraj was struck by a bullet which passed through his body and touched his spine. The wretched man lay on the track in agony and when they tried to lift him, he cried out with pain; meanwhile a party of Turks were approaching on a trolley, coming from a

nearby station; they had to make off and Farraj could not
be carried.

"We could not leave him where he was, to the Turks,
because we had seen them burn alive our hapless wounded.
For this reason we were all agreed, before action, to finish off
one another, if badly hurt, but I had never realized that it
might fall to me to kill Farraj.

"I knelt down beside him, holding my pistol near the
ground, by his head, so that he should not see my purpose;
but he must have guessed it, for he opened his eyes and
clutched me with his harsh, scaly hand, the tiny hand of these
unripe Nejd fellows. I waited a moment and he said 'Daud
will be angry with you', the old smile coming back so
strangely to his grey shrinking face. I replied 'Salute him
from me'. He returned the formal answer 'God will give you
peace', and at last wearily closed his eyes".

* * *

God did not give Lawrence peace. He had the impression
that he was forever climbing up a wearisome slope. He was
mortally tired of the Arabs, of Arabian affairs and of himself.
He was supported by his burning will-power, by his pride
and by his sense of humour, which was in no wit gay but
bitter and often sneering, and which allowed him always to
see the ridiculous and inane side of himself and of everything
around him.

He felt himself drifting further and further from his fellow
countrymen, but he could none the less perceive with lucidity
the barrier which separated him from the Arabs, a barrier of
race, religion and sensitivity. In camp, he kept aloof. Plunged
in a morose reverie, he read untiringly the three books which
he carried about with him, an anthology of English poets,
Malory's Le Morte d'Arthur, and an Aristophanes, a mixture
of lyricism and sarcasm, the two sides of his character.

Finding escape only in violent action, he carried out alone,
or almost so, a number of raids on the Turkish lines and on
the railway; more than anything else he plunged into the
devastating solitude of the desert. He has left us sparkling
descriptions of the infinite sands of the Nefud, of the chalk
mountains of Moab, of the magnificent canyon of Rumm,
but above all else he understood the essence of the desert,

and has grasped better than anyone else what it is that these empty spaces mean to certain minds. He wrote that, "To the thinkers of the Town the impulse into Nitria had ever been irresistible, not probably that they found God dwelling there, but that in its solitude they heard more certainly the living word they brought with them". Perhaps in this lies one of the keys to his strange destiny.

But in the desert, also, he was pursued by phantoms. The inner voice became a tumultuous nightmare, and he saw again, in anguish, the Moor executed by his own hand, the tortures of Deraa, the wounded at Tafileh dying in the frozen night, and Farraj lying on the cinders waiting for the *coup de grâce*. This war filled him with horror as did the sudden flushes of cruelty which he often felt rising within him. He realised with fear that he had within him the stuff and the tastes of a killer: "Blood was always on our hands", he said with horror. "They had had enough of corpses!" One night, crossing the line alone a long way in front of his guard, he came across a Turkish soldier asleep. The man threw a panic-stricken glance at the pistol which the Englishman held in his hand, and then looked sadly at his rifle which he had left a few yards away. Lawrence said in a low voice, "God is merciful", and passed on. The little Turk was man enough not to shoot him in the back.

* * *

His position in Arabia was obviously something of a very particular kind, considerable but fragile. The importance of his rôle, the initiative which he was allowed, the prestige which he enjoyed with the Arabs were sufficient to turn the head of any man of thirty. The English officers were perfectly aware that without being the official head of the British mission, it was he who directed almost entirely the policy and strategy in this theatre of operations; he enjoyed Allenby's confidence, and during his visits to G.H.Q. he discussed the plans of campaign with the great man alone. As for the Arabs, from self-interest but also from admiration, and subjugated by his extraordinary personality, they seem to have adopted him almost completely. He always wore Arab dress, even when visiting the English headquarters; by strength of will,

suppleness of mind and his ability to imitate, he had acquired
not only the appearance but also the mentality of an Arab.
Seeing him in constant intimacy with the grand seigneurs of
Mecca, the Arabs were not far from considering him as one
of themselves.

On one occasion Feisal had him taken to Mecca. He walked
around the town and went to the Suks to buy a golden dagger,
the ornament usually reserved for the descendants of the
prophets. It was a scandalous thing; they had had to hide it
from King Hussein and did not dare talk about it openly, but,
in fact, it had taken place. A Christian had perhaps never
before been thus admitted to the Holy City, and a similar
situation had perhaps never before arisen among the
Muslims.[1]

Certainly he knew the value of the homage of the Arabs
and the dangerous fragility of the sentiments which they
expressed, but he took a keen pleasure in this game and was
to allow himself to be caught in its toils. He had always been
vain, and had always loved disguises; to impress the English
and the Arabs he played at Oriental princes; the title of
Sherif was in the end to obsess him, he always carried his gold
dagger, and we know from Ronald Storrs that on one of his
little-known exploits he had himself called the Sherif Hassan.[2]

Those who saw him at that time describe him living in his
tent, dressed in splendid white silk robes, seated on a rich
carpet, reading or meditating in magnificent isolation, surrounded only by his mercenaries, who guarded him closely.

*   *   *

In the midst of these violent and contradictory sentiments
one thought haunted him: what would be his moral position
with regard to the Arabs and Feisal, but above all with regard
to his more intimate friends, Nasir, Ali Ben el-Hussein, and
to those autonomists of Syria whom he had known for years
and whom he had visited in the course of his secret missions,
and of the mysterious friend who waited for him at Damas-

[1] Lawrence is very discreet about his journey to Mecca, but he speaks
of it, however, in his letters of the 25th of September, 1920, the 25th of
May, 1923, and the 27th of May, 1927. Ronald Storrs was convinced
that this visit had taken place.
[1] *Orientations*, p. 538.

cus? He had promised to everybody, in order to galvanise
their energy and stimulate their faith, more than he had any
right to promise; the basis of his propaganda had been that
the Arab world should create itself and, for corollary, the
Arab world for the Arabs. Now he knew perfectly well that
the Allies would never allow this last point to take effect.
England and France had colonialist intentions, the one on
Mesopotamia, the other on Syria. What would become of the
promises of total independence preached to the soldiers whom
he had sent to fight? The remorse of having been in whatever
degree the artisan of an imposture gnawed at his heart. In
his pride he considered himself engaged on a personal project,
and he forgot the Arabs' innumerable failures to keep faith,
the mediocrity of their efforts, their venality, their vacillations and their duplicity.

On the 16th of August he realised that he was thirty years
old. He was at the wells of Bair, preparing for the autumn
offensives, amongst a crowd of English and Arabs. He isolated
himself for several hours to discover, with cruel lucidity, the
reason for his existence. Who was he, and where was he
going? He analysed himself unsparingly. No casuist has gone
further in self-criticism; no psychoanalyst has better dissected
the recesses of the subconscious; no detractor has ever been
more severe in judgment than he was of himself in the course
of this searching of his conscience.

"Four years ago," he said to himself, "I had meant to be
a general and knighted when thirty. Such temporal dignities
(if I survived the next four weeks) were now in my grasp . . . ",
but it gave him no happiness and he felt no desire for them.
At heart he was vain, with, God forgive him, a conscious
vanity controlled by the intelligence, but vain none the less.
"There was a craving to be famous; and a horror of being
known to like being known."—"The hearing other people
praised made me despair jealously of myself . . . I began to
wonder if all established reputations were founded like mine,
on fraud?"

Yes, all his work was one vast imposture. He had at the
same time deceived Allenby, Clayton, Feisal and the Arabs by
his perpetual double game: "I must have had some tendency,
some aptitude for deceit. Without that I should not have

deceived men so well, and persisted two years in bringing to
success a deceit which others had framed and set afoot. . . ."

Besides, he had a base soul: "I liked the things underneath
me and took my pleasures and adventures downward. There
seemed a certainty in degradation, a final safety . . . the force
of things, years and an artificial dignity denied it me more
and more", but he kept a delicious memory of the days of his
youth when he had freely degraded himself, mingling with
the *canaille* and the dregs of Syria and Egypt.

The aims which he pursued were worth no more than himself, and in order to achieve them he had voluntarily lost his
European soul, without having gained an Oriental soul in
exchange. "A man who gives himself to be a possession of
aliens leads a Yahoo life, having bartered his soul to a brute-
master." Feisal was a puppet. "I served him out of pity, a
motive which degraded us both . . . " and Syria was no more
than a mosaic of tiny tribes without bond of race or religion,
and without any common notion of patriotism—a heap of
rootless bazaar-keepers and scoundrels.

It was for this that he had sacrificed himself for years, but
what was the moral value of his sacrifice? There is no cause
worth the sacrifice of oneself, for everything is useless. The
sole value of sacrifice is to elevate the voluntary victim; and
it is the victim alone who profits; it is, then, a further act of
pride and of egoism. "There was nothing loftier than a cross,
from which to contemplate the world. The pride and exhilara-
tion of it were beyond conceit. . . . To rescue simple ones from
such evil by paying for them his complicated self would be
avaricious in the modern man. . . ."

But clearness of insight has never prevented men from
acting in conformity with their nature, their duty or their
passions. He had begun and he must continue. Allenby at
this time was preparing for the final offensive: Lawrence
wished to play his part in it and lead Feisal to Damascus, as
he had promised himself.

*   *   *

The defeats of the Allies in the West and the weakening
of the English forces in the Orient had their effect on the
politics of the Sherif's army. One day Lawrence learnt from

the Intelligence Service in Cairo that Feisal was negotiating the terms of a cease-fire with the Turks, and perhaps of an alliance with the Ottomans against the Allies.

The bitterness of a man who had given himself body and soul to the Arab Movement, when confronted with this treason, can be imagined. We do not know with what counter-mines he managed to interrupt the parleys nor what arguments he used with Feisal, but the defection of the Emir, whose fortune he had made, must have been a terrible blow to his pride.[1]

It was absolutely necessary to get out of the impasse, to think of some action which would again change the general aspect of the Arabian war as had done the march on Wedj, and Feisal's installation at Aqaba. Lawrence searched furiously for a solution to these problems but he was up against the inconsistency of the Bedouins, the desire of the Sherif's officers to carry on the war in their own way, and often the incapacity of his English colleagues to follow his overbold ideas.

He states in his memoirs that he had at this time envisaged a general effort on the part of the Arabs which would have carried them to the Hauran and even to Damascus. Leaving only a screen of troops in front of Maan, he would have pushed his regulars forward in the direction of Amman and Jericho in order to make contact with Allenby installed on the crossings of the Jordan, while a powerful offensive by the nomads would menace Deraa and Damascus. Only the internal quarrels of the Arabs and in particular Hussein's jealousy of Feisal would have prevented him from undertaking these operations.[2]

It must be repeated that these were only day dreams. At no time, neither at the beginning nor at the end of 1918, were the Arab partisans in a position to furnish such an effort. It does not seem that they would even seriously have tried. No

---

[1] The story is told by Liman von Sanders (*Five Years in Turkey*, p. 313), by Brémond (p. 291) and by Lawrence himself in the *Seven Pillars* (Ch. CI), where, as always in defence of the Arab cause, he declares that it was something quite natural. Feisal had the right to protect the interests of the Sherifs' followers and to quit the game if the affairs of the Allies were in jeopardy.

[2] *Seven Pillars*, Ch. XCVII.

one can doubt the furious courage of the Arabs, a virtue
which they have demonstrated in twenty wars, but this courage only appears when their passions are roused, when their
hunger for power or for gain is involved, or their religious
fanaticism. Now it is clear that their hearts were not in this
war, and that on the whole they fought feebly.

Meanwhile the summer of 1918 brought changes in the
general situation of the Palestine army and allowed Allenby
to prepare the final offensive in which Lawrence and the
Arabs were going to be able to play their part.

The Camel Corps

In July 1918, Allenby summoned Lawrence to a conference in which he explained to his staff the next of his projects for the autumn.

In France, the three German attacks at the beginning of the year had not succeeded in breaking through the Allied front. They were now enjoying a breathing space, and the troops that had been withdrawn from the Palestine army were beginning to be sent back again. The General was training up the newly-recruited units, for the most part Hindu, which he had been allocated; at his disposal were seventy or eighty thousand combatants and nearly six hundred guns. With a force of this size he had decided to take the offensive in September.

Facing him were forty or fifty thousand Turkish soldiers, strengthened and officered with Germans and Austrians. The experience of the war had shown that against an entrenched enemy, disposing of artillery and machine-guns, an attack could only succeed if the assailants were about three times more numerous than the defenders. Allenby, however, decided to attempt the venture by manœuvring the Turks in such a way that at the point at which he would try to make his break-through, the ratio of the opposing forces would be distinctly to his advantage.

His plan was inspired by the one that had enabled him to conquer Southern Palestine and Jerusalem a year previously: with a series of feints and manœuvres and by planting false information he intended to mislead the enemy into massing the bulk of his troops to the east along the Jordan, then after a brief artillery barrage, push his infantry against the defences of the coastal region, breach the line and hurl through his cavalry.

The rôle assigned to the Sherifs' army was a double one. On the one hand it was to attack around Maan in order to

draw off to the east as many of the enemy's troops as it could;
on the other, at the time of the offensive, commandos of camel-
troops or machine-gun carriers were to take to the desert and
destroy the railway north of Deraa, the only route by which
the Ottomans could send reinforcements and equipment to
the threatened areas of the Palestine front.

As far as we can ascertain, Lawrence must have put forward the following points: the Sherifs' army was not capable
of mounting a worth-while attack on Maan. It was itself under
the threat of a Turkish offensive and Feisal was so worried
that he was thinking of negotiating with the enemy. He must
be helped in one way or another in order to avoid a collapse
on this flank which would have altered the whole appearance
of the front and the equilibrium of the opposing forces. Lawrence could take care of the demolitions around Deraa, but
he needed reinforcements in order to carry out a diversion of
any significance on the Arab sector of the front.

There remained the political aspect. They had to think of
the future positions of England and France in the Levant,
and Allenby as much as Lawrence was attentive to this question. It was indispensable that a contingent of the Sherifs'
army should enter Damascus in order that it could be said
that the Arabs had liberated their future capital. Lawrence
would organise a small column strengthened with English,
Egyptian and French detachments, but officially commanded
by the Arabs, which would move up to the east, past the
enemy's left flank, and which if the allied offensive was successful could make a spectacular entry into Damascus, with
an important bearing on political propaganda for the future.

It must have been very disagreeable for Lawrence to admit
that he was powerless, with the Sherifs' army as his only asset,
to play the rôle which had been assigned to him. They were
back again to the old question, so often debated, of sending
European units into Arabia. After two years of futile discussion, they had to determine upon this solution if the plan of
the Commander-in-Chief was to be carried out in its entirety.
It was decided that the Palestine army would detach two
companies of the Camel Corps to the Arab army, and that
this contingent would carry out around Maan and along the
enemy's eastern front offensive activities which would con-

vince the Turks that the British command was going to make
its main thrust to the east of the Dead Sea and of the Jordan.

"Do not forget," said Allenby to Lawrence, "that I am not
giving you the Camel Corps, I am lending it to you temporarily. Send it back to me at the beginning of September. Try
not to lose me too many people, as I need all my men for
the offensive. As for your Arabs, they don't appear to be
able to do very much, and all I ask of them is that they
remain in front of Maan and make an appearance, with partisan attacks on the enemy's left flank in the area of Deraa,
on the 16th of September precisely." And the great man
added: "Three men and a boy with pistols, I ask no more
of you."

Lawrence returned to Aqaba to let Joyce and Young know
these new dispositions. Three hundred English camel-men
were going to arrive and operate for a month and a half to
the east of the line; the supplies must be hastily organised
for a raid of six hundred miles which would take them first
to the south of Maan and then by the wells of Bair as far as
Amman, where they would attempt to destroy the tunnel and
the viaduct of the Hejaz railway. They must from now on
also start thinking about the organisation of the column of
Feisal's troops, which at the end of September would cut the
railway lines around Deraa, and if the English attack was
successful, march on Damascus.

Joyce and Young were astounded. To employ English
troops was in complete contradiction to the evangelism
preached by Lawrence since the beginning of the campaign.
It seemed to them to be an incomprehensible and shocking
volte-face. Joyce told his colleague so, with some asperity, and
informed him that the reactions of the Arabs, unprepared for
this new policy, might well be disastrous; further, the im-
promptu organisation of supplies for two columns in succession across the immense spaces devoid of all resources seemed
to him impossible with the means of which the base disposed
and with the delays that could be foreseen.

Lawrence took the protests of the two officers very lightly.
He would, he said, take care of softening the reactions of the
Arabs to the arrival of the Camel Corps; the English would
only just touch on Aqaba and would then disappear into the

desert, and he would guide them for some of the way in
order to avoid incidents. As for the organisation of supplies,
that was for Joyce and Young to sort out; that was what they
were there for: he had himself solved more complicated
problems whilst on the move, and besides professional
soldiers understood nothing of this campaign and allowed
themselves to be blinded by the problems of administrative
routine; they always went too high in working out food for
men and forage for animals, forgetting that in a war of
movement the troops should live off the land. He cut by a
half all the estimates that were put in front of him. For
several weeks relations were fairly strained between the three
officers. Lawrence left Joyce and Young to their calculations
and retired to his tent, where his exasperated colleagues saw
him reading *Le Morte d'Arthur* all day, with a superior smile
on his lips.

Having left the Suez Canal on the 23rd of July, the Camel
Corps arrived at Aqaba on the 30th; it was commanded by
Captain Buxton, of the Sudan Civil Service, calm, cheerful
and friendly; the men, hardened by years of campaigning in
Sinai, were magnificent soldiers who asked for no more than
the chance to fight. Lawrence gathered the English around
a camp fire and explained the situation to them: they were
in a semi-savage country whose touchy and xenophobic inhabitants would probably give them a cool welcome; all incidents were to be avoided and if anyone was offensive "they
should turn the other cheek"; he would himself, moreover,
lead them for some of the march and smooth over friction
with the natives. Then, allowing the Camel Corps to be in
contact with the Sherifs' men for the least possible amount
of time, he took them off towards Wadi Itm, by which he
was to reach the gorges of Rumm, and then the station of
Mudowwara, south of Maan, the objective of the first attack.
The English unit was supported by the Hindu machine-
gunners and the machine-gun carriers.

Although they had tried to keep the march of the Camel
Corps a secret, their progress was not entirely uneventful.
All along the route the column was the target of odd rifle
shots, and at the wells of Rumm a brawl nearly took place
between the English and the Howeitat Bedouins, furious at

seeing their precious water removed by strangers; but all
things considered there were no serious incidents and Lawrence, obliged to rejoin Feisal for a difficult tribal negotiation, was able to return without too much anxiety, leaving
Buxton alone to carry on with the expedition.

Marching with these English soldiers had stirred in him
some contradictory sentiments. The routine of this troop, its
uselessly complicated equipment and its strict discipline
irritated him, but he discovered with astonishment that it
was deliciously relaxing to be with these simple, cheerful
men of his own race. His thoughts turned inwards bitterly,
and on his life spent constantly scheming with complex and
fugitive Orientals; it would have been good to submit to a
simple discipline, to be surrounded with trustworthy comrades, and to forget his indecisions, his scruples and dilemmas.

The men of his guard laughed at the English camel-men,
seated awkwardly in their saddles; Lawrence, annoyed, dryly
told his Ageyls that he could easily find in this troop of
Europeans forty soldiers who would ride better, fight better,
and support hardship better than no matter what group of
forty men chosen from Feisal's army.

Having left Buxton, he returned to Aqaba "through the
high-walled Itm, alone now with six silent, unquestioning
guards, who followed after me like shadows . . . and a home-
sickness came over me stressing vividly my outcast life among
the Arabs, while I exploited their highest ideals, and made
their love of freedom one more tool to make England win".

Buxton made for Mudowwara, the station that Feisal
had vainly attacked six months earlier, and arrived there on
the 8th of August. A few minutes' fighting sufficed to make
him the master of the place, losing no more than fifteen men
and taking a hundred and fifty prisoners. Then, still accompanied by the machine-gun carriers, he went north to carry
out the second part of his mission at Amman. En route
Lawrence rejoined him. His presence was useful in avoiding
difficulties; the natives were not exactly welcoming and the
supply depots were found to be insufficient, a part of the
provisions sent on by Young having been stolen by passing
caravans. Lawrence took the situation in hand; he had a
good understanding with Buxton, a direct, calm man of

whom he had no jealousy. Obliged to live more frugally and to pasture their animals, the English camel-men lightened their equipment and adapted themselves to the ways of the Bedouins; their progress became faster and more supple and to Lawrence's joy they went at the pace of a raiding party.

The column passed through Bair, and then on the 20th of August reached Muaggar ten miles south of Amman, where it was to destroy the great bridge and the tunnel on the Hejaz railway; but news of the raid had spread through the desert and the English found the line solidly held and the country combed with patrols. The camel-men wanted to attack but Lawrence refused. Allenby had enjoined him to avoid useless losses, he hated having people killed, and in his opinion the stake was not worth risking the lives of these fine soldiers. The principal object of the expedition had been attained, since the Turks, made uneasy, had reinforced their troops to the east of the Dead Sea. The enemy would find traces of a large column, heaps of boxes of preserves and the wheel ruts of numerous vehicles; the exaggerated reports of the nomads would do the rest and the Turkish command would remain convinced that the English were preparing a large-scale operation on their eastern flank.

The historian, however, is indeed tempted to ask whether Lawrence was not in fact disgruntled to find three hundred Europeans achieve with relative facility that which the Sherifs' army and all the Bedouin partisans had not been able to do for so many months, and whether he did not put an end to the operations of the Camel Corps for this very personal reason.

Lawrence took the Camel Corps back by Azrak and Bair as far as Aqaba, whence the camels went on to Beersheba, where they arrived on the 6th of September. In forty-four days they had marched fifteen hundred miles at a time when the heat makes any expedition in the Syrian desert extremely punishing.

Lawrence had been indefatigable. He had, as we have seen, followed Buxton's column for a part of the expedition but he had left it twice to deal with matters in which he felt that he was indispensable. With Joyce he had travelled by car down the track between Rumm and Azrak to find

out if the armoured cars could use it during the operation
which he was planning. At the beginning of August he
had taken part in Feisal's negotiations with Nuri Shalaan,
the Sheik of the Rualla Bedouins. Nuri had till then
refused to declare for the Revolt; his territory was to the
south and east of the Dead Sea and he was exposed to
Turkish reprisals, but the old Bedouin, sensing that the tide
was turning, had finally come to a decision. His adhesion
to the Movement took place with some solemnity; Feisal
sent a car for the Sheik and his suite to bring them to Jefer
and held a vast palaver in his tent in Lawrence's presence.
A large number of Rualla chiefs accompanied the potentate
of the nomads of the north who until then had been the
stumbling-block to Feisal's policy in Southern Syria. "It
seemed incredible that this old man had freely joined our
youth. For he was very old, livid and worn, with a grey
sorrow and remorse about him, and a bitter smile the only
mobility of his face . . . a red light glittered into his eye-
sockets and made them look like fiery pits in which the man
was slowly burning."

Once more, during a long and difficult ceremonial interview Lawrence played the rôle of negotiator with these
reserved and rapacious allies. He spread forth the treasures
of his diplomacy, distributed gold and received doubtful
promises.

After the Ruallas came the chiefs of the Hauran and of
the Druze mountains, with their followers mounted on little
Syrian horses carrying bandoliers over their shoulders; they
brought to the Revolt the adhesion of the settled people of
Syria; in this new phase of the war, horsemen were replacing
camel-men, and the peasants of the north came to mingle
with the camel-born nomads; the rapidity of these transfor-
mations gripped Lawrence's heart, and Damascus seemed
within his grasp, but as he was well aware, this success that
was now so close would not have for him the savour which he
had known in two years of struggle, suffering and hope.

Around Deraa

THE march on Deraa, followed by Feisal's entry into Damascus, was to be the crowning achievement of Lawrence's work. He has related these battles in a breath-taking epic which constitutes one of the finest parts of the *Seven Pillars*, but we cannot quite believe his version of the events, a version that is rather too poetic and in which much talent and many political considerations have to some degree obscured the reality. We must reconstitute the facts with the help of other documents, a fairly simple task moreover, thanks to the Official History and to the stories of the other witnesses like Young[1] and Pisani.[2] To re-establish the truth only increases Lawrence's stature as a fighter and leader, and reveals his extreme ability as a politician, but it seriously weakens the legend which he had striven to create of the Sherifs' army.

* * *

Allenby wanted to see the Arab army which he had supported for so long participate in the general advance of the English troops. Lawrence himself wanted a victorious Arab army to enter Damascus.

But there was no Arab army.

Three thousand of the Sherifs' men were struggling on the Aqaba front and were with difficulty containing the enemy in Maan; at any moment they were expected to be routed, and a fighting contingent could not be levied from this slender force. As for the nomads and the Syrian insurgents, they were an annoyance to the Turks, but they were too anarchic and indecisive a mass to be able to undertake military operations without support.

The only dependable elements of which Lawrence could dispose and from which he could expect coherent action were

[1] Young, *The Independent Arab*.
[2] Pisani, Rapport au commandant Cousse du 3 Novembre 1918: *Les Armées françaises dans la Grande Guerre, t. IX*, volumes d'annexes.

the units foreign to the country: the Gurkhas, the Egyptians, Pisani's North Africans, the English machine-gun carriers and the Ageyls of his guard. With these shock troops and a few Bedouins duly rewarded, he could, thanks to his knowledge of the desert and his skill in lightning raids, achieve the cutting of the railway lines around the turn-table at Deraa, which was what Allenby wanted. But for the political reasons which we know, it seemed to him indispensable to have some of the Sherifs' regular troops with him, were they only as extras in a skilful stage setting, in order to be able to state later that Syria had been liberated by Feisal's soldiers.

*   *   *

With these as a basis, Lawrence made up his column. A few hundred of the Sherifs' troops were to give the expedition a national character, the real backbone of the contingent being supplied by the Gurkhas, the machine-gun carriers, and paradoxically by the French.

Joyce and Young were busy with the organisation of supplies for a thousand men, numerous animals and a dozen armoured cars on a long trek across the desert. Intermediary depots between Jefer and Bair had to be created, a strict schedule laid down, and a certain discipline imposed on the drivers of the two caravans of more than six hundred camels each, who were to carry the munitions, the food, the fodder, the petrol, the tents and the explosives along the interminable track. Young, a scrupulous and fussy man, was living on his nerves, hustling the English and Arabs and giving everybody a frightful time. Lawrence watched his nervous restlessness jeeringly, and the sarcasms which he bestowed on an excellent associate were exasperating to that irascible Indian Army officer.

At the end of August everything was ready and they were about to send off the different échelons of the column to the north-east, in particular the four companies of a hundred regulars each, which made up the Sherifs' part of the expedition, when for different reasons but at the same moment, Feisal's officers and soldiers both mutinied.

It was for Lawrence a tragic disappointment, and a little farcical also; the Arabs were refusing to participate in a plan so carefully designed in order to give them, despite everything, the leading part.

Once again he was everywhere at once and almost single-handed succeeded in saving the situation.

The revolt of the Sherifs' officers was the least serious: their access of bad humour was provoked by an outburst from the Sherif Hussein. The king, jealous of his son Feisal, had without any warning published some startling things in the *Kibla*, his official journal. Feisal, he said, was a rebel son, and the ranks and distinctions which he had conferred on his officers were null: "Fools were calling Jaafar Pasha the General Officer commanding the Arab Northern Army, whereas there was no such rank, indeed no rank higher than captain in the Arab Army, wherein Sheikh Jaafar, like another, was doing his duty."

This bombshell caused quite a stir among Feisal's officers, who were covered with braid and honours. These indignant parasites brought in their resignations *en bloc,* and to calm their anger Feisal had to negotiate, telegraph to Mecca, and persuade the irascible old gentleman to go back on his declaration. In the end Lawrence, who was running the radio set, altered the signals, pretended that the king had made excuses and calmed the storm.

It was more difficult to end the mutiny of the soldiers. The troops had plenty of cause for complaint, for they had suffered heavy losses before Maan, they were commanded in the Turkish fashion, with trafficking in the pay and provisions, and the fatigues and dangers were allowed to fall on the least resourceful. The anti-English propaganda of the Turks made headway with these primitives who thought themselves betrayed, cried out that all was lost, and that Feisal and Zeid were going to abandon them. The gunners aimed their pieces at their Colonel's tent and none of the Arab chiefs dared go and parley with the mutineers.

Lawrence alone had the courage to take the situation in hand. He mixed with the mutineers, threatened, joked and made promises. In order to quieten the rumours he obliged Feisal to show himself to the troops and to drive through the camp in a car. Stiff, icy and distant, the Emir drove through in the green Vauxhall which had been given to him by

Allenby, and the presence of this formal mannequin, the incarnation of a powerful and high ideal, reassured the simple warriors. Calm returned and the English were able to set the column on the march for which they had prepared for so many weeks. Everyone was on tenterhooks, and every minute counted. Allenby's offensive was fixed for the 19th of September: Lawrence had promised that the destruction of the communications around Deraa would take place on the 16th or 17th at the latest. Every hour's delay would risk ruining the whole plan.

*   *   *

The column was composed as follows:

Four hundred regulars of the Sherifs' forces commanded by Nuri Said and Joudad Bey.[1]

Thirty-five Egyptian sappers under the command of Captain Peake and in charge of demolitions.

Thirty Gurkha machine-gunners under the command of Captain Scott-Higgins.

About forty Englishmen who made up the crews of five armoured cars equipped with artillery and machine-guns, and a few transport vehicles.

A hundred and forty North Africans commanded by Captain Pisani and Lieutenant Leimbacher and constituting a battery of four mountain 65s transported on mules and provided with 2,000 shells, a platoon of machine-gunners, a section of engineers and a small sanitary detachment. As N.C.O.s, the French unit had Sergeant-Majors Souquet and Segala, Sergeants Reveau, Mathieu, Zamith and Dauadi, and an Army Doctor Montero.

All these troops were mounted on camels (one for two men), for crossing the two hundred miles of desert which separates Aba el Lissan from Azrak, where they were to concentrate. It was arranged that two aeroplanes would be detached from the Egyptian army and put at the disposal of the column at Azrak.

Officially the expedition was commanded by Nuri Said,

[1] The figure given in Pisani's official report. Young speaks of five hundred and fifty Sherifs' men in the march from Aba el Lissan to Azrak. We may imagine that one hundred and fifty remained at this base and did not take part in the operations around Deraa.

the European staff being constituted by Lawrence, Joyce,
Young, Stirling, Winterton[1] and Pisani. The French were
officially to take their orders from the English. Sherif Nasir
and Auda had joined the expedition; their presence during
the course of the advance was to help with the recruiting of partisans among the nomads as among the village
dwellers.

*   *   *

On the 30th of August and the 2nd of September, the
indefatigable Young had got the column off, in two échelons,
and it took a dozen days to cross the desert. With incredible
effort, and much cursing and swearing, he had more or less
kept to the pre-arranged schedule. The sheepdog of an un-
tamed flock, he ran yapping up and down the track, jolting
about in a little Ford, and hustling on the camel-men, the
mule drivers and the stragglers. Lawrence reached Azrak with
Nasir and Winterton in his command Rolls, the Blue Mist,
whose unbreakable chassis could withstand the jolting of the
desert for which its makers had certainly never designed it.

Going back up the two long caravans which were making
their way up the track Lawrence felt overwhelmingly sad.
This crowd, this commotion in a country that was meant for
an almost religious peace, seemed to him a sacrilege. Something eternal and sacred was being brutally violated and
destroyed: "Now the desert was not normal, indeed it was
shamefully popular. . . . " It was with a heavy heart that he
arrived at Azrak, where he at last found silence and solitude.

Alone with Nasir and a dozen English, he tasted for a last
time the calm before the days of commotion, effort and danger
which awaited him, a calm in which he could weigh up the
risks of his enterprise.

The whole operation was insanely daring. He has spoken
in his book of the "Arab Army": in reality it was no sort of
army that he was bringing into action, as this word implies
large numbers, fire power, protected lines of communications, resources in supplies and munitions, and the possibility
of entrenchment which the slender contingent that he led
certainly did not have. Until then he had, in pursuance of

[1] Winterton came from the Camel Corps.

his 'maritime' tactics, harassed the Turkish flank with light
mobile camel-borne groups, capable after the battle of scatter-
ing and vanishing into the desert. This new expedition was
something quite different. The Sherifs' infantry were not
nomad camel-men, but Syrian peasants, slow moving, laden
with equipment and knowing nothing of the desert, the
column was heavy and vulnerable, and if engaged by a force
of any size armed with modern machine-guns and artillery,
it would court disaster. If Allenby's offensive did not succeed,
they would probably be massacred during their retreat by
the Turks and by the natives: their march from Aba el
Lissan to Azrak was already very risky and to continue it
north behind the Turkish front was an even more hazardous
operation.

What is more, Lawrence was leaving a very precarious
situation on the front at Maan. The Turks had begun an
offensive against the Sherifs at Tafileh and the Arabs were
falling back; Hornby tried as best he could to delay the
enemy in the area of Shobek. A man without Lawrence's
iron nerve would have been paralysed by this threat to his
flank. When he heard about it as he was driving from Aba
el Lissan to Azrak, he lost nothing of his composure and said
simply that the enemy troops committed at Maan were so
many soldiers who would not oppose Allenby in the west, and
that he was pleased that the Turks had made this mistake.
It was true, but it needed a leader of unusual courage and
strength of character to reason with such coolness.

Lawrence and his handful of companions stayed alone at
Azrak for several days. Out of touch with their own people,
they could have been at the mercy of the smallest Turkish
patrol: Winterton, uneasily scanning the desert, expected at
any moment to see enemy horsemen appear; Lawrence, accustomed to solitary raiding, affected tranquillity and unconcern. In this relaxation between two big efforts he found
great ease of mind. He soaked himself in solitude, and in it he
regained his strength.

Towards the 10th of September, the oasis was invaded by
the crowd of fighting men who were concentrating there. The
two échelons of the column arrived in good order; the North
Africans with nose-bags and arms, "like merchants of the

four seasons", Lawrence's guard returning from the pasturing
grounds of the Hauran, the machine-guns, the aeroplanes.
The partisans came in to join the regulars: Auda, Nuri
Shalaan, the other nomads and Tallal with the Druze horsemen; the Bedouins thronged the place, and Lawrence, afraid
to let this crowd of plunderers loose among the villages of
Syria, sent back to the desert many of the volunteers and
only kept three hundred of the Bedouins with him, chiefs
for the most part, whose presence with him proclaimed further the pan-Arabic nature of the expedition. With miracles
of diplomacy he had arranged that the clans, split by ancient
vendettas, should make peace for this offensive which he
hoped would be the last. With the skill of a stage producer
he had created the image of a unanimous Arab world marching towards its liberation.

Feisal had arrived at Azrak in order to be shown to the
troops, and he walked through the ranks, aloof and ghost-
like, before returning to his tent where he awaited events;
whilst Nasir joined Lawrence in order to represent the nobility of the Sherifs in the uncertainties of an hazardous affray.

Once more the presence of so many of his fellow men
induced in Lawrence a strange depression. His nerves, which
had stood up so well to danger and solitude, now failed him.

"The crowd had destroyed my pleasure in Azrak, and I
went off down the valley . . . and lay there all day in my old
lair among the tamarisk, where the wind . . . told me I was
tired to death of these Arabs. . . .

"Today it came to me with finality that my patience as
regards the false position I had been led into was finished.
A week, two weeks, three and I would insist upon relief.
My nerve had broken, and I would be lucky if the ruin of
it could be hidden so long. . . . "

He was experiencing now that troubled anguish which all
commanders know when they have cast the die, and are about
to hazard their forces in battle. The next day he had regained
his energy and clear-mindedness.

There is in youth a wonderful resilience and all these
men were marvellously young, young like Bonaparte's soldiers
in Italy. There were few among the Arabs as among the

Europeans who were over thirty; many were less, and in the memoirs which some of them have left us of those heroic days, one can feel their insouciance and gaiety continually breaking through. They were keenly aware of the formidable dangers which threatened them: of dying wounded in the desert, of having their throats cut by the Bedouins, or of being hung by the Turks; but they could not help seeing in this war the adventure of which they had dreamed since they were Boy Scouts. Lawrence, concentrated and tense, had his hours of unconcern. Young, the sage, tells amusingly of his marches between Bair and Azrak, mounted on a mule, chatting with Pisani who told him the stories of his Moroccan campaigns, the hard blows, the absinthe and the native girls. They made fun of Scott-Higgins' Gallic moustaches, Peake's red beard, Pisani's round-topped kepi and little goatee. Nuri Said was quite one of the party of Europeans: a fine youth, always ready and eager, he had a courage that was equal to every test, a perfect impassivity under fire and a sense of humour. In his revolver holster he carried a flask of whisky, and would offer the English what he called 'calories' so as not to outrage the principles of his religion. Of them all it was he who ran the greatest danger, because had he been taken he would immediately have been executed by the Turks; nevertheless, throughout the expedition he was always foremost in advocating the most daring plans.

We can understand that Lawrence should wax lyrical in evoking these hours of enthusiasm. "It felt like morning and the freshness of the world-to-be intoxicated us." It is the cry of a youthful soul. Other men, remembering the horrors of this war, discover with astonishment that for them also it is tinged with the joyful light of their youth.

* * *

Lawrence's intention was to cut the line in three places round Deraa. Close to this town another line branches off the Hejaz railway, crossing Palestine by way of the Yarmuk and reaching the sea at Haifa. By destroying the railways to the north, south and west of Deraa, they would isolate this centre and prevent all communication by rail between the Ottoman front in Palestine and its bases.

On the 12th of September, Lawrence sent Peake and Scott-Higgins, with the Egyptians and the Gurkhas, to carry out the first part of his programme and cut the line between Amman and Deraa; he then sent the rest of the column on towards the north. He joined it by car the next day at Giaan el Khunna, close to Umtaiye, only to learn bad news: Peake had not been able to reach the railway line, which was guarded by Bedouins still faithful to the Turks, he had not dared to engage the nomads in a pitched battle, and he had brought back his troops without having accomplished his mission.

This failure compromised Lawrence's whole plan. Quick action was called for. He reflected for some hours, disappeared all night to make a reconnaissance, and then assembling his companions he announced that he would go alone with an armoured car and a small Rolls-Royce truck to effect the destruction of the track. By making a lightning raid he was sure of taking the Turks by surprise and of blowing up one or two culverts in a place of which he knew; he added that this little operation would be amusing. Young replied that he at any rate saw nothing amusing in such a desperate enterprise: that Lawrence was completely mad, but that after all it was by follies of this kind that he had taken Aqaba and achieved his other successes. Joyce and Winterton refused to allow their comrade to expose himself alone and they accompanied him in a second armoured car, whilst Lawrence set off in a truck crammed with explosive, and driven by the driver Rolls, with whom he had already made so many raids.

The three vehicles went jolting off along an incredibly bad track, heading for a place on the line where Lawrence knew that he would find two little structures. Whilst Joyce and Winterton were attacking with a machine-gun the small fort which guarded the culverts, he went right up under the arches, and calmly placed the charges in position, with the assistance of Rolls who had come to join him. If a bullet had touched the two hundred pounds of gelignite which the two men were handling it would have blown them to pieces. Whilst the attack on the little fort was continuing, Lawrence carried on working with a deliberation and care that terrified his companion, and by the time he had finished Joyce

and Winterton had despatched the defenders of the fort; five
or six Turks had surrendered, and the English withdrew in
order to watch the blowing-up of the line. By the morning
of the 16th of September they had rejoined the column.

The cutting of the line to the south of Deraa had been
achieved, and they had now to effect its destruction to the
north. During the raid the column had advanced slowly
parallel with the line and almost within sight of a town in
which were concentrated around three thousand troops, including some German and Austrian units. The English were
continually expecting to see patrols from Deraa advance towards them. In fact the enemy were demoralised and panic-
stricken by rumours that eighteen thousand Bedouins were
coming to attack them, and they had besides been severely
shaken by air raids; they remained inactive and instead of
doing anything, feverishly entrenched themselves where they
were.

*   *   *

For the second demolition, Lawrence had chosen a point
less than six miles to the north of Deraa. Such was the bold-
ness and impudence of the plan that the Turks had not
thought of strengthening the guards on the posts so close to
the town. On the morning of the 17th of September, the
regulars and partisans attacked the fortified post which protected the bridge of Tell Arar. The Turks defended themselves well and repulsed the assault, killing a Rualla Bedouin;
Pisani's 65s were brought up and a few shells put an end to
their resistance. The Arabs hurled themselves on the fort
and to avenge the death of their comrade massacred all the
occupants.

Lawrence immediately posted a body of troops and a section of 65s on the small hill which dominates the track to the
west. Thus protected, the English and French demolition
teams destroyed the line for a considerable distance. Then
leaving the guard on the Tell under Joyce's orders in order
to safeguard his retreat, Lawrence set off to the west to carry
out the last of the pre-arranged operations on the Deraa-
Palestine line.

The whole country was seething. Liman von Sanders was

16

sending reinforcements up to Deraa, and the Turks in an
effort to hit back sent out their available aeroplanes to try to
strike at these mysterious troops who were destroying their
communications. The slow-moving Sherifs' column and the
bands of nomad camel troops, discovered in the open desert,
were heavily bombed, but extricated themselves without
much loss, Pisani's little 65s were turned into anti-aircraft
guns and compelled the aeroplanes to fly higher. A bomb
meanwhile had fallen quite close to Lawrence, wounding
him on the arm, but it was no more than a scratch; despite
the attack from the air he pushed his men feverishly towards
the station at Mezerib.

Here again, the Sherifs' men under Nuri Said, and Pisani's guns, had the measure of the Turks' resistance, and
whilst the English were busy with destroying the line, the
regulars and the partisans hurled themselves on the station,
which was crammed with equipment and supplies. The
frenzied mob almost knocked down the walls of the sheds
and on that day the Arabs plundered more than ever before.
Fifty of the regulars, gorged with booty, deserted in order to
carry to their mountain villages whatever they had been able
to rifle.

*   *   *

The column had left Azrak on the 12th of September, and
by the evening of the 17th it had accomplished its mission,
having cut the three railway lines which radiate out from
Deraa, thus completely isolating this place from all communication with the north, the south and the west. This destruction deprived Liman von Sanders' Germano-Turk general
headquarters, set up at Nablus, of the possibility of receiving
reinforcements, as of evacuating his equipment in the case of
retreat. Having achieved such effective results Lawrence
should have been able to return to the east of the line, and
there in relative security await the development of the English offensive, of whose issue he was still ignorant.

However, he refused to stop at this prudent solution and
wished to exploit the advantages of the situation to the maxi-
mum, throw the Turkish rear into disorder, and above all
make use of the passage of the Arab column in order to raise

the people and create a vast indigenous movement against the Ottomans. After the attack and the destruction of the station at Mezerib he decided not to rejoin the body of the expedition which had stayed with Joyce to the east of the line until after he had made a tour to the west of Deraa through the middle of the enemy position.

Lawrence himself, Young and Pisani have each separately written an account of the vicissitudes of this long march through the Ottoman lines.

Lawrence, immersed in what he was doing, beset by a thousand problems, and trying to be everywhere at once, has left us a confused and colourful chapter, a kaleidoscope of feverish, heroic and chaotic days.

Young remained attached to the column of foot and artillery, and mounted on his mule he covered these fearful marches amongst exhausted soldiers; often left without orders or information by his companions, he has retained of these days the memory of a somewhat frightful nightmare. The whole business seemed to him absurdly imprudent, almost pointless, conducted any old how and without the most elementary precautions. Less given than Lawrence to pro-Arab lyricism, he watched with disgust the plundering and the exactions of the Bedouins, and he noted that many of the settled people of Syria were showing little enthusiasm for the national cause and that they did not turn against the Turks until they were completely routed. He tells us that as they passed through some of the villages the exhausted column found the villagers hostile, trigger-happy and ready at the least sign of weakening to throw themselves upon them. A grumbling philosopher, he criticised these disjointed operations but played his part without weakening, reserving for himself the most thankless but by no means the least dangerous tasks.

The honest Pisani kept a journal on the march, the official account of his mission. This document, which has neither the oratory of Lawrence's pages, nor the humour of Young's, has the advantage of being clear, precise and complete as the regulations require, and allows us to follow step by step the progress of the column from Aba el Lissan as far as Azrak and throughout the march around Deraa. He gives us exact

figures on the strength of the forces engaged, the shells and
the cartridges carried and fired, the number of pack animals,
and indicates the date and the timing of the operations. The
colonial artillery captain seems to take no pride in what he
accomplished, but he shows quite distinctly his conviction
that with his artillery and machine-guns he was the backbone
of the whole expedition.

*   *   *

Having bivouacked in the station at Mezerib, an unsafe
place, at the mercy of a surprise attack from the Turks or
from the populace, the column took the whole of the 18th to
accomplish the twenty miles of the march around Deraa; it
was ceaselessly harassed by the enemy air force; the two
fighter aeroplanes which Allenby had assigned to the Sherifs'
force had been brought down and the bombing from the air
severely tried the slow-moving caravan; in order to recross
the line on the evening of the 18th of September, they had
to take the station at Nisib, and the little forts which guarded
the track, by assault; when they at last thought themselves in
shelter on the other side of the track, some guns mounted on
trucks sent from Deraa came and sprayed the weary soldiers
with shrapnel, and inflicted on them further losses.

Lawrence was everywhere at once, wore himself out, and
exposed himself more than he should have done. He himself
carried out the demolitions around Mezerib, attacked an
aerodrome in an armoured car, took on with a machine-gun
a train loaded with troops, and untiringly helped Nasir in
his propaganda with the Syrian insurgents, passing his nights
with the dissident chieftains who came in from all sides.

In the disorder of this mad ride he had to keep the nomad
partisans in hand, for loosed into this settled country and
sniffing plunder, they became quite uncontrollable; the old
instincts reappeared, and it needed all Lawrence's authority
to prevent their exactions and stop the old vendettas between
rival clans who had temporarily made peace from flaring up
again and causing internal strife; the personal guard, mad
with excitement, thrown into a fever by the rapine, no
longer retained its old discipline; at the end of the raid,
during the assault on the Nisib station, the mercenaries re-

fused to attack and Lawrence did not dare to coerce them. They had reached the point, he said, when the soldiers were as dangerous to their leaders as to their enemy.

It was only in the evening of the 19th of September that the flying column came back to Umtaiye, a few miles to the east of the line, where the remaining detachments had stayed with Joyce. In safety at last, the Sherifs' men, the English and the French were able to draw breath and reform.

Lawrence considered that Allenby's request for "three men and a boy with pistols" in front of Deraa had been largely satisfied.

*   *   *

Leaving the column in the relative security of Umtaiye, Lawrence returned to Azrak by car and from there he went by aeroplane to Allenby's Headquarters. He had to have news of the offensive, find out his orders and whether he could bring back to his contingent supplies of food, munitions, petrol and spare parts for the vehicles which, after weeks of churning through the sand, the basalt screes and the shelves of lava, were in a pitiful state.

Joyce also left the expedition and returned to the front at Maan, taking with him the Egyptians and the Gurkhas. The column, reduced to three hundred and fifty regulars, the English armoured cars, one hundred and forty French and the partisans, remained under the orders of Nasir, Nuri Said, Young and Pisani.

On the 21st of September Lawrence was at Ramley at General Headquarters and found Allenby on the flood-tide of victory and very pleased with life. The English offensive had been a terrific success. The Turkish front had collapsed; the cavalry, driving across the plain of Esdrelon and then that of Escharadon, had outflanked all the enemy defences; Liman von Sanders with the whole of his staff had almost been captured at Nablus; they had taken ten thousand prisoners and a hundred guns; the 7th and 8th Turkish Armies in the west were no more than a flock of fugitives; the 4th Army, in the east, was preparing to disengage, to evacuate Maan, Amman and Deraa, and to retreat towards Damascus. Three cavalry corps under the command of Generals Chauvel,

Barrow and Chaytor had been launched towards the east to cut off its escape route.

Allenby was counting on the Arabs to harass the retreating Turks. He gave Lawrence two fighter aeroplanes to free himself of air attacks and a Handley-Page loaded with all the necessities for which the column, remaining close to Deraa, was crying out.

On the morning of the 22nd, Lawrence landed at Um el Surab, a little to the east of Umtaiye, where he once more found his companions.

Damascus

"THE Arabs will possess with all sovereignty whatever they conquer by force of arms," said a declaration from Cairo in June 1918. It was now necessary to lead the Arabs right to Damascus, to create at least the fiction of a victorious Arab army liberating, by its own efforts alone, the capital of Syria. All Lawrence's activities during the days that followed were to be directed towards this end.

For this achievement he had no more than three hundred and fifty regular soldiers, of whom several were ready to desert in order to return, in the general chaos, to their villages in the Hauran, but the partisans whom he had taken so much trouble to stir up in the course of the past months were at last going to weigh in the balance.

When it became known that the Turks were in retreat, the Bedouins came in from all over the desert, eager for the spoil; they hoped not only to rob the routed Turks of their clothes and their arms, but to hold to ransom the people of the settled countries, from whom the fear of the Ottoman police had kept them away so long. The villagers who had remained hesitant until a few days previously were now burning to shoot their ancient oppressors in the back; from the Lebanon to the Druze mountains, the insurgents crowded in to join the Sherifs' column in the hope of gigantic plunder. It was this mob of which Lawrence intended to make use in order to harass the retreating Turks and to bring into Damascus on their heels a force that was undeniably Arab.

Lawrence was with his column on the enemy's flank; the 4th Turkish Army was disengaging all along the line which it had occupied, between Maan and Deraa, to the east of the Dead Sea and the Jordan; the advance of the English cavalry threatened to cut it off from its base, and the demolitions carried out by Lawrence and the Sherifs' troops had deprived it of the railway with which to evacuate troops and equipment.

The Arab–Allied contingent had done its work brilliantly and could now have taken up a less hazardous position, but a passive rôle seemed to Lawrence to be a tactical and political mistake. He sensed that one could dare everything against an army that had been routed and that a few men could bring off the most spectacular success against soldiers in flight. He wanted the little Sherifs' force to be in the centre of the fray and to take an active part in it. He who was so careful of his soldiers' lives was going to throw them in at the most exposed point of the fighting, since from the political point of view it was a gamble worth taking.

On the 24th he learnt from a message brought by aeroplane that the 4th Army had started to move north. He immediately sent Feisal instructions to launch on Deraa all the nomads whom he could get together and to send emissaries into the villages to call the volunteers to arms. He decided to station himself the following day with the regulars and Pisani's guns somewhere between Lake Tiberias and the railway line, and by blocking the Turks' line of retreat, to stop or slow down the enemy until the arrival of the English cavalry which was marching on Amman and Damascus.

Such a project with all the risk it involved provoked some diverse feelings among his companions. To try and impede the march of scores of thousands of men with five or six hundred soldiers and four guns seemed mad. Young in particular energetically opposed his colleague's plan; supported by Winterton and Pisani, he declared with heat that in his opinion the column had accomplished its mission and that it was folly to risk it aimlessly in the midst of all these units now surging back of which many were still in fighting trim. He pointed out that Lawrence was accustomed to the mobility of camel troops, and had not taken account of the slowness of the regulars, who were already very tired; leading their pack camels and their mules they could march at no more than two miles per hour. The idea of placing themselves across the line of retreat of an entire army was so absurd that it was like a "man who puts himself in the path of a hunted lion instead of shooting at it from the flank".

The discussion was lively. Young was to the point, outspoken

and not inclined to mix his words. The most experienced
officer of the group, he considered himself responsible for
its operations. He looked on Lawrence as an amateur strategist and did not hide the fact that he regarded him only as
the liaison agent with Feisal and that he doubted his right
to command the whole column.

The discussion can be imagined; the little group gathered
under the tent at night, lost in a hostile solitude, exposed to
every danger, and weighing formidable decisions, whilst in
the distance can be heard the crash of the enemy's débâcle.
The Arab officers listen silently to a debate on which everything will hang.

Winterton is hesitant, tempted by the boldest party; Lawrence turns to Pisani and asks whether he will follow him.
The Frenchman begins to laugh and replies that the enterprise seems to him to be quite mad, but that he is a soldier,
trained to fight, and he will go. Young would like to pursue
the discussion further, but Lawrence cuts him off. "It is time
to go to sleep," he says, "we will start at dawn tomorrow."

*   *   *

But the next day, the 25th of September, the column did
not strike camp, as the Sherifs' troops were tired and uneasy,
and took a long time in getting on the march. Young returned to the charge; if Lawrence was to persist in his intentions, at least he should do it with the minimum of risk. He
begged him to cross the railway line as soon as he could, if
possible in the evening of the same day, before it was overrun
by the retreating Turks, and he asked him, besides, not to
take up a position on the principal route along the railway
line, but on high ground where the infantry could entrench
itself and resist the flood of the vanquished. Nasir then
suggested that they should establish their regulars at Sheik
Saad, a village situated to the north of Deraa, built on an
eminence halfway between the two tracks which run from
Deraa and Mezerib to the north.

The column did not get under way till the afternoon and
the march parallel to the line was torture for Young. The
soldiers dragged themselves along at a mortally slow pace
and they could see with the naked eye the grand route to the

north covered with assorted Turkish units heading for Deraa; many of these detachments were marching in good order and did not convey the impression of a débâcle.

The column covered sixteen miles on that day with great difficulty. At the level of Tell Arrar, it tried to cross the line, but finding it firmly held, had to continue on its way. It came to a halt finally at Ghazale, and camped to draw breath. The chieftains and the soldiers were in need of a night's rest, but the intractable Young extorted from his colleagues the promise that they would get on the march again as soon as the moon rose. Whilst his exhausted companions slept on the bare ground, Young spent the night on his feet, his watch in his hand, "tortured at the idea of the confusion into which a night attack would throw their little contingent". With the assistance of Nuri Said, he succeeded at the given hour in setting the troops on the march again; they crossed the track without harm and reached Sheik Saad on the morning of the 27th.

*　　*　　*

The whole country was in an unparalleled state of excitement. The Bedouin bands had joined the Movement, and four or five thousand partisans, on camels or on horses, under the command of Nasir, Auda and Nuri Shalaan, were roaming about everywhere. The command of the outflanked 4th Army, threatened at Amman by Chaytor's cavalry, at Deraa by Barrow's and deprived of its railway line, had given orders to each of its units to retreat individually and by its own means, and the plain gradually became covered with groups of varying size and importance, more or less vigorously commanded, trying to reach the north; in this confusion the Bedouins were rifling their prisoners, and having stripped them, brought them into the Sherifs' army: more than a thousand captives, exhausted, hungry and half naked, were now weighing down the expedition.

*　　*　　*

Lawrence strove to put some order into this turmoil. Riding ahead of the column with the camel-men of his guard, he prepared the over-excited populace for the arrival of a

semi-European force of khaki-clad soldiers, which the natives
might have attacked in mistake for Turks; he directed the
Bedouin bands on to the important objectives, and calmed
the quarrels between the clans, whose excitement had been
raised to fever pitch by the battle, and who were threatening
to kill each other.

On the morning of the 27th, an aeroplane brought a message to tell him that two large-sized columns were marching
in his direction: four thousand men emerging from Deraa
were retreating along the track, and two thousand others
were heading for Damascus by the western route from
Mezerib which passes through the village of Tafas. At the
same moment the inhabitants of Tafas, horrified by the
Turks' approach that would mean the inevitable destruction
of their village, desperately requested help from the Sherifs.

Lawrence hastily assembled his infantry, Pisani's guns,
Auda's Bedouins and some armed peasants and rushed towards Tafas. He arrived too late. The wave of Turks had
passed on, and all that was left of the village were ruins and
a frightful carnage. The sight of the tortured bodies was
ghastly. Lawrence and his companions were overwhelmed,
and the partisans like the regulars, despite their inferiority
in numbers, went after the retreating column bent on destroying it.

They were taking on several Turkish regiments, with
cavalry and infantry, marching in good order, and covered by
a stoutly commanded rearguard armed with machine-guns
and composed mainly of Germans. They attacked the enemy
from all sides; Auda, the old lion, threw himself furiously
into his last battle, the nomads whirling round the enemy
units, panicking them with incessant fire; Pisani brought
his guns up to the front and sprayed them with shells; his
65s constituted the only protection of the little Sherifian
contingent, and when the enemy cavalry attempted a
turning movement, it was their shrapnel that managed to
stop them.[1]

In the end the Turkish column allowed itself to be cut in
two and a terrible butchery commenced. Almost the entire

[1] "Our guns had the best part, but it was a warm thing," is all that
this modest soldier says in his report.

enemy detachment of two thousand men was annihilated, with the exception of the Germans, who, better commanded, managed to reach the north. The Sherifians had arrived at the point at which all fighting men lose control, when cruelty is piled on cruelty by adversaries who are determined to avenge cruelties still worse. Every enemy soldier they met they butchered; in an orgy of murder the Arabs finished off the wounded and killed even the beasts of burden that had fallen on the road; two hundred prisoners were brought together and exterminated *en masse* with a machine-gun. "For the first time and with my orders, they gave no quarter," says Lawrence in his account. One would like to think that his taste for sacrifice compelled him to accept the responsibility for atrocities that he could not prevent, and that he gave no such order.[1]

At the same time Nasir was subjecting the eastern column to a similar fate. He had always been the bravest of the Sherifs, the true warrior chieftain of the Arab Revolt, and on this day he surpassed himself, leading the Rualla and the Anezeh Bedouins without respite against the dislocated and retreating enemy; in the evening the harassed fugitives were unable to make camp, for the Bedouins had fastened on to them and gave them no repose; more than two-thirds of the six or eight regiments which had left Deraa in the morning of the 27th of September were massacred before reaching Damascus.

*　　　*　　　*

Lawrence was living in a tragic and exalted dream. He was attaining the end for which he had worked so hard for two years. Damascus was within his grasp and the Revolt was at last inflicting crushing losses on the Turks. Drunk with fatigue, with nervous exhaustion, with the violence and inhumanity of what he had seen, he assembled his column as best he could and brought it back towards Deraa.

The town had been evacuated by the enemy, but the Bedouins and the peasants had rushed in to plunder. The

[1] Young expressly says (*Independent Arab*, p. 251) that Lawrence and a Sherifian officer, Ali Jaudat, vainly tried to prevent a group of prisoners from being massacred by the Bedouins.

demons were unleashed and the whole countryside was put
to the sword; the Turks were not the only people to suffer
from the violence of the savages whose instincts had been set
free; terrible chaos reigned in Deraa, and the partisans were
holding to ransom and cutting the throats of their sympa-
thisers as of their enemies. Young, Winterton and Pisani had
great difficulty in preventing the massacre of the thousand
miserable prisoners which they had dragged in with them. It
was in this incredible confusion that Nasir installed himself
in the town hall and officially took possession of the place
in the name of the Sherifs' army.

This was the situation when a few hours later General
Barrow, at the head of his Indian cavalry, arrived in the
outskirts of Deraa after a week of bloody fighting. The meeting between Lawrence and the General did not go very
smoothly. Barrow found it difficult to consider as allies these
primitives whose cruelties and depredations were throwing
the town into confusion, and the handful of ragged, hirsute
officers who hid their uniforms beneath their filthy burnous
meant nothing to him. He was reluctant to accept the idea
that authority in Deraa should belong to Sherif Nasir and
not to him, the English General, who was arriving at the
head of a victorious division in good order. The British
soldiers felt a strong antipathy for the Bedouins, whom they
regarded as plunderers and robbers. During these final
battles the English had been seen to allow surrendered
Turkish units to keep their arms and then get down shoulder
to shoulder with their prisoners in order to resist the attacks
of the natives.[1]

Barrow was then annoyed by the situation which he found
in Deraa, and Lawrence did nothing to calm his uneasiness.
He "had adopted with him what, I am told, was his usual
attitude towards British Generals, a mixture of schoolboy
cheek, with an assumption of omniscience and of being in
General Allenby's confidence which Barrow found extremely
trying",[2] and relations between the two men were very
strained during the advance on Damascus.

Lawrence was now feeling the reaction of these exhausting

[1] Wavell, *Palestine Campaigns*, p. 250.
[2] Young, *loc. cit.*, p. 252.

days. He allowed his force to go on, staying behind to camp
for a last time amongst the men of his guard as in the uncertain days of the solitary raids. Rolled in his coverlet he
slept on the ground in the restored calm and beneath the
unmoved stars of the beautiful Syrian sky. Once more his
servant Abdullah came at dawn and knelt down close to him
to offer him the morning bowl of rice. But the simple joys of
wartime companionship had lost their savour, victory had
spoilt the soldiers, their new assurance and their boasting
exasperated him; he struck camp and left again for the north.

The fighting on the road to Damascus was coming to an
end. Some enemy units, harassed by the Bedouins, were still
desperately resisting. Lawrence accompanied by Stirling
passed the English cavalry and went on his way. Finally
Damascus, the pearl of Syria, appeared before him with its
cupolas, its minarets, its gardens on the mountainside des-
cending in the east to the sands of the desert. A horseman
galloped towards them holding out a handful of grapes and
shouting: "Damascus salutes you!"

*   *   *

The two Englishmen stopped to wait for the Sherifians
who had stayed behind, and at the gates of the city, the
object of their desire, they had yet a further adventure:
whilst they were washing themselves in a stream some Bengal
Lancers appeared, and taking them for enemy fugitives, took
them prisoner; with a lance at their buttocks and somewhat
ill-treated, they were marched off and it was only when they
had reached Regimental Headquarters that they were set
free.

*   *   *

These heroic and confused days were responsible for all
the misunderstanding that was to poison Syrian politics in
the years to follow. Henceforward the Arabs could say and
perhaps believe sincerely that they had destroyed a Turkish
army and taken Damascus with their own troops, forgetting
the English offensive which alone had made possible their
advance. Feisal's demands at the Peace Congress and the
Franco-Syrian war had their origin to a large degree in this

march of the tiny Sherifs' contingent and in the general levy of the partisans, which Lawrence had wanted and organised.

As early as the fall of Deraa, Feisal had left Azrak and held himself in readiness to play the rôle which had been assigned to him. The stage setting had been carefully arranged between Lawrence and the Commander-in-Chief. The Australian troops and the regiment of French spahis which had reached Damascus and had started to penetrate the city received orders to withdraw, and Feisal's triumphal entry into the Syrian capital was then arranged.

Nasir and his Bedouins, followed by Feisal and Lawrence, marched with the Arab troops in procession through the streets of Damascus, where they received a delirious welcome, and the Emir, assisted and instructed by Lawrence, started work on setting up an independent Arab government destined to rule the whole of Syria.

But here again there were a thousand obstacles to the realisation of T.E.'s old dream. After the first acclamations, the Damascenes, horrified by the excesses and the savagery of the chieftains of the Hejaz and of the Bedouins became more aloof. Opposed groups were struggling for power: the Sherifians, the Druzes who remained secretly pro-Turk, and the partisans of Abd el-Kader, that Sheik of Algerian origin who in the previous year had betrayed the Allies at the time of the Yarmuk bridges affair. Abd el-Kader tried by main force to take possession of the town hall; there were violent scenes between him, Nasir and Lawrence whom the Algerian denounced to his co-religionaries as an Infidel and a tool of European imperialism. The squabble became a brawl, the Algerians turned out of the town hall spread out through Damascus, arousing the Syrian population against the Sherifs, and to the war with Turkey there succeeded the slaughter of the rival Arab factions. The Sherifs' men swept the streets with bursts of machine-gun fire and numbers of the rioters were added to the already lengthy death-roll of the war.

In this bloody confusion a thousand different things had to be thought of, and all of them were urgent. Lawrence, always when he was needed, helped the Arabs, novices in the art of administration, to organise a police force, food supplies, and the lighting of the town and even to re-establish the railway which for two years he had worked so persistently to destroy. The Allied officers were astonished to see this little man, half-English half-Bedouin, busying himself with a thousand mysterious problems, freely approaching the Commander-in-Chief, and pursuing a complicated policy for the benefit of the natives, which constantly brought him into conflict with the British military autorities.

His position had never seemed more ambiguous and it was difficult to tell whether he was defending the interests of the Arabs or those of the Allies. And as a result of this equivocal situation in which he seemed to take pleasure during these troubled hours, he had one last and bitter experience.

He had tried to put the Damascus hospital into some sort of order; there were a thousand sick men dying there of dysentery, and the stench was appalling. With the assistance of a few Turkish doctors and a handful of prisoners, he was struggling desperately with this revolting task, when an English doctor with the rank of major entered the hospital. Disgusted by what he saw, the officer went for the little man in the native robes who seemed to be responsible for this appalling filth. "Scandalous, disgraceful, outrageous, ought to be shot! . . ." he screamed at him. Lawrence burst out laughing in his face and the enraged major slapped him and walked out, burning with anger. Lawrence passed his hand across his face. This farce was the end of the epic, this blow struck by an imbecile was the conclusion of the victorious cavalcade.

His powers of resistance, moral and physical, were at an end. He had achieved what he had promised himself that he would accomplish, but the end which he had so ardently pursued did not have the appearance for which he had hoped. The scenes of massacre at which he had been present and in which he had taken part remained before his eyes. The victorious Arabs were different men from those who for two years had been docile instruments in his hands; their appetites, their independence, their talk and their native pride disconcerted him. The apprentice sorcerer was discovering the world to whose creation he had contributed, and this world filled him with repulsion and fear. He went to find Allenby and asked for leave to go away immediately.

The General was astonished, resisted and then acquiesced. On the 4th of October, three days after the entry of the Sherifs into Damascus, Lawrence returned to Cairo, and then without bothering to collect his papers and books, he went back to England.

PART III

The Peace

THE best-known part of Lawrence's career will always be, by
virtue of its epic and romantic nature, the Arabian War.
However, his political and diplomatic rôle during the three
years that followed the armistice was important, and it has
left a mark that cannot be under-estimated in the history of
Franco-British relations, one could say in the history of
Europe.

When the Peace Congress opened at the beginning of 1919,
a thousand thorny questions presented themselves to the
treaty-makers: that of Arab independence was one of the
most confused, and even if England and France had attempted to solve it in a spirit of amicable co-operation, it
would have been difficult to settle.

The documents which they had to base it on, signed at the
dictate of successive situations, were contradictory. The following are the principal of them.

I. The English promise to King Hussein in 1915, committing themselves to recognition of the independence of
the Arabs if the Lord of Mecca would rebel against the Turks.

II. The Sykes–Picot agreement of 1916 on the distribution
of zones of influence amongst the English, the Russians and
the French, in the areas which they hoped to remove from
the Ottoman Empire.

III. A declaration made in Cairo in June 1918 by the
High Commissioner in Egypt by which the latter promised
to certain Syrian individuals "that the Arab Zones liberated
by the military action of their inhabitants would be entirely
independent".

IV. President Wilson's fourteen points, of which the
twelfth proclaimed that the basis of future treaties would be
the right of people to self-determination. This declaration
had given rise to great hopes in the Orient, and it was very
widely diffused.

V. An Anglo-French declaration of the 9th of November, 1918, which, with the object of calming the anxieties of the people of Syria and Mesopotamia, promised the Arab populations of these countries "to show favour to indigenous governments and to guarantee the normal functioning without interference of the governments which the people themselves should elect".

In these documents, the Arabs—represented at the Congress by Feisal—the English and the French could each on their own account find material for the support of their different and incompatible claims.

Feisal wished to obtain the complete independence of the Arab countries.

The English had a very definite desire to colonise Mesopotamia from Mosul to Basra, and if they supported Feisal's ambitions in Syria, it was less out of friendship for him than an attempt to prevent France from gaining a foothold in the Levant. Lawrence, in a report, said bluntly that the Levantine coast ought to be "England's Monroe zone", in other words that England did not wish any other nation to establish itself in a place that she did not believe she could herself colonise openly.

France, out of motives that were far from being entirely sentimental, and doubtless failing to estimate the difficulties of the task which she was undertaking, wished to install herself in Syria and Cilicia.

These opposing ambitions, all based on official documents, were to give birth to a frightful imbroglio and a quarter of a century of sterile strife.

The causes of Lawrence's actions during the years which followed the armistice are complex. Personal passions, pride, motives of a moral order, others of a sentimental order, patriotism, and an unreasoning hatred against France were all mixed in his mind. Besides, one feels that he is the prisoner of what throughout the long months had been his exclusive goal. A man who has completely devoted himself to an enterprise ends by identifying himself with it, by giving it a value that is absolute. For him good and evil are what is good for his work and what is opposed to it.

Lawrence was certainly not the anti-colonialist of principle

which people have wished to make of him. A deep believer
in the greatness of his country, he wished, legitimately, to
see the influence of England extended across the world. "It
will be a sad day when our Empire ceases to grow," he wrote
somewhere. He had never shown any particular affection for
people who had been colonised, he had contributed to the
stamping out of Egyptian nationalism, and did not seem to
worry very much about the fate of the Irish; for the Hindus
he had only contempt. But where the Arabs were concerned,
he was a fierce partisan of the right to self-determination. It
was an attitude more passionate than doctrinaire, born of
circumstances particular to him.

To have led into battle an ally so little enthusiastic as
Feisal, he would certainly have had to make a number of
promises; many more promises in fact than his government
had authorised him to make, and he felt personally committed. His position must have been more delicate still with
relation to the Syrian nationalists. Since the happy days of
Carchemish during which he had so deeply fraternised with
the natives, Syria had become his second fatherland; he was
also involved in Syrian separatist movements, and had
perhaps been a member of a secret society. Could he abandon
his friends to a foreign power?

But if he felt indignant at the idea of delivering his dear
Syria to France, he had no wish to see her escape from English
influence. If he had differences of opinion with the British
colonials, it was over methods. He regarded the old colonialism as dangerous and out of date and he was convinced that
England ought only to attach to herself the countries which
from henceforward she was to bring under her control, by
ties that were much more supple and more liberal, by creating dominions and associated states, and not subject countries. It was a humane idea, perhaps prophetic, but difficult
to achieve in 1919. Despite the hypocrisy of the propaganda
it was necessary to have the courage to say that Europe could
not renounce colonialism without renouncing herself, for her
entire social and economic structure was based upon it.
During the four last centuries she had conquered a part of
the planet and had organised herself to exploit it. She could
no more do without the raw materials which she obtained

from her overseas possessions than she could dispense with
the markets which she had thus created for her manufactured
goods. She had a vital need for large areas in which, although
not admitted as a friend, she could reign as mistress, in other
words of colonies.

It was with these imperious if not legitimate necessities,
enormous political and financial interests, that Lawrence
found himself at grips. England and France were much more
interested in drilling oil wells, buying cotton, selling rails
and motor-cars and miles of cloth, than in making justice
rule upon the earth. But in this particular case they were
embarking on a dangerous adventure, and it was on this
point that Lawrence, better informed, saw with clarity.

The Middle East was not a backward, easily conquered
area. The populations of these ancient countries, upheld by
ancient cultures and an extremely lively religion, were much
less backward than the English and the French supposed. In
thinking that we could easily install ourselves in Syria, we
were making the same error as the British in treating the
Egyptians as semi-savages, and in using "Order first, justice
if possible" as a system of government on the banks of the
Nile. But if the principle of these colonies was dangerous,
the struggle between the Europeans, the colonising powers,
was more dangerous still.

The Peace Conference

LAWRENCE left the Palestine front, scarcely stopped at Cairo and embarked for London. For his haste in leaving Damascus he gives only vague reasons. Sometimes he speaks of his extreme fatigue, sometimes of his desire to leave the Arabs to organise themselves without his assistance in order that they should arrive at political maturity more quickly. On the other hand he said to Liddell Hart: "It had finished, what better reason? . . . The East was sucked dry. . . . What was in my mind, as I went towards London, was to begin again—as a junior officer—in France, learning the new way of war." In the *Seven Pillars,* he declares that a few days of political power at Damascus had given him such a taste for personal authority that he had become afraid and had preferred to fly. David Garnett thinks that, more simply, he had understood with his quick insight that the war was finished and that it was at London that he would from now on be most useful to his Arab friends.

Before he left, Allenby had promoted him to Colonel. "It was I who asked him for it," he was to say later, "in order to be able to get a sleeper from Tarento and travel by rail. Below the rank of colonel, one had to travel either on a very slow train, or else in a troopship which took fifteen days by sea." "It is my Tarento rank," he added to show that he attached no importance to military hierarchy.

He landed in London a few days before the Armistice and was able to witness the mad joy of a nation delivered from war. It is scarcely possible that he took part, tense and solitary as he was, in that gigantic funfare, for hardly had he arrived in England than he went to work, made contact with politicians and set out to achieve the success of his own personal views on the future status of the Arab countries. As early as the 4th of November he was called before the Eastern Commission of the English Cabinet. He explained his ideas and submitted a memorandum in which in four or five pages and in a style that was anything but official, but that was full of force and colour, he related the origin of the Revolt, and the evolution of the war, and gave his views on the way in which he envisaged the establishment of the peace: in broad outline, complete liberty for the Hejaz, an English mandate for Mesopotamia, the territory to be conceded to France to be reduced to the minimum and almost the whole of Syria to be given to Feisal with the maritime outlet of Alexandretta and without any French control or protectorate. The Arabs were agreeable to the projected creation of the Jewish home, but on condition that it was subjected to English control.

These proposals could but please the British Cabinet, as they left in entirety the idea of the Israeli State which they had at heart, and they blocked the French expansion in the Levant, which for historical reasons that we know was extremely unpopular in England.

Besides at this time public opinion in England was violently anti-French. It seems a paradoxical fact, after the common sacrifice and the battles fought side by side, that it should have been so, but it is undeniable. The prolonged contact of the two armies had not produced happy results; between the great leaders there had been constant friction; the night of Doullens had been forgotten; the English privates and even the officers, who had submitted to inhuman suffering and danger, imagined in an obscure way that these sacrifices had been imposed on them for the sole benefit of the French. "Anti-French feeling among most ex-soldiers amounted almost to an obsession," one English veteran was to say.[1] Perhaps it is impossible for two peoples of an advanced civilisation to live side by side. Close as their customs are, they can in the end only perceive their differences. A similar phenomenon occurred in the last war, when large forces of Americans were stationed in England throughout its long years.

The Syrian affair became a fixation for the victims of francophobia. British opinion did not understand why England should abandon to her ancient ally, now once more her colonial rival, the countries taken from the Turks by a British army with much heroism and at the cost of heavy

[1] Robert Graves, *Good-bye to All That*, p. 363.

losses; even before the end of the war, Georges Picot, having
landed at Beirut as French High Commissioner in Syria,
found himself in conflict with the English authorities, who
exhibited the greatest possible repugnance to handing over
to him the administration of the country; Feisal, feeling that
he could rely on British arms, and morally supported by
English advisers, refused to accept a French tutelage of any
sort or to evacuate the Sherifs' troops from the territories
reserved to France in the Sykes–Picot agreement about which
he affected to know nothing (legitimately, since he had had
no part in it). It was open conflict.

* * *

During the month of November, friction between the
Arabs and the French increased. In Feisal's entourage the
extremists wished to resist France's pretensions by force of
arms. The Emir, indecisive and frightened, sent an S.O.S. to
Lawrence and the latter had him invited to London by the
British Government in order to discuss the situation. On the
26th of November Feisal, transported by an English warship,
landed at Marseilles, accompanied by Nuri Said, Rousten
Haidar and two or three Syrian notables. Lawrence was
waiting on the quay.

France, immediately after the Armistice, was in a state of
great confusion, and no provision had been made for this
sudden appearance. Our representative in Cairo, slightly
panic-stricken by the news of this journey, had telegraphed to
the Grand Sherif Hussein "that the Emir Feisal would be
received in France with the welcome due to the son of a
friendly allied sovereign, but that his government was astonished that they had not been previously informed about this
visit. It was impossible to consider the Emir as charged with
a mission to the French Government of which the latter had
not been informed."

A purely formal protest but one that was lodged in the
wrong quarter, since the Emir had not taken orders from his
father for some time, and the latter complained bitterly about
it.

The French Minister for Foreign Affairs, caught off balance, was at a loss to know what to do with this importunate

guest. Recourse was had to Colonel Brémond, who was found in a headquarters in the neighbourhood of Gand, and charged with this delicate mission on the spur of the moment. They advised him to be extremely reserved with Feisal, enjoining him not to discuss any question of importance with him and not to bring him to Paris without fresh orders.

The Minister knew that Lawrence was with Feisal, and one paragraph of his instructions was concerned with him:

"With Lawrence you must be precise and show him that he is on the wrong track. If he comes as a British colonel, in an English uniform, we will welcome him. But we will not accept him as an Arab, and if he comes disguised, then he has nothing to do with us. . . . "

Brémond missed Feisal's arrival at Marseilles, but caught up with the Arab delegation at Lyons where it put up at the Hotel Terminus. Beneath a leaden sky in a November drizzle the protagonists of an intrigue begun in the heat of Arabia met again . . . Feisal, Nuri Said, Lawrence, Brémond. "Lawrence," says the Colonel, "never left Feisal; he wore his strange white dress, and it must be said that it did not have a very striking effect. . . . "

The old struggle was reopened, close-fisted, paltry and futile. Brémond, seeing that Lawrence was wearing Oriental clothes, communicated to Feisal the views of his government on the subject of the English officer. Without a moment's hesitation Feisal replied that Lawrence would leave without delay. He sent for him and told him himself of this decision. Lawrence said to Brémond's representative: "You are getting rid of me, I shall leave this very evening." "He did not consider the possibility of staying in an English uniform," adds the Colonel, who does not seem to realise the ridiculous, odious, useless and dangerous clumsiness of this little scene.

Brémond took care of the Emir throughout the official journey: the Lyons Chamber of Commerce; gifts of silks; Strasbourg still half mad after its liberation; a review of the troops; the decoration of the Emir with the order of Grand Officier de la Légion d'Honneur; Verdun. Even for a man who had seen the battlefields of the Dardanelles, this slaughter that stretched as far as the eye could see and the enormous breaches made by the 400s in the masonry of the

Douaumont fort were impressive. A people that could carry on such a struggle were not to be ignored; the Sherif revised the ideas which Pisani's meagre contingent had given him on the prestige which France enjoyed. He took the Colonel's arm and said to him: "We are comrades in battle, we have made war together." Lawrence left them, Jeanne d'Arc prepared to be sacrificed by a Charles VII of the Hejaz who knew without a deep study of history that ingratitude is the first duty of princes.

Finally, Brémond was authorised to bring the Arab delegation to Paris. He made the journey from Bar-le-Duc to Paris in the old personal coach of the Kaiser, and was sumptuously housed in the Continental.

Between an evening at the Opéra where the Emir, impassive in the first row of the stalls, heard a performance of *Marouf*, an Oriental tale, and a lunch at the Foreign Ministry, Feisal was presented to President Poincaré, dry, courteous and hurried. But little of this contributed to solving Syria's problems. On the 9th of December the Emir left again for Boulogne. The ship was waiting at the quay and Brémond saw Lawrence come down the gangway in his white costume looking "small and shaven beneath the cloudy sky, like a Catholic choir boy".

"Would you like to come with our Arab friends? We should be delighted to have you in England," said Lawrence to Brémond with his half-smile. The French Colonel bowed: "Unfortunately I cannot accept. My mission is at an end, I am returning to my post in Belgium," he replied.[1]

* * *

Lawrence took the Emir to London, and in December 1918 they toured England together. More official visits, chambers of commerce, monuments. Feisal was presented at Westminster to King George V. Lawrence was with him at this audience and one of the members of the Royal Household was

[1] I have followed Brémond's account (pp. 310 to 317 of his book). Later, Lawrence denied having worn Oriental dress in France (Liddell Hart, p. 386). It is, however, difficult to doubt what Brémond says, as he is a man of indisputable sincerity and honesty of mind.

astounded to see a British officer appear before his sovereign dressed in Oriental robes. "When one serves two masters, is it not right to wear the uniform of the least powerful of the two?" was T.E.'s reply. He was showing off, and it outraged English dignity. Quite legitimately, as the English idea of nationality is of something indivisible, but Lawrence probably only wished to shock a man who, being conventional, had irritated him.

Feisal was taken to the Foreign Office, where he attended some important conferences. Syria's claims had to be drawn up and preparations made for the Peace Conference which was about to open in Paris early in 1919.

At this congress, France at first refused to accept Feisal as the representative of a Syrian state founded in the chaos of war and whose actual form and frontiers she was disputing. Feisal lacked the support of his jealous and suspicious father, who cursed the son that was eclipsing him. England alone backed him and did what was necessary to have him admitted to the Conference. Hussein was swiftly brought to reason and appointed his son as the representative of the Hejaz at the Congress, whilst Clemenceau was persuaded, by the personal intervention of English and American diplomats, to go back on his refusal. Feisal and the Arab delegation which he led thus had an official seat at the Congress. Lawrence went with the Emir as his mentor; he was part of the Foreign Office delegation, and no one could object to his presence.

We know the confusion that reigned at this conference, solemnly opened in the great Salon de l'Horloge in the Quai d'Orsay on the 19th of January, 1919, and prolonged by long and confused discussions right up till July. The Arabs had a *succès de curiosité,* and their white robes, a splash among the lounge suits and the khaki and sky-blue uniforms, alone struck a picturesque and exotic note during the stifling and interminable sessions. Feisal's tall immobile silhouette, his icy distinction, demanded attention. The Americans looked with tenderness on this messenger of the oppressed and misunderstood races whose champions they had made themselves. "Feisal was not without resemblance to the pictorial representations of Christ," said Colonel House in a book which he published later.[1] And he added quite seriously: "But a Christ who could have shown his worth in battle", which proves that he was misinformed on the Emir's war career.

At the grand opening session, Feisal's turban of rose silk, studded with diamonds, attracted attention. The Emir's object was to obtain enormous propaganda for Arabia out of this congress of twenty-seven nations and he avoided wearing the braided European uniform that he had ordered from a Savile Row tailor.

* * *

Indefatigably Lawrence strove to defend Feisal's and the Arabs' point of view, and their conception of an independent Syria which they were striving to create. He had rapidly learnt his way around the Babel that was the Congress. Just back from an exile of several years in the desert, he was *au fait* with every intrigue, and knew the names and the propensities of every important individual. Lost in the enormous British delegation which occupied the entire Hotel Continental, he managed, however, to gain the ear of the great and overworked leaders, to whom he explained with ardour his thesis. He laid siege to Lloyd George, who listened to the clear and vigorous exposition of a man who had the gift for dissecting a problem. The old Welsh politician appreciated the humour and the subtlety of the Irishman; their Celtic minds were terminals between which there jumped an electric current. He had a long interview with Balfour, the apostle of Sionism, and brought him on to his side, persuading him against all probability that the Jews and the Arabs would get on well together and form the solid framework of a paradisium in the Near East. He even managed to approach Clemenceau, and as we find in an article by Winston Churchill,[2] he had several interviews with the French Prime Minister, who would have lent an attentive ear to his surprising interlocutor. We have no account of the interviews between these two strong and original personalities. The 'Tiger' was probably captivated and half convinced: he was

---

[1] *What Really Happened at Paris: The Story of the Peace Conference, 1918, 1919.*
[2] Churchill's article in *Lawrence by his Friends.*

not good at resisting the dangerous charms of the intelligence and it is a fact that he always showed more favour to Feisal and his claims than did his colleagues.

But the stage on which Lawrence had to struggle was of a different size from the one on which he had acted so brilliantly in the Levant. Enormous and formidable interests were at stake and the questions that were debated had names like the Left Bank of the Rhine, the Disarmament of Germany, Reparations, Poland, Austria, Hungary, Oil, and the Interallied Debts. Innumerable minorities, until then unknown to the man in the street, equally oppressed, equally seething with revolt, raised their heads and claimed legitimate, obscure and complex rights. Arab independence was but a small part of the pandemonium in which harassed, overworked men tried in a few months to settle problems insoluble since the Middle Ages.

Lawrence was not to achieve a victory for his cause. England would have liked to have evicted France from the Syrian coast, but did not wish to renounce her plans of colonisation in Mesopotamia, and for the negotiators the two questions were linked.[1] The discussion dragged on in sordid haggling, and the rights of self-determination became somewhat blurred in the course of these palavers. "Since the Syrian question raises so many difficulties, let's have the Sykes–Picot treaty cancelled, and let the French have the Saar," said Field-Marshal Henry Wilson[2] bluntly. The British financiers wished to see their country in control of the oilfields of Mosul, which in the hasty carve-up of the Sykes–Picot agreement had been placed under French authority; against the cession of the naphtha wells by France, England bartered Feisal and Syrian nationalism.

But the discussions were sharp and the allies of yesterday were now quarrelling bitterly. The close co-operation of the

[1] Young, with his clear and honest mind, remarked in his book: "The position was in fact that while Colonel Wilson was fighting for the unity of Iraq at the expense of Arab independence, Feisal and Lawrence were fighting for Arab independence at the expense of the unity of Syria. Wilson failed to realise the necessity for keeping faith with the Arabs as much as Lawrence under-estimated the necessity for keeping faith with the French." (*The Independent Arab*, p. 291).

[2] *The Memoirs of Field-Marshal Sir Henry Wilson*, Vol. II, p. 168.

battlefield was a thing of the past. If he did not win his case, Lawrence contributed to setting England and France against each other, and to creating that moral rupture whose evil influence was to last throughout the next quarter of a century. Public opinion in the two countries was aroused, and knowing nothing of the problem, became passionate; the Syrian question, of little significance at the opening of the Congress, now assumed a monstrous importance, poisoning Franco-British relations and adding to the many exasperating obstacles over which the unfortunate peace-makers stumbled.

When on the 6th of February Feisal came to plead his cause before the Council of Ten, Lawrence acted as his interpreter and secretary, and addressed the delegates in English, Arabic and French. There was a confused discussion: Feisal spoke of "the hundred thousand warriors which he had thrown against the Turkish army and of the twenty thousand killed in the Arab armies", figures that are clearly Homeric. Stephen Pichon, Clemenceau's assistant, delivered a discourse in which he spoke of the Crusades. "The Crusades? but which of us won the Crusades?" Feisal is supposed to have said. If the *mot* is not apocryphal, it shows a greater sense of humour than one is tempted to attribute to the Emir, but is it not more likely a quip of Lawrence's attributed to the Arab?

Lawrence felt that everything was slipping through his fingers. Syria was going to be cut up into two zones: one a French colony and the other in theory free, but in reality bound to France. The relief of English by French troops had started, and Feisal was thus losing his only support. The promises that Lawrence had made to his friends, perhaps imprudently, but to which he had lent all the weight of his personality, were not going to be kept, and he would not admit to having been a party to imposture and treachery. He felt mounting within him a ferocious hatred of France which the humiliation of Lyons and Brémond's abrupt behaviour had only fanned into a flame. In desperation he tried one last expedient which was not without a certain grandeur. He attempted to interest the King of England personally in the Arab cause.

He had been called to London to receive from the very

18

262 T. E. LAWRENCE

hands of his sovereign the Order of the Bath, awarded to him after the taking of Aqaba. Before the ceremony he asked for an audience with King George V and told him that he could not accept this honour. He had, he said, during the war undertaken some engagements in the name of his country with regard to the Arabs, engagements that were not going to be fulfilled; thus he had been involuntarily a party to a shameful action and could not receive a decoration on this score. How could he wear the Orders of the Allies, since if it came to the point he was ready to rejoin the ranks of the Arab army and fight in order to defend Arab independence against the French, and if necessary the English?

Disconcerted, the King could only bow to so firm and unusual an attitude, but he retained, as one can easily imagine, a painful memory of this scene.[1]

Lawrence returned to Paris and renewed his efforts. As a last hope he tried to interest Colonel House in Feisal's cause, and at the end of March he obtained for the Emir a meeting with President Wilson's right-hand man. Feisal and Lawrence during a discussion in which Lawrence acted as interpreter, went so far as to suggest the establishment of an American mandate on Syria. House listened with sympathy, promised to hasten the despatch of a commission of inquiry to the Levant, but refused to commit himself.

Throughout these months of strife Lawrence hardly ever left Feisal, who with his delegation was installed in the Avenue du Bois.[2] He advised him, encouraged him and strengthened the often weakening will of this Oriental who was lost among so many strangers, and swamped in the unknown world of the West. In the morning, to take him away from the haunting memory of the interminable sessions of the Congress, he took him to bathe in the lake of the Bois du Boulogne. One day Pisani on his way through Paris came to see his old battle companions, and we have a photograph of Feisal taken in front of the steps of a French house, posing

[1] The King told the story to Ronald Storrs during a private audience, and said, "There was I left, holding the box in my hand."
[2] Now 72 Avenue Foch, close to the Villa Said. The premises have been altered and enlarged since then in order to house the Canadian Legation.

between Nuri Said and Lawrence in a khaki uniform and wearing the agal on his head, side by side with the colonial artillery officer with his kepi and his goatee beard.

In the enormous crowd at the Congress, Lawrence by the end became fairly well known. Sometimes he wore the Sherifian head-dress with his English uniform, sometimes his Arab clothes. He was introduced to the important men. Churchill lunched with him and was captivated; a year later he was to remember this reserved and subtle youth and to make use of his services for a mission in the Orient. One day he was introduced to Foch. The Generalissimo, harassed and bad-tempered, affecting that air of an old soldier behind which he hid his personality; Lawrence, thin, ironical, but impressed at being in the presence of the man who had led the Allied armies to victory. "Well, young man," growled Foch, "it seems that you are going to take command of the Arab armies and make war on us in Syria?"

"Certainly not, mon Général," replied Lawrence, "unless however you yourself take command of the French forces. In that case of course I could not decline the honour. . . ." "Take command myself?" Foch is supposed to have said. "Not on your life, I would be much too frightened of losing!" The veracity of this dialogue cannot of course be guaranteed.[1]

Amidst all this feverish activity, these plots and intrigues, this continual tension, Lawrence had started to write his memoirs of the Arabian war. For months the book had been boiling up inside him. He wished to raise an imperishable monument to the Revolt and the Arab Campaign. In this book he would say what he—a soldier and a poet—had seen and felt; he would tell the story himself and paint the reflection of the events on his sensitive and restless soul, but his work would also be an instrument of war, with the help of which he would plead his friends' cause by making known to the public their heroism, their sacrifices and the justice of their aspirations.

[1] Later on, no doubt because of his bitter disappointments at the Peace Congress, Lawrence spoke of Foch with sarcasm. "He was no more than a frantic pair of moustaches," he said. In his correspondence with Liddell Hart, he judges the Generalissimo's military talents with scorn, a point on which he agreed with his biographer, as Liddell Hart's opinion of Foch was extremely unfavourable.

It was in the villa in the Avenue du Bois-de-Boulogne that
he devoted himself to the writing of his memoirs. It is a little
surprising to think that it was in Paris, beneath the uncertain
sky of a spring on the banks of the Seine a few yards from the
house in which Anatole France created Jerome Coignard and
Monsieur Bergeret, that a book was in part written, English
in form, and impregnated to its depths by a scorched and
tormented East, but in which there is no trace whatever of
the atmosphere of France.

The spring of 1919 ended without having brought any
solution to the problems of Syria.

British opinion remained violently opposed in principle
to our claims, but it began to grow tired of Feisal. In
Mesopotamia, the English had to repress revolts as violent as
those which were impeding the establishment of a French
mandate in Syria, and they were beginning to think in
London that the ultra-nationalist propaganda of Damascus
could be as inconvenient for England as it was for France.
In the East politics and religion are closely connected, and
the agitation of the Sherifians was spreading to all the Islamic
countries; Egypt rebelled against the English protectorate, and
in India the Muslims rose with such violence that the British
authorities had to indulge in brutal and bloody repressions.[1]

In order to make clear what the exact feelings of the
Syrians were towards the French mandate, the Americans
proposed sending a commission of inquiry into Syria. The
French refused to join this delegation, the English equally
abstained; the pilgrims from beyond the Atlantic, who were
proposing to visit countries of which they were somewhat
ignorant, where they would ask imprudent questions, meet
the individuals who were the least qualified and often the
most questionable, were entangling the subtle threads of
ancient European policies and threatening to upset some very
delicate balances, and they made the British very uneasy. An
American delegation had toured Ireland in the same way,
greatly to the displeasure of the English, and had encouraged
dangerous aspirations in that country.

Fundamentally, no one among the innumerable delegates

[1] On the 13th of April, 1919, at Amritsar, 379 Hindu rioters were
killed in the repression directed by General Dyer.

of the twenty-seven countries that met at Paris, each concerned with his own problems, had any real understanding of this Syrian business which was setting against each other two of the principal protagonists of the Congress. It was not a simple problem: not all the Syrians were francophiles but then they were not all francophobes. It was true to say that some of the Arabs had behaved like heroes, but without constant impulsion from the Allies it was clear that they would have done nothing. Many of the Arabs had been and remained pro-Turk. Shekri Ganem was a puppet in the hands of the French, and Feisal in the hands of the English was scarcely worth more. In this sea of incertitude and contradictions everybody foundered.

Feisal, discouraged, lost in an immense whirlwind and unable to make himself heard, left for Damascus, where his brother Zeid, immature and lacking in character, was making a poor attempt at running the interim government. Lawrence also left Paris and went to England. He was, besides, called back to his country by a bereavement: early in April 1919, his father had died. At Oxford he found an empty house: his father and two brothers had gone. Amidst these ruins his mother retained her icy stoicism, and was planning to leave for the Far East with her eldest son, the doctor, and there devote herself as a missionary to religion and charity. Lawrence wandered through the sad home. To the family sorrow there was added the crumbling of his Syrian hopes; his mother saw him for hours on end sitting immobile in an armchair silently sifting his morose thoughts; his moral honesty, his pride, the passion that he had for Syria, the humiliation of having lost face with men for whom he had been or thought he had been for several years a hero, a leader, a sort of prophet, all this mingled within him. At Paris he had seemed to everyone to be in possession of his dynamism, of his quickness and power of intellect; the inaction after the defeat left him unbalanced. He had had these depressions before: after his torture in Deraa his companions had noticed a sort of split in his personality, and he himself has noted that in Arabia at certain particularly tough moments, he had felt that "madness was very near"; but the iron strength of his will had always enabled him to surmount these weaknesses.

At Oxford his mind had nothing to occupy it, and he felt that he was losing his balance.

Suddenly he decided to leave for Egypt. His pretext was that he was going to look for the documents and personal objects that he had left in Cairo; probably he was obeying the imperious desire to see again that Near East to which he was drawn by every fibre of his being.

Aerial Interlude

IN a less eventful life than Lawrence's, the journey which he made by air from France to Cairo would form a single romantic chapter in itself. Wishing to get to Egypt, he discovered that two squadrons of Handley-Page heavy bombers were being urgently sent to that country in order to help in repressing the insurrections which were breaking out everywhere. General Graves, the British Air Representative at the Congress, procured him a seat on one of the aeroplanes, and in the middle of April he took off from an aerodrome near Carvin[1] for the Nile Valley.

The equipment of the Allies, after the long battle of 1918, was in a terrible state of repair and long sea crossings were a difficult undertaking for the aeroplanes of that period. The aeroplane in which Lawrence was travelling nearly turned over at Pisa, barely reached Rome, and whilst landing at Centocelle in the twilight, crashed into a quarry. The two pilots were killed, Lawrence broke his collar-bone and several ribs and was cut all over. A few days in an Italian hospital more or less put him right again; meanwhile the aeroplanes were arriving one by one on the Italian aerodrome, and Lawrence, his chest encased in plaster, his arm in a sling, was on the first to leave.

The English machines, after a landing at Taranto, set out for Athens by way of Albania. At Valona there was another delay. The Handley-Page motors had to be inspected, and the aviators camped on the ground. To the technical accidents, and the boredom of being stranded on a strange coast, there were added financial difficulties. Most of them had only a little Italian money, which the Albanian peasants were loath to accept, but an unexpected currency was established between the British and the natives, empty petrol cans. Throughout the Eastern Mediterranean at this time, the

[1] In Northern France.

four-gallon tin was replacing the ancient amphora. The Nausicaas, the Rebeccas and the Agars went to the well carrying on their heads these horrible metal receptacles, and dishonouring the classical countryside. The Albanians, wishing to keep up with the fashion of the day, exchanged figs, milk and eggs with the aviators, for the white metal cans.

At Athens, reached with great difficulty (the aeroplanes had to go round the mountains as they could not go over them), they stayed for further long weeks. One hop took what was left of the two squadrons to Crete, where several of the machines refused to take off and more days were lost in repairing them.

By way of Sollum and the Libyan coast, the first Handley-Pages finally arrived in Cairo in July, but the laggards were still coming in one by one, weeks later.

Lawrence bore with equanimity the hardships, now tragic, now grotesque, of this long-drawn-out escapade.

He seemed indifferent to the consequences of his wounds, accepted the delays and privations, slept on the ground beneath the wing of the aeroplane, and joked with the mechanics. He spent almost all his time in writing. It was between France and Italy, against the roaring of the propellers, that he wrote the introduction to the *Seven Pillars*. Later he found the hum of the big Rolls engines in the rhythm of his phrases.

* * *

Lawrence's visit to Cairo has remained rather a mystery, and one wonders whether he was involved in some negotiations of his own. His personal luggage was usually limited to a little linen and a tooth brush, and it is astonishing that he should have made so long a journey to recover these few things. His journey had been kept a secret, but news of it filtered through to the Foreign Office, who fearing that he might go to Syria and further embitter relations between England and France, telegraphed to the General Staff in Egypt to forbid him to take any inopportune initiative. Allenby thundered, and demanded that he be brought to the Residency dead or alive, and Colonel Wavell (Rommel's future adversary) was charged with finding him. But Law-

rence was not to be found until the day when he was run
into by chance in the lounge of Shepheard's Hotel, enigmatic
and smiling. "Syria?" he said innocently, "I have not the
slightest intention of going to Syria; at the end of the week
I am catching the boat to England."

* * *

Lawrence returned to Paris, and then, at the end of the
summer of 1919, to Oxford. He was extremely tired. He was
suffering as a result of his accident in Rome; one of his lungs
had been perforated by a broken rib. He stayed in order to
rest himself at home with his mother, who was frightened by
his state of moral and physical exhaustion.

When in September 1919 Feisal came back to London to
ask the English once more for help against France, Lawrence took no part in the negotiations. The principal conference at which the Emir pleaded his cause was attended by
Lloyd George, Lord Curzon, Bonar Law, Allenby, Ronald
Storrs, Cornwallis and Stirling, but Lawrence was not
present. The War Office, like the Foreign Office, no longer
wished to see him involved in this affair, to whose embitter-
ment he had contributed. Lloyd George even had him discreetly told that he did not wish to see him in too frequent
contact with Feisal.[1] The mandate on Syria was about to be
granted to France, that of Mesopotamia to England and the
British were just about to obtain from our country the Mosul
concessions, and it was thus a bad moment to choose for
increasing tension with the French; besides, England had
learnt with much displeasure that part of the subsidy which
she had granted to the Grand Sherif Hussein was being used
through the intermediary of Feisal to support the revolts in
Mesopotamia. The Emir was received with a certain frig-
idity, he was advised to settle the matter with Clemenceau,
and as soon as they could they got rid of him.

Lawrence, however, did not remain completely aloof to
what was going on. He wrote a long letter to the *Times*,
going through point by point the arguments which he had
used at the Congress of Paris, but since it contained passages

[1] Draft of a letter from Lawrence to Lloyd George dated the 19th of
September, 1919, published in the *Correspondence*.

that were too violent it was not published in its entirety. He had a talk with an American called Yale, who tried to find a solution to the Syrian question, drew up a memorandum for the Foreign Office, and addressed a letter to Lord Curzon. But all this achieved nothing, and it seemed that he was for ever to be turned out of the affairs of the Levant.

These days of uncertainty and regret left an indelible mark on his character. It seems that the moral disorder, the neurasthenia which was to make havoc of his life, dates from this period. His hatred of France had become something morbid. He attached the French Croix de Guerre with which Pisani had decorated him to the collar of Hogarth's dog.

The Goddess with a Hundred Mouths

WE learn from the earliest sources that it is difficult to disband an army after a long campaign; the *Odyssey* is the story of the troubled demobilisation of a captain and his soldiers who after years of fighting are unable to return to a peaceful life, and whom war pursues beyond the war's end.

The soldier when freed, divests himself with difficulty of the character of a warrior, in which he has had a cruel but exciting time and above all a life with a simple and well-defined aim, a sort of moral comfort in servitude. Discipline is a hard pillow, but one on which heads in torment love to recline. What is more, the rediscovery of the fatherland, left so long before, seems to the demobilised soldier a sad disappointment. During the chaos of war the ideals for which he left to fight have not remained intact. He feels a foreigner in his own country, and finds that the community which he had defended is ruled by profiteers and greybeards. With bitterness he thinks: "Rome is no longer Rome."

*　　*　　*

Lawrence tried to start a new life as a civilian. He settled at Oxford: some friends of his had obtained for him at the beginning of 1919 a research fellowship at All Souls. It carried an assured income of £200 and rooms in the University buildings—the vital minimum.

This institution left him with much liberty. There were no strict rules to oblige him to keep any set hours in Oxford, London was not far away and he could keep in touch with the numbers of friends, of whom many were in high positions, that he had made during the war years and at the Peace Conference. Hogarth, his spiritual father, was again Curator of the Ashmolean and he saw him often.

He could perhaps have found equilibrium in some civilian occupation, were it not that circumstances for which he was not directly responsible turned his life upside down. Overnight he became one of the most famous, perhaps the most famous man in England.

Until then he had enjoyed a limited notoriety among a circle of soldiers, officials and diplomats of whom many appreciated and greatly admired him while others detested him cordially, but he was neither more nor less well known to the public than an infinity of other men—heroic figures or great leaders—who had distinguished themselves in the war. Suddenly he became a national hero.

This sudden and vast renown was the result of the sensational advertising given to him by the lectures of an American journalist, Lowell Thomas. First in the United States, and then in London, Thomas gave a series of film shows, which he accompanied with a commentary and which were an immediate and prodigious success in every English-speaking country.

Lowell Thomas had been sent in 1917 by the American Government to the Western Front as a war correspondent. He was to send back to his country propaganda articles on the great things that were being done by the Allies, with the aim of encouraging the United States to enter the war. He next visited Allenby's staff in Palestine and Ronald Storrs, then the Governor of Jerusalem, introduced him to Lawrence as he was on his way through that city. The sight of an English officer dressed like a Bedouin filled him with enthusiasm. This picturesque personality and the stories which were circulating about him promised to make good copy; he had some interviews with Lawrence, who always on the watch for any publicity which could help the Arab cause, suggested that he come to Aqaba, and himself applied to Allenby's staff for a pass for the journalist.

Lowell Thomas knew his trade well, but he exercised it in the rather flashy way for which the gentlemen of the press are sometimes reproached. He wished before everything to please his public and was more interested in sensation than in strict accuracy. He spent a few weeks at Aqaba, and gleaned some anecdotes from the men at the base, which he adapted to suit himself. Lawrence encouraged rather than moderated the journalist's enthusiasm. He allowed himself to be copiously photographed in romantic poses by Harry Chase, the photographer who accompanied the American traveller, and furnished him with tendentious information on the war aims of the Sherifians, on Feisal's political and military virtues, on the disinterested and almost idyllic character of the Bedouins, and finally on his own personal rôle. After an excursion to the site of Petra, of which he brought back some excellent photographs, Lowell Thomas returned to America.

A little after the armistice the journalist organised a series of performances in New York, half cinematograph projections and half lectures, in which he related his memories of the Allied front; those which dealt with the war in Palestine and Arabia were the best received, for they revealed some romantic episodes of which the public until then had heard nothing. They were entitled rather audaciously: "With Allenby in Palestine and Lawrence in Arabia."

An English impresario, Percy Burton, having seen one of these spectacles, was astonished to learn in America of the great deeds of the British armies in the Levant of which England was almost completely ignorant; he brought Lowell Thomas to London, where the latter, starting in September 1919 and right up to January 1920, repeated his lectures at Covent Garden, and then at the Albert Hall. The performances were organised like circus parades in order to impress the crowds. The band of the Welsh Guards, engaged for the event, played military airs, and the lecturer spoke in the 'clair-de-lune' décor of a Thomas Beecham opera Its success was enormous. The whole of London rushed to see the films of the American, to which more than a million people came in the capital alone: Cabinet Ministers, generals, and men of the world went like the populace. Lowell Thomas was for four years to take his spectacle round the entire British Empire, and to make a fortune out of the venture. As for Lawrence, he suddenly emerged from obscurity and in England he became a household name.

The immense popularity which he found himself so suddenly enjoying filled Lawrence with mixed feelings. It is impossible for a man of thirty-two to become the idol of his country without being profoundly moved. He had always been, in contradiction to the strong sides of his character and his sharp critical sense, extremely vain, and had always had a certain taste for acting and an incorrigible puerility, and he was intensely flattered by his renown while he feigned to suffer from it and to despise it. He pretended to fly the world, refused invitations, complained loudly that he was pursued by the press, that he was treated like a strange animal, but this invincible glory attracted him. "He hid himself from the public admiration by concealing himself beneath the projectors," Lowell Thomas himself was to say later, piqued by the fact that a man who owed to him his celebrity spoke of him in a very cavalier fashion. In that year Lawrence was the most photographed, the most painted, the most sculptured man of the British Empire. He lent himself to this intensé iconography, went to see his portraits which stocked the exhibitions and adopted advantageous poses in front of them, but vanished with sham embarrassment when the crowd had acknowledged his success. He now found himself on an equal footing with all the most important men, the politicians, the generals, the explorers, the writers and artists, all happy to meet the "famous Colonel Lawrence" and to talk to him. There was nowhere in the British Isles where he was not welcomed with eagerness. He claimed that the fuss made of him by the "wild American" who had turned him into a "matinée idol" was insupportable, but if we are to believe what Lowell Thomas himself said, difficult to check but which has a ring of truth, he went to the first performance of the production that was devoted to him and he returned more than five times to delight in a spectacle of which he was the star attraction.

Not only did he make no effort to put right the inaccuracies and the obvious exaggerations of the lecturer, but having learnt that Lowell Thomas was writing a book about him he went to see him several times and supplied him with the basis of it. It even seems, after comparing some of the text, that he read to him some passages from the *Seven Pillars* which he was then writing. When the American became anxious over the authenticity of some of his activities, Lawrence would say good-humouredly: "Come, come, you must know that History does not consist of the truth." The idea of

creating his own legend, his saga, his myth amused his sardonic mind.

All this log-rolling did not go without provoking some
reaction from the men who were better informed or who had
a more highly developed critical sense than the general
public. Young, in his memoirs relates that he went with
Lawrence to the first session of Thomas Lowell's lectures.
At a given moment the film showed a group of British officers
at Aqaba, with the following sub-title: "They helped him
in the rear, but they did not go with him to the front."
Young, indignant, said to his comrade: "You are not going
to allow him to leave that in!" Lawrence promised to have
it put right, but later when Young went to see the performance again, he found that the sub-title had not been altered.

To attempt to analyse why Lowell Thomas's cinematogra-
phic lectures were so great a success, or the enormous and
quite exceptional celebrity which they gave to Lawrence, is
to be confronted with a very complex issue.

First, the American had great talent and his devastating
style attracted the crowd. He was speaking to a people who
had always been keenly interested in exotic countries and
with everything connected with its colonial Empire, and
besides he presented, united in one man, the two types
which have always played a great part in the folklore and
literature of a colonising country, and in particular of
England.

First that of the European, the friend and upholder of
primitive peoples whom he subjugates with his prestige as a
white man, his authority and his justice, who counsels the
brown and black sovereigns and leads them towards civilisation (it is the type that one finds often in Kipling, and in the
Sanders of the River series of the popular writer Edgar
Wallace).

Next the character almost equally as artificial and quite as
classical, the secret agent, the super-spy, who speaks and
dresses like a native, who can blend with the exotic crowds,
who spies out everything and who can snap his fingers in the
face of the enemy, mystify him and ridicule him. At his best
he is the character of Kim, while his popular brand is repre-

sented by the infinite number of heroes of adventure novels so common in Anglo-Saxon countries.

To the romantic attractions of the American's films there were added others that were due to contemporary events: the attention of British public opinion, impassioned by Anglo-French rivalry, was drawn to the Palestine campaign, and Lawrence's rôle such as it was presented, flattered the Englishman by appealing to his prejudices and to his belief in his own rights.

More subtly finally, Lowell Thomas's spectacle gave satisfaction to a popular sentiment, the anti-militarism bred among men who for four years had been submitted to the harsh discipline of the British Army, in which a very high barrier existed between officer and man, and in which the ordinary soldier was perpetually harassed and punished for small details of clothing and turnout. It was very agreeable for men who had been demobilised to see Lawrence disregarding all the old military taboos, laughing at staff and senior officers, and at the useless and irritating formality. This inspired leader, without rank or almost so, a war-time officer and not a professional soldier, led a people to victory, and made owls of the pompous men in gold braid. His hair was too long, he wore his tunic unbuttoned, he forgot to put on his belt and often, to show his contempt for uniform, he even dressed like an Oriental. The English soldier felt himself avenged for four years of constraint.

All this explains a phenomenon which by its violence surprised Lawrence himself; he became the cynosure of a crowd of adulators, and he literally no longer belonged to himself; it is not to be doubted that he drew, as is natural, enormous pleasure from this nation-wide renown, that he lent himself to it and even did everything to increase it; it is also certain that his sensitivity suffered from it as well as his savage taste for liberty. In any case his life, his whole destiny was overthrown by it.

Oxford—1920–1921

BEING a national celebrity does not constitute a profession and Lawrence had to think about his career. The All Souls fellowship gave him a breathing space in which to look for the way, but he had great difficulty in organising his life; he wished to enjoy his glory and to escape from bondage, two things that are difficult to reconcile, and he did not do it well. Among the young heroes who encumbered Oxford, where they were taking up the studies that the war had interrupted, bearded submariners, colonels of twenty-five and fighter pilot aces, he was by far the most celebrated, and everyone wished to meet him; about this time he made a large number of friendships that were to last all his life, but cultivating his notoriety took most of his time.

Everyone who saw him at this time felt the same reaction. They expected to find themselves before the imperious self-assured hero of Lowell Thomas's films, a sort of warrior arch-angel, and they found a skimpy little man, who looked incredibly young, a boy, they said automatically, badly dressed and retiring, and whose timidity betrayed itself by a nervous smile and a sort of embarrassed giggle. But then if he liked his audience, he became animated; in his eyes there appeared that fire, that irresistible magnetism which he seemed to be able to switch off at will like an electric current; in his words and in his posture could be seen the leader. The classic beauty and nobility were discovered in the face that at first seemed banal, and it was also often noticed with uneasiness that he had an unusual gift of insight, the piercing intuition of a man who sums up and weighs his interlocutor, and leaves him amazed to find his most secret thoughts laid bare.

Among the crowd of men to whom he was introduced in Oxford and London, Lawrence was most attracted by the artists; poets, painters and musicians seemed to him to have been endowed by heaven with a mysterious and almost sacred faculty, and he seemed to be sincerely unaware that he himself, often much more than those whom he looked upon with a religious admiration, had received the marvellous gift. He made friends with Robert Graves, the half-brother of that Philip Graves who had been his colleague in the Arab Bureau. Graves was a fairly bizarre character; as an officer in an élite regiment of infantry he had been through a very tough war in the trenches; he was trying to recover from a wound he had received on the Somme and from which he was still morally and physically shaken. He was a thin, sickly youth with a broken nose and a nervous mouth. Hypersensitive, he was almost without balance or will-power and his erratic way of leading his life as a civilian contrasted with the fine service he had given in the war. He had married an out-and-out intellectual and militant feminist, during a spell of leave, and had several children; at twenty-five he was leading a needy life while trying at the same time and without conviction to carry on his studies, to write poems and novels and to keep a family that was already numerous. But he was a real poet whose verse, although of varying quality, touched the younger generation and Lawrence, for love of his poetry, saw him frequently.

At this time also he met the painter and sculptor Eric Kennington, whose work will always be closely linked to his glory. Kennington had first fought as an infantry soldier and had then become one of the official painters to the Army and had brought back from the front some striking sketches. He was thirty-two or thirty-three, the same age as Lawrence. He was an uncouth man who with his rebellious hair and broad shoulders owed to his Scandinavian forbears the appearance of a Viking pirate. But this cheery fellow was an artist to his very depths and his works had a keenness of line, an hallucinating power of evocation which would have made one think of Daumier or Degas or Toulouse-Lautrec, if their complete originality had allowed of comparison. Lawrence saw an exhibition of Kennington's in London, bought several sketches and left his address. The painter came to see him in Oxford, and as often happened had great difficulty in recognising in the self-conscious little whipper-snapper who greeted him, the young god of the war whom he had seen in the films. But the two men rapidly summed each other up and reached an understanding. Lawrence said with embarrassment, "I've written a book ... a poor thing without illustrations to help it through. ..." At the end of this conversation, Kennington was to leave for Trans-Jordania, there to make sketches of the old companions of the Revolt, of the Arab sheiks, the English officers and the simple cutthroats of the guard, the sketches that illustrate the *Seven Pillars*, and which fit in so well to the book that one cannot imagine it without them.[1]

Lawrence made friends with another painter of talent, Augustus John, whose portraits of him and of Feisal had a great success. The friendship between John and T.E. must have been fairly troubled, as the painter has given Lawrence a rather unusual and rather unpleasant look—perhaps the one which he knew—he accentuates the acting in his posture and a disturbed side of his nature which one does not find in the other portraits of T.E.

Lawrence made the acquaintance of Bernard Shaw, of the novelist E. M. Forster and of Siegfried Sassoon, and he renewed his friendship with Vyvyan Richards, the companion of his youth. With the latter he planned to set up a press and to publish books of an impeccable typography. He bought from a relation of his father a few acres of ground in Epping Forest, at Pole Hill, and decided to build a house there, for which the book he was writing would provide the necessary money; in the hermitage of Pole Hill the two friends would print the works of Conrad and Heredia; Lawrence would publish the *Theocritus* of his dreams in his own workshop.

The men who came to see him in Oxford found him in a rather sombre room in All Souls, poorly furnished but enriched with some fine panelling. On the wall there was the portrait of Feisal by Augustus John and a bell taken from a railway station in the Hejaz. Lawrence took no part in the life of the University, refused to go to the formal dinners, but was not beyond from time to time reminding people of

[1] During a sitting in Amman, Kennington was nearly assassinated by one of his models, Mahmas, the member of the bodyguard whose portrait figures on p. 292 of the *Seven Pillars*.

his presence. He organised a strike of the college servants, pompous and traditionalist officials that might have been caricatures, but who were, also traditionally, badly paid, and who were no doubt astonished to find a leader in this member of the University who conformed so little to the secular ideals of their profession.

For all that he did not feel very much at ease in Oxford. He was accustomed to other surroundings, to men more complex, more uncouth, more free. The petty formality of the University irritated him, stifled him, and besides he was incessantly harassed by money troubles. The income from the fellowship was slender; now he loved to receive his visitors in noble style, and could not resist the desire to help his friends who were in financial difficulties. To have played for three years at being a sovereign and to have kept up a guard of ninety warriors equips a man poorly for a scant life with the income of a petty official. Fundamentally Lawrence, who could be content himself with practically nothing, was greatly in need of money. He must have inherited a certain sum from his father, but the purchase of Pole Hill, and the expenses which he incurred from this time on for the illustrations and the preliminary impression of the book which he was preparing, had absorbed his capital. He was perpetually short and complained about it in his letters to his friends.

In London he found a more congenial atmosphere. He had made the acquaintance of the reputed architect Herbert Baker, who put at his disposal a large attic over his offices in Barton Street, Westminster. It was in this refuge which very few people knew about that Lawrence perfected the work of his life which he had begun in Paris in 1919, *The Seven Pillars of Wisdom.*

Cairo—Jidda and Amman

February 1921—February 1922

DIVERTED from the affairs of Syria, Lawrence could not take his mind off the fate of the Arab States. Writing his book on the campaign brought back incessantly the same thoughts. The crumbling of his dream filled him with immense bitterness.

With the help of his celebrity which opened every door and which impressed influential people, he laid siege with his usual skill and stubbornness to a number of politicians, and in particular Lloyd George and Winston Churchill whom he had known since the Congress of Paris. He persuaded these men that he alone understood anything about the Arab problems and behind the scenes he prepared for his re-entry into the politics of the Near East.

During the year 1920, events in Syria and Mesopotamia took a very disquieting turn for England and France alike and it appeared to the British Government that the decisions of the Peace Congress to which Lawrence had been so passionately opposed, had created in the Levant a very thorny situation for the titulary nations of the mandates.

Furthermore England discovered that events in Arabia had repercussions in every Islamic country, and that a clumsy policy pursued in Mesopotamia would risk damaging her position in Egypt and India.

At the root of the intense ferment in the Near East were diverse and equally powerful currents: Arab Nationalism which several years of propaganda conducted by the Arab Bureau had exacerbated; a religious reaction: contact with the infidel drove the Muslims, sustained by a faith that was strong and alive, to rise against the invasion from Christian Europe; finally there appeared an unexpected sentiment among the élite, that very élite that had been the most separatist, regret for the Ottoman Empire.

All the rulers of the new States born of the dismemberment of that Empire had had a Turkish upbringing, and remembered with nostalgia the life of Constantinople and discovered (as the ex-subjects of Austria-Hungary were discovering at the same time) that nations recently and hurriedly improvised were economically unbalanced, too small, too poor and enjoyed a lower standard of living than they had when they had formed part of a larger whole that allowed of exchange and compensation.

This malaise fostered both social troubles and xenophobia and the two European occupying powers suffered from them equally. There is at this time a definite parallel between the difficulties of the English in Iraq (from now on the official name of Mesopotamia) and those of the French in Syria, and at the Congress of Damascus which was held in March 1920, the Arabs protested as violently against the English expropriations as against those of our country. This Congress named Feisal King of all Syria, and Abdullah King of Iraq. England managed to prevent Abdullah from claiming his throne and taking part in the imbroglio, but she was as directly involved as her colonial rival.

We know how things turned out in our mandate. Feisal had never ceased to oppose our pretensions in Syria. Surrounded by extremist elements over whom he had little control, he pursued a policy of pin-pricks against our administration, and the English advisers who were with him did not hold with moderation. The French representatives in Syria were as clumsy as Feisal was tortuous and indecisive; they were besides divided amonst themselves, since the French soldiers and civilians did not get on together.

To re-establish order in the Levant, a soldier of repute, General Gouraud, was sent there. The old warrior of the Sudan had a simple mission: he had to maintain security and protect his troops and that prevented him from losing himself in the subtleties of Oriental politics. Feisal refused to allow the French the use of the railway line from Rayak to Aleppo which was indispensable for our troops who were then engaged in operations against the renascent Turkish army, and Gouraud sent an ultimatum to the Emir; not having received any reply during the time appointed, he marched his regiments against Damascus.

Feisal in his usual way hesitated and wavered. It seems that he gave in to the ultimatum, but that his reply did not reach the French in time. His entourage was for war, and he did not dare prevent it, but he did not have the courage to put himself at the head of his troops. The Sherifians, commanded by a Turkish general, Azmi Bey Youssef, were completely defeated at Meyssaloun, forty miles from Damascus, in an engagement in which both sides had fairly heavy losses and in the course of which Azmi Bey was killed.[1] The French entered Damascus on the 21st of July, 1920.

It was Nuri Bey, Pisani's old comrade in battle who had drunk his "calories" with the colonial captain at the time of the raids around Deraa, who brought the capitulation of the Sherifians to Gouraud. Feisal fled to Palestine, beneath the wing of the English. All this was a very great pity. The French rejoiced to see the disappearance from the Syrian scene of a character who owed all his loyalty to a rival country, but they took no account of the long years of trouble to which they were committing themselves.

It would probably have been easy enough to win Feisal over to our cause by the grant of a few concessions and financial advantages; more able diplomats would have avoided the extreme decisions that embittered our relations with the Syrians and deprived us of the intermediary of a native prince between us and our new protégées. It is curious to find that among the numerous French authors who speak of this episode in the history of our Levantine mandate, Colonel Brémond alone defended Feisal. He knew the faults of the Sherif extremely well, but he declares quite distinctly that the expulsion of a man with whom right up to the last moment it was possible to treat was a political blunder.[2]

*   *   *

In Mesopotamia things had reached exactly the same point.

[1] In homage to a courageous adversary the French buried Azmi Bey amongst their own dead.
[2] *Le Hedjaz*, p. 346.

The country was administered by Colonel A. T. Wilson, a man of probity, energy and humanity, but imbued with the old colonial principles. He tried to apply in Iraq the system of government that was in use in India. A desperately hard worker, surrounded by a team of devoted and courageous, but on the whole rather inexperienced officers, he found himself up against a host of religious, social and economic problems, the new nationalism of the people and the fanaticism of the Muslim. He found that free Syria, the kingdom of Feisal, was undermining the English mandate as much as the French, and he learnt with bitterness that the agitators whom he had arrested had been sent and paid by Damascus.

In the summer of 1920, the nomads of the Euphrates rose, and bloody methods had to be employed to reduce them. More than fifty thousand men were immobilised in Iraq and the occupation was costing thirty million pounds a year. In England the post-war economic crisis was beginning and the British taxpayer complained bitterly. The Cabinet in London realised that they must get rid of this burden as soon as possible.

The Minister for Foreign Affairs, Lord Curzon, was a 'tough' imperialist who did not seem the man to carry out a policy of appeasement in the Near East, and Lloyd George, the old schemer, decided that by withdrawing the affairs of the Levant from the Foreign Office and passing them to the Colonial Office he could entrust it to Winston Churchill, then Under Secretary of State for War and much more diplomatic. A Near East department was created in which Churchill surrounded himself with specialists such as Clayton, Hubert Young and Meinertzhagen, Allenby's assistant in Palestine. He asked Lawrence to join this service as "Political Counsellor".

Lawrence, sensing that Churchill needed his help, begged to be excused. He could not accept, he told the Minister, unless he was allowed considerable latitude and unless Churchill promised him that he would to a large degree satisfy the Arab aspirations. Some effort was made to appease him, and he entered the Colonial Office in 1921. Perhaps his decision was hastened by the fact that Feisal, kicked out of Syria by the French, was in London, where he had come to seat himself on the threshold of the British Empire; for Lawrence he constituted a living remorse.

*   *   *

Churchill's first decision was to assemble a conference at Cairo, in March 1921, of all the competent authorities. Around the table there sat, with Sir Percy Cox the Governor of Mesopotamia, Clayton, Cornwallis, Young, Jaafar Pasha, Gertrude Bell, Trenchard of the Air Force, and Lawrence. They discussed the measures to be taken in order to calm the agitation in Iraq whilst giving the country an autonomous government, without at the same time losing political control of the regions in which the oil flowed. As a form of government they chose constitutional monarchy, and since they had to endow the new kingdom with a sovereign, Feisal was put to a referendum of the Iraqis. A few million illiterates were in the course of 1921 to vote for a constitution and to elect by plebiscite a king.

There remained the question of the security of the country. It was necessary to protect both the young State and the commercial and industrial establishments which the English were founding at Mosul and Baghdad against the turbulent nomads and against Turkey. It was decided that this police rôle should be taken by the Air Force alone and that almost all the occupation troops should be withdrawn from Iraq. This last idea probably came from Lawrence who knew the possibilities of aviation in the desert. A few squadrons were stationed along the Euphrates, and they would, it was hoped, replace in a more economical fashion the heavy and costly ground forces.

*   *   *

Such dispositions were skilful and wise. They show yet once more that England is better than France at extricating herself from a bad business and cutting her losses without allowing her decisions to be influenced by considerations of vanity. In the course of these negotiations Lawrence was in frequent contact with Churchill, who himself whimsical, original and unconventional in character, appreciated these qualities in others. "He is a fine animal, but he cannot live in captivity," said the Minister. The two men had become fairly intimate, since in their final correspondence T.E. addressed the Minister of State by his Christian name, Winston.

This return to the Levant brought Lawrence back to an atmosphere in which he was thoroughly happy. He made a journey into Trans-Jordania, saw again many of his war-time companions and old soldiers of his guard. He was welcomed with enthusiasm by these men who for years had looked on him as their omnipotent and invincible leader; they pressed around him in order to touch his coat and the horsemen cavorted about, threw their weapons in the air, fired shots and shouted unceasingly: "Aurens! Aurens!"

One decision of the Cairo Conference had in effect given birth to a principality in this desert country, and Abdullah, who was available and whose ambitions had to be appeased, had been given the crown of a little buffer State, situated at the juncture of Arabia, French Syria and the restless State of Palestine.

In Cairo, surrounded with admiration and respect, Lawrence schemed and intrigued. The other English delegates watched his acrobatics with astonishment and some disapproval, and they found that in order to arrive at his ends he did not hesitate to depart from the strict paths of truth. His Oriental cleverness was shocking to their English ethics. To a large degree he obtained satisfaction from the results of the meeting. In helping to give Feisal a crown and Iraq a fairly large measure of autonomy he had the impression that he was reforming the decisions of the Congress of Paris against which he had striven so fiercely.

Later on he convinced himself that at the Cairo Conference he had been the *Deus ex machina,* the great and only leader. Winston Churchill makes the position clear with great tact but with great firmness,[1] by saying that Lawrence was no more than one of the members of his team of advisers and that he was grateful to him for restricting himself to the job of a "humdrum official", a member of the rank and file, and for not having played the part of a lone wolf. The great statesman adds: "I have dwelt upon this part of his activities

[1] In *Lawrence by his Friends,* the article by Winston Churchill.

(in Cairo) because in a letter recently published he assigns
to it an importance greater than his deeds in war. But this
is not a true judgement."

In the spring of 1921 he returned to London, but after a
few weeks he had to leave again for the Levant. The Cairo
Conference had not in fact settled everything in the Arab
countries and a number of difficulties remained to be
smoothed out. Hussein was at war with the Emir of the
Nejd, Ibn Saud, whose bands were penetrating as far as the
neighbourhoods of Mecca and Medina. The Grand Sherif
requested help, but refused to follow the advice of the
English and seek an agreement with the Saudites. The
British did not know which of these two Oriental sovereigns
to support. They had representatives in both camps and
wished to arrive at some compromise, but Hussein was un-
governable. He cried that the Allies had deceived and betrayed him, and that he bitterly regretted not having stayed
on the side of the Ottomans, forgetting of course that the
ingratitude of the British found expression in royal crowns
for himself and for two of his sons. In spite of English representations he continued to administer what remained to him
of the Hejaz along barbarous lines and his methods of expedi-
ting justice horrified the Europeans. They had to bring him
to a less intransigent attitude. England secretly wished to
conclude a treaty with him making him into a semi-
protectorate.

Lawrence was sent as an envoy to Hussein and arrived at
Jidda early in July 1921, but he had never managed to get on
with the Grand Sherif and he failed in all his attempts at
negotiation. The old devil used all the tricks that had exhausted the patience of Ronald Storrs, Wilson and Brémond;
he roared, stormed, sulked, and in the middle of the negotiations went and shut himself up inaccessibly in Mecca, leaving
Lawrence to grill in the stifling climate of the Red Sea at the
height of summer. Everyone who had dealings with Hussein
was left with the same impression: the cantankerous old man
had a distinction and a sincerity which compelled respect,
but they had to recognise that narrow, authoritarian, capricious and medieval in piety as he was, there was no longer a
place for him in an Orient that was in the process of trans-

formation. Exasperated, Lawrence had to break off the negotiations and return to Cairo.[1]

There another mission awaited him. Trans-Jordania, that region which, outside the Fertile Crescent to the south of the Dead Sea, is composed almost exclusively of arid mountains and desert steppes, and which extends from the Gulf of Aqaba as far as the Jebel Druze to the east of the Jordan depression and of the Dead Sea, had been as we know placed under the sovereignty of Abdullah. What remained of the Sherifs' army and of the Syrian extremists who had fled Damascus at the time that our troops entered that city were surrounding the Emir, and the new State had become a hotbed of anti-French intrigue. Making use of the sheiks of the Atrache family, Abdullah tried to take possession of the Jebel Druze and he had even struck against Sueida. Between the French troops and the Arab bands there were frequent skirmishes. With the State of Israel relations were equally bad: Arab–Jewish friction, which was later to take on the tragic proportions which we know, had begun to appear, and the Emir carried on with his Jewish neighbours a veiled struggle which closely resembled that which he pursued with the French. Trans-Jordania was thus a definite danger point for the fragile equilibrium of the Near East.

By an irony of fate Lawrence was deputed to Abdullah in order to abate the excesses of an Arab nationalism which he had done so much to excite. He remained in Trans-Jordania till the end of 1921 as "chief British Representative" and it is not easy to tell exactly what his activities were. Churchill says briefly, "I sent him out to Trans-Jordania where sudden difficulties had arisen. He had plenary powers. He used them with his old vigour. He removed officers. He used force. He restored complete tranquillity", which although it indicates

[1] Three years later the Grand Sherif Hussein was expelled from the Hejaz by the Wahabites of Ibn Saud. He was to die in Cyprus almost in penury. The Arabs had treated him worse than had the Allies. Abdullah, who was assassinated in 1951, was the grandfather of Hussein, the present ruler of Jordan. The late King Feisal of Iraq, who recently met his end in such tragic circumstances, was the grandson of the Feisal of this story, and Nuri Said who died with him, was Lawrence's comrade in battle.

the importance of Lawrence's mission, is very vague, and one would like to have more details.

Lawrence had never been fond of Abdullah and to humble his pride must have been quite agreeable to him, but to have to restrain Arab reprisals against the French occupants of Syria must have wrung his heart. Without documents or precise information, it is impossible to accuse him of having helped to foment the revolts and murders which at this time troubled Southern Syria and in particular the Jebel Druze, but it is very difficult not to allow suspicion to fall on him. Most of our soldiers and our Syrian officials are convinced that during his stay in Amman he did not cease to act against us by means of propaganda and even with arms. His hatred against France was intense. Was this man with his terrible gift for organising political agitation and guerilla warfare, at the root of the Druze revolt which was to break out two years later and cost so many French lives? It is undeniable that this insurrection was supported and financed by Trans-Jordania, that Sultan Atrache and his partisans found arms, money and a refuge in Amman, Azrak and Deraa and that the rebellion ceased in 1926, when the French command in Syria finally obtained from the English officials around Abdullah that the Druze raiding parties should no longer be allowed into and supplied in Trans-Jordania.[1]

* * *

At the end of 1921 Lawrence came back to England. From now on Near East politics to which he had given himself with such ardour no longer seemed to interest him. He went to find Winston Churchill and hand in his resignation.

The statesman tried to keep him on, promising him the most important positions if he remained in the Colonial

[1] In June 1920, when interviewed by a French journalist Berthe George-Gaulis, Lawrence made the following statement: "In order to punish France for having forbidden the landing of troops in Alexandretta, England immediately organised anti-French propaganda in the Levant"; and he added "Since you are so determined to go into Syria, a Syria will be prepared in which you will be unable to live. That will be my personal task." (*Angora, Constantinople, Londres* by Berthe George-Gaulis, Paris, 1922).

Office.[1] Lawrence refused; his work was finished, he said, the Arabs had received their due, and he wanted his liberty.

In the end as his chief delayed the official acceptance of his departure he went to the Ministry no more, and no longer drew his salary. In July 1922 he ceased to belong to the Colonial Office.

He had besides, ever since his return to England, but one preoccupation: to finish his book. He had continued writing it during his stay in the Near East: at Jidda, during the bitter negotiations with Hussein, in Amman where he had rediscovered the atmosphere of the war years; and finally in London in the attic in Barton Street where he worked without interruption, with no fire in the winter and dressed in a flying-suit. He was haunted by the need to deliver himself of this enormous piece of work, at once a witness, a polemic and a confession, and which for three years had been boiling over inside him. He had to put the finishing touches to the manuscript and then exorcise himself of it by getting it printed.

What then would be the aim of his life? Nobody knew. He had said on several occasions that he would join the Royal Air Force as an ordinary airman, but his friends considered that this statement was a whim and a paradox.

[1] Winston Churchill expressly says in his contribution to *Lawrence by his Friends* that he had envisaged for him a post of governor. "The greatest employments are open to you if you are to pursue your new career in the Colonial Service ... Governorship and great commands were at my disposal."

"*The Seven Pillars of Wisdom*"

"Le personnage principal est un miroir."

THUS as we have said, Lawrence started to write his book in Paris early in 1919, while he was with Feisal at the Peace Congress. The tension of these periods of diplomatic struggle alternating with moments of despairing inaction acted on him like a ferment compelling him to deliver himself of a work which he wished to make into a burning plea for the Arab cause. During his journey to Cairo, then again in Paris, and finally in Oxford, he continued to write feverishly. Towards the end of 1919 he had almost finished his labour.

In November 1919, on his way from London to Oxford, he took with him almost the whole of his work, eight books out of the ten, and having got out at Reading in order to change trains, he left his portfolio on a chair in the station buffet. Despite every effort it was impossible to find the mislaid manuscript.

It is easy to imagine what must have been the feelings of a man who has lost a book into which he has put so much of himself. He had destroyed almost all his documents as he had written it and he felt that he would not be able to reconstitute the book.

As usual he gritted his teeth against adversity and joked about it. "I have lost the damned thing", he wrote to Hogarth. But Hogarth, who had seen some of the manuscript, keenly insisted that he immediately write it again. Hogarth's influence on Lawrence had always been very strong and this book was the flesh of his flesh. With the aid of his prodigious memory and basing himself on a few notes which he had kept, he compelled himself to recommence the enormous task. He devoted the early part of 1920 to it. Taking refuge in Barton Street with his friend Baker, he plunged like a madman into this work, his nerves taut, engrossed in the effort, reliving the epic in a sort of nightmare which kept him at his table for long hours at a stretch, scarcely eating, seeing nobody and finding his relaxation only in nocturnal walks through the sleeping streets of London. The work was again complete when Lawrence entered the Colonial Office in 1921.

He was not, however, satisfied with the new version which had been completed too hastily, almost as fast as he could wield his pen. He took it with him on his journeys to the East, to Cairo, to Jidda and then to Amman in order to revise it. After leaving the Colonial Office, he devoted himself to this work, and in the course of the summer of 1922 he was finally able to bring out a preliminary impression of this third version. He entrusted it to a local newspaper, the *Oxford Times*, who set it up in linotype and printed eight copies of it. These were the proofs of the *Oxford Edition* which Lawrence showed to a few of his friends and to his companions of the Arabian war like Buxton, Alan Dawnay, Bartholomew, and Wavell or to the artists like Edward Garnett, Bernard Shaw, Thomas Hardy, Robert Graves and Kennington.

He had a strange inferiority complex and a troubled and distressing modesty about this book. He entrusted it to his friends wrapped in a veil of mystery, with nonsensical reticences, excuses, and complicated explanations. To each he let it be understood that he was the first to hear about it. He begged for opinions and advice with a modesty that was either real or feigned, but which was very out of place considering the importance and the powerfulness of the work.

All his friends expressed their admiration. Bernard Shaw was with difficulty persuaded to attack so large a manuscript. Mrs. Shaw read it first, and won over, she compelled her husband to read it. The old writer was full of enthusiasm, and from then on he did not cease to encourage Lawrence to publish his work. The eight copies issued by the *Oxford Times* passed from hand to hand, and Gertrude Bell, having heard about this extraordinary book, asked to read it. As all the copies were out it took a long time to find one for the use of the explorer, and it occurred to Lawrence to produce a limited edition of it in order that a larger circle of interested people might be able to see it. But he hesitated to publish a work in which the subjective was so closely intertwined with the objective. For a long time he equivocated. At first he thought of publishing an edition in America in order to be able to make enough money to retire to some Thebaid and live as he wished. "The book to build the house," he said at the time. He thought also of only publishing an abridged edition of his memoirs, and the critic Edward Garnett strove to condense the *Oxford Edition,* reducing it to half its length. "To publish or not to publish?" Lawrence repeated incessantly. His letters to his friends are full of hesitancy, and make one think at times of Rabelais' Panurgos asking of all the winds whether he should marry or not marry. Bernard Shaw, with his vigorous moral health, played the rôle of Brother John in the debate: "By God! Marry!" It was no good Lawrence saying, "Books are not meant to be read. They are to be written only"; at heart he could not escape from the almost general rule that every artist must have an audience and suffers if he keeps to himself that which has cost him so much effort to exteriorise.

After much wavering, he decided to print a hundred copies of the *Seven Pillars* in extenso, illustrated with sketches which since 1919 he had had executed by the best artists, and which would be sold by subscription at the high price of thirty guineas.

Lawrence as we shall see had at this time become an ordinary soldier in the British Army, and before publishing a definitive edition of his work, he rewrote it entirely for the fourth time in the fairly extensive leisure which the service allowed him. It seems that Shaw and his wife gave him much assistance with this revision: they were able to give him the benefit of their lengthy literary experience and of their practice of getting things into print, without interfering with the powerful originality of the author or stepping too hard on his corns. This work took Lawrence three years (1923–1925), and it was only in 1926 that the subscribers' edition of the *Seven Pillars of Wisdom* appeared. Because of his taste for complexity and in order to confuse the bibliophiles, Lawrence carefully dissimulated the number of copies issued. There were probably a hundred to a hundred and twenty. An almost equal number was given to

20

the Englishmen who had taken part with him in the Arab campaign.

The success of the *Seven Pillars* was immediate and unanimous. Some copies were resold several times and reached astronomic prices, five or even six hundred pounds. People would offer five guineas per week in order just to be able to read it. On the other hand the edition had been produced with such care and lavishness and the blocks for the coloured reproductions had cost so much that as a financial operation it incurred a heavy loss; Buxton, who had become a bank director and who had guaranteed the affair, was in danger of losing a large sum.

To meet this deficit, it was decided to produce an abridged edition of the *Seven Pillars* for the general public, and Lawrence hastily cut out everything in his work which in his opinion was too subjective or too realist. Thus was born *Revolt in the Desert*, which was published in 1927 in a general English edition and was translated into several languages. The success of this production enabled the loss on the luxury edition to be wiped out and much more, but Lawrence had no wish to profit from this sudden fortune. Once more he had changed his mind and refused he said, to make money out of his glory and out of all the blood that had been spilt during the Arabian war. Once the debit on the subscribers' edition had been paid off, the profits of the operation, about £15,000 it was said, were given to Army charities. In 1935, after Lawrence's death, the full-length edition was reprinted and put on sale to the public.

It is difficult to give an opinion of a work which, with all its faults, long-windedness, omissions, obvious inaccuracies, and passionate bias, remains without any doubt one of the finest books of our generation. Through its complexity it escapes analysis; to appreciate its originality, its faults and its power alike, one must hold it in one's hand.

We have seen that at Carchemish Lawrence had written on Seven Cities of the Orient, a work which he destroyed in 1914. He had entitled it *The Seven Pillars of Wisdom*, drawing his inspiration from a verse in Proverbs: "Wisdom hath builded her house, she hath hewn out her seven pillars"

(Proverbs ix. 1). This fine title, which had remained unused, never ceased to haunt his memory, and he made use of it for his new work.

This title, with all its poetic content, places the *Seven Pillars* on the level on which it was conceived, not on that of wisdom—never was a book less wise—but on that of lyricism; further, Lawrence was thus able to connect the story of his war experiences with his former life, heavily charged for him with the memories of a carefree and happy youth in a Syrian Arcadia.

Above all else, the book is in fact a work of art, a literary monument. To underline his aesthetic intentions, Lawrence had placed a poem of Shakespearean inspiration at the beginning of his work with an introduction which transports us to the highest summits of sensitivity and fervour. These are the first movements of the *Pathétique*. The reader is warned, he is on the threshold of an epic and not of a staff report.

This tone is maintained throughout the *Seven Pillars*. The story is told with control, the excitement is gradually built up from the opening of the situation right up to the feverish pages of the final battle and the triumphant entry into Damascus. In truth the work has the sweep of an epic poem or of a tragedy. Spell-bound by this seething work, the reader comes across successively philosophical considerations, stories of battles and diplomatic negotiations, descriptions of landscapes, and portraits and confessions of brutal accuracy. The size of the work, the multiplicity and diversity of the subjects of which it treats could have made of it an incoherent jumble, but throughout its thousand pages the interest never sags for a moment, so skilful are the transitions and so powerful the architecture.

The style, sometimes too laboured and taut, has a flawless solidity. Lawrence has the mastery of language, of the evocative word full of suggestions and echoes. He handles the familiar, the scholarly, the trivial, the classical, and the crude without ever losing his distinction. It is difficult to find prose that is more colourful, more vibrant, and more full of imagery. The vast and dense vocabulary, steeped in the ancient sources of the language, brings it close to the

Elizabethans, and for a Frenchman recalls the vigorous authors of the end of the Renaissance: Montluc and d'Aubigné or yet Retz.

The profundity of the introspection and the nakedness of the confessions make one think of Rousseau or rather of Proust or Gide. Though a book on war it contributes to our researches into the obscurities of the human heart. In the course of a painful quest into a rent and complex self, and behind a screen of dignity and gravity can be perceived some very dangerous problems; few authors have described the troubled twistings of the serpent with so much penetration and sincerity.[1]

The book when it appeared struck a new note: its balance between romanticism and naturalism was the essence of a new form of literature. Traditional in form, the *Seven Pillars* is in many ways revolutionary. The public of the time, especially the English public, was not accustomed to so much precision in the depicting of the horrors of war nor to such confessions of the inner life. In the pages of the *Seven Pillars* one sees in detail men killing other men with their hands; the veil of modesty which the majority of authors of war books have drawn across the technical details of the immense collective murder is withheld. Certain passages in the *Débâcle* by Zola, certain episodes in *Feu* by Barbusse had alone attained to this degree of horror; but still one felt of these two authors that their literary gift was greater than their personal experience, that they had held neither the knife nor the machine-gun which Lawrence, the intellectual and artist, had handled in twenty engagements; no great writer had ever told how he had executed one of his men at point-blank range, finished off a wounded comrade, been successively tortured and sodomised by a squad of soldiers; no veteran of the trenches had revealed what happened after an attack or analysed the state of his soul.

Thirty years ago, these accounts plucked at fibres that were not accustomed to vibrating. Into the *Seven Pillars* he

---

[1] There are curious analogies between Lawrence and Gide. Faced with a sentence like "I punished my flesh cheerfully, finding greater sensuality in the punishment than in the sin, so much was I intoxicated with pride at not sinning simply," it is not easy to tell which of the two authors wrote it.

dragged in the musty smells of homosexuality, of cruelty, and of death. A certain sadism mingled with the stories, a sadism which had been carefully expurgated from the accounts of the other war writers, who by tacit consent presented themselves as martyrs and paladins that were not supposed to have known such troubled sensations.

Lawrence proved to be the forerunner. Before Malraux, the Koestler of *Darkness at Noon*, Kafka and Jean-Paul Sartre, before the writers of the Resistance and those who described the Nazi and Soviet atrocities (without speaking of recent commercial novels, hybrid offsprings of brutality and pornography), he invented a style which was to be largely exploited by a whole generation of writers.

*　　*　　*

So much art was not expended gratuitously. Immersed in his work, living in the hallucinating world of the writer in the process of creating his work, Lawrence allowed himself to be carried away by purely aesthetic considerations, but he never lost sight of his aim, his plea for the Arab cause, and his service to the nation whose champion he had made himself; he never hesitated before an exaggeration, an omission or if necessary a lie.

When very young he had once said to one of his brothers who was in the process of studying history, "Political poems are the only thing not dry in History." In writing the *Seven Pillars* he wittingly composed a political poem, a work of propaganda as tendentious as *Renard, The Song of Roland,* Shakespeare's *Henry V* or Napoleon's *Mémorial.*

Now it is not possible for a writer to be at once the painter of a large lyrical fresco, an inflamed partisan, a faithful memorialist and also the recorder of the confessions of a soul in torment. One must of necessity ask what is the historical value of a testimony in which truth is quartered on so Procrustean a bed.

If we are to go by what Lawrence himself said, this value would be definitely questionable. In the first introduction which he wrote for the *Seven Pillars* he allowed himself to say some disturbing things. "It seemed to me historically needful to reproduce the tale, as perhaps no one but myself in Feisal's army had thought of writing down at the time what we felt, what we hoped, what we tried." And further on: "In these pages the history is not of the Arab Movement, but of me in it."

And he finished with: "I began in my reports to conceal the true stories of things and to persuade the few Arabs who knew to an equal reticence. In this book also, for the last time I mean to be my own judge of what to say."[1]

The reader must choose between three such contradictory professions of faith.

Bernard Shaw realising that these preliminary statements would remove all credence from the work, persuaded Lawrence to suppress them, but T.E.'s brother, with some naïvety, published them posthumously to the great concern of future historians.

It does not seem, however, that we ought to take literally lines that were written from differing motives, and despite the author's imprudent statement we can consider that the *Seven Pillars*, cross-checked and verified with other writers, and brought into focus by a critical mind, remains a relatively accurate story, and the only one which can give us any idea of this complex, multifarious and confused movement called the Arab Revolt.

It will always be possible to raise doubts on the authenticity of a number of incidents related in the book and to which there was no other witness than the author himself. We appear, however, to have a proof of the veracity of the story as a whole, which for being indirect is none the less a strong one. It is the attitude of the officers and the soldiers who, having been Lawrence's companions during the war, came to know the *Seven Pillars of Wisdom* in 1926.

We know that Lawrence sent a copy of his work to most of the Englishmen who had been with him in Arabia; now none of them ever raised a protest against the author's allegations. This silence is all the more significant since Lawrence dealt with some of them rather unkindly. Such colleagues as he had treated badly had a fine opportunity for getting their own back. Now, if some have had reservations to make on points of detail or have criticised the character, the methods,

[1] *Oriental Assembly,* pp. 142–146.

the strategy, or the political views of the author, nobody has said that he did not play a major rôle in the campaign, nor above all that he boasted of personal exploits which he did not accomplish. The tacit acquiescence of Allenby, of Clayton, of Storrs, Newcombe, Joyce, Young, Wavell and Dawnay, to speak only of them, guarantees the authenticity of the work. They might possibly have let a few inaccuracies go out of a spirit of comradeship or for political reasons, but their tolerance, if it existed, must have had its limits, and one cannot for a moment imagine soldiers and officials of that quality keeping a conspiracy of silence in order to cover up for a braggart or an impostor.

It is none the less indispensable for the historian to watch his steps carefully if he does not wish to fall into the traps which the author, with diabolical cunning, has placed in his path. Anyone who wishes to write an account of the Arabian war cannot do without the *Seven Pillars*, but he would have to use it with the care with which he would handle a palimpsest.

In fact, if one studies it at all closely and attempts to escape the powerful influence of a writer who is almost inspired, one is compelled to realise that Lawrence, by the skilful use of emphasis, by altering perspectives, by exaggerations and often omissions, has managed to falsify the truth every time he has found it necessary to support his doctrines and satisfy his prejudices.

A critical study of the *Seven Pillars* from the angle of the military operations will certainly be undertaken one day. It will have to be based on the English official documents buried in the files of the War Office and the Colonial Office, and inaccessible to a Frenchman. It will probably reveal a number of errors of detail on points of secondary interest, and will discuss theories of tactics and strategy *ad infinitum*, but it will above all reveal the fact that Lawrence, carried away by his passions or attentive to his political aims, has exaggerated the importance of the facts which he relates out of all proportion to their relationship with the general picture of the military situation in the Levant.

In the course of the present essay a number of adjustments have been made and some serious omissions pointed out. It is pointless to mention again how ungenerous is Lawrence's silence on the help which the French contingent gave to the Arab campaign. One can understand his embarrassment in admitting that a Corsican captain, a hundred and fifty North Africans trained in the French Army and four 65s forged in Creusot had been indispensable to the epic ride of the Sherifians to Damascus, but one finds that he treated the Egyptians and the Hindus who went with him on the raids on Yarmuk and Deraa just as badly. The Gurkhas in particular were soldiers of a proverbial courage and loyalty; those that served in the Arabian campaign certainly showed their traditional qualities. It would have been fitting to have done them honour.

But these omissions are minor ones compared with that which in the *Seven Pillars* gives a totally erroneous idea of the surroundings in which the Arabian war unfurled.

With a strange obstinacy Lawrence has voluntarily minimised and almost conjured away the burning religious problem which is in the background of all these events, for there is nothing in the Muslim world, whether it has to do with politics, with war or with the personal life of men, that escapes from the ever-present hold of religion.

He speaks of religion with much skill at the beginning of his book, but in a general way that removes from it all actuality; in reality he never dared to tackle the problem, saying once and quite incidentally that he had not come across any fanaticism in the Hejaz, and that the profundity of national sentiments dominated religious preoccupations. He knew quite well how untrue this statement was. In Islam, the Faith is never forgotten: it colours all life and all action, and comes before everything else. He was better placed than anyone to know the difficulty of bringing Muslims and Christians together, and of establishing a real co-operation between men who were separated by a formidable barrier obvious to the least sensitive of men the moment they come in contact with Mahommedans. He knew that the biggest obstacle not only to all colonisation and mandate but also to all alliance between Arabs and Europeans would come from religion. Faced with so thorny an issue, Lawrence evades it, and skips over the essential in silence.

So large an omission removes much of the weight from a book that is otherwise remarkable. It is all the more to be deplored since Lawrence, with his unique knowledge of the Moslems, could certainly have given us some penetrating views on a problem which for more than a millennium has bedevilled so large a part of the civilised world.

* * *

Can we really blame Lawrence for not having told all about these feverish and difficult years? Just as he related the facts in a broad, dramatic sweep which makes the reading of his book more gripping, so he had to give a certain unity and coherence to the character of his Arab heroes, to their doctrines and their actions, without which they could not have the sympathy of the reader.

It is probably impossible to tell the history of a revolt completely and faithfully. All dissidence is of necessity tainted by the twin evils of civil war and treason, with their odour of fratricide. Such a movement can be exalted as a whole by reason of the loftiness of its aims, but the details are necessarily sordid and shameful: hesitations, lapses, the strength of material interests, denunciations, the settling of accounts, the *volte-faces* of the heroes of the future sagas. To galvanise a Resistance and create a Maquis, the forces of legality and morality must be dispensed with and the demons be given their head; the official histories, the enshrined histories of nations, never dare to sully their pages with the unexpurgated account of these underground struggles. Lawrence must very quickly have realised that he could not allow so dangerous a truth to escape. Prudently he passes over much in silence, and he but scarcely alludes to the sad treasons which never ceased to hatch in the Arab army. But often beneath the veil which the too respectful son has thrown across the details of the Revolt, he is unable to prevent the appearance of ghastly teeming reptiles.

In fact, the devil which he had within him did not allow him entirely to dissimulate the truth that he wished to hide away. The delirium of confession held him, and the morbid need to tell those things about which he had the greatest desire to remain silent. Every artist is disarmed before the truth, not for moral but for aesthetic reasons. All art is founded on truth. Transposed and modified it remains the point on which the artist and the human touch. It is the points of truth which constitute, amidst themes that are imaginary, the strength of masterpieces.

Lawrence was too much an artist to escape from this law. He always ends, having tried to hide everything, by revealing the truth, and almost all his lies are contradicted by parallel confessions. His most exalted heroes, the Arabs, Feisal, and even his own person, he manages to depict as he really saw, with his cruel clearness of insight. And this is why the *Seven Pillars* appears to have been written beneath the sign of contradiction. Hagiography is mingled with the most ferocious criticism, and every purple patch is destroyed with some caricature; if we know how to use this key, it is almost impossible, in these too skilful and too passionate pages to deceive ourselves.

*　　　*　　　*

Should we regret this bias, this dangerous virtuosity? As an impartial witness Lawrence would have given us an accurate account of confused battles in a secondary theatre of operations. Subjective, partisan and violently egotistical, he leaves us a work of art, a monstrous but unique book which is a combination of *War and Peace, The Confessions* of Jean Jacques Rousseau, and the *Châtiments* of the old Victor Hugo and which has a much greater chance of survival than the sincere accounts of so many of the actors of the war, more faithful but lacking in genius.

The Poem of Dedication in the "Seven Pillars of Wisdom"

to S.A.

I loved you, so I drew these tides of men into my hands
      and wrote my will across the sky in stars
To earn you Freedom, the seven pillared worthy house,
      that your eyes might be shining for me
          When we came.

Death seemed my servant on the road, till we were near
      and saw you waiting:
When you smiled, and in sorrowful envy he outran me
      and took you apart:
          Into his quietness.

Love, the way-weary, groped to your body, our brief wage
      ours for the moment
Before earth's soft hand explored your shape, and the blind
      worms grew fat upon
          Your substance.

Men prayed me that I set our work, the inviolate house
      as a memory of you.
But for fit monument I shattered it, unfinished: and now
The little things creep out to patch themselves hovels
      in the marred shadow
          Of your gift.

S.A., the Begetter

Some erudite people have tried to persuade us that Dante's Beatrice was a classical riddle, a cryptogram, a fantasy with numbers and not a being of flesh and blood. No one has believed them. The work of great artists is lit by their loves. It seems that we can understand Michael Angelo, Rubens and Beethoven better since we knew about the Countess Colonna, Helen Fourment and Theresa of Brunswick.

Lawrence's life is also dominated by a love to which he attributed so great an importance that he published the *Seven Pillars* beneath its invocation. He has signified this ardently loved being only with the initials S.A., creating one of those enigmas that are the despair and the joy of the specialists of literary history.

The book opens with a very fine poem, in which he addresses a dedication to an unknown for whom he declares he has achieved his exploits, to whom he has consecrated his efforts for the liberation of Syria, and for whose disappearance at the very moment of victory he weeps. The terms in which he expresses himself are burning: "I loved you . . . that your eyes might be shining for me when we came . . . Love, the way-weary, groped to your body . . ." We know neither the name nor the sex of the being for whom these passionate lines were written and to whom the last lines of the work are obviously addressed, in which the author declares: "The strongest motive throughout had been a personal one, not mentioned here, but present to me, I think, every hour of these two years. . . ."

Biographers, commentators and readers have sought to pierce the mystery of S.A.'s identity, but no definite answer had been found to the enigma which Lawrence deliberately left to posterity. The clues that we have for its solution are rare and contradictory; here are the essential:

In a letter to Buxton, dated the 22nd of September, 1923,

Lawrence wrote: "S.A. was a person, now dead, regard for whom lay beneath my labour for the Arabic people. I don't propose to go further into detail thereupon." That was clear enough. Clear also was what he said to Liddell Hart in conversation: "The personal motive (for devoting myself to the Arab cause) was S.A., but S.A. croaked in 1918." During the same conversation he added: "Of the two initials, one corresponds to a person, the other to the name of a place", which is more obscure.

As for Robert Graves, Lawrence seems to have taken an evil delight in misleading him. On the faith of information given to him whether by T.E. himself or by his friends, Graves had written in his book *Lawrence and the Arabs*, published in 1926, that S.A. must have been a certain Sheik Ahmed with whom Lawrence would have had a "blood brotherhood", and this Ahmed would have died of typhus in 1918. Lawrence, to whom Graves submitted his manuscript, corrected the sentence with this note: "You have taken me too literally, S.A. still exists, but out of reach, because I have changed."

Lawrence's brother has added still more to the entanglement by writing in a note in *Oriental Assembly* (p. 26): "It is believed that his personality (Sheik Ahmed's) supplied the largest element to the figure of S.A. to whom the *Seven Pillars of Wisdom* is dedicated. 'An imaginary person of neutral sex' according to a note of the author's." As A. W. Lawrence does not reproduce the author's note, one is slightly disconcerted by this strange statement, the expression "of neutral sex" being pretty baffling, since we are concerned with someone to whom the writer addresses himself in such ardent terms.

There remains the text itself to throw light on the question. The verses are very fine, the closing sentences of the book are full of a moving fervour; but neither the one nor the other give anything away, and it is impossible to tell whether he was addressing a woman, a man or even a symbolic entity, Syria for example, represented as an adored being.

With such slender evidence it is difficult to form an opinion. S.A. will join the long list of enigmas in the history of letters. It is all the more improbable that the identity of the dedicatee will never be discovered as Lawrence has visibly covered up his tracks, it is a part of his life which he wished to keep secret, and he has done the necessary to ensure that the mystery remained impenetrable, defending it with a mesh of lies.

What to believe? One can admit that S.A. existed, that Lawrence experienced in Syria a love which went deep in his heart, and that the object of his love died before the end of the war: despite his taste for poetic lies, it would be very extraordinary that Lawrence should have invented so sad and complicated a story out of nothing and for a joke.

Nothing in the tone of the preliminary poem gives away S.A.'s sex; but Lawrence always declared forcibly that he was not physically attracted by women, and we know that he had a great need for male companionship; all his affections, almost without exception, had been masculine. Among those who knew him there seems to have been a unanimous agreement to think of S.A. as a man.

Graves and A. W. Lawrence identify S.A. with Sheik Ahmed (Dahum). We know that Lawrence had a very intense friendship for this ephebe, with whom he lived at Carchemish, travelled in Syria and Sinai, and whom he even had to stay at Oxford. We could imagine that when he organised his spy network in Syria from Cairo, he made use of Dahum and installed him in Damascus. It is he that he would have seen either in this city or in the neighbourhood at the time of the raid of June 1917 which he surrounds with so much mystery. S.A. could be Dahum and the problem would be solved.

This identification, however, is not entirely satisfactory. It seems strange that Lawrence should have based his mystical ardour for achieving the liberation of the Arab people on a small, semi-illiterate donkey-boy who, brought up in the outlandish village of Jerablus, could scarcely have had nationalistic feelings of much conviction. It would above all appear very suspicious that Lawrence should have advanced a name even to his intimates whilst he was taking such minute pains to dissimulate the least details of the identity of his mysterious loved one. The very fact that he allowed this opinion to gain credence inclines one to believe that it is erroneous. One would imagine the enigmatic Ganymede rather as appearing with the features of a young Damascene intellectual whom Lawrence would have known at the time of his contact with the Syrian revolutionaries, a literate bourgeois or some aristocratic Arab enthusiast for the national cause, a man of the type of Sherif Nasir or of that Nezib with whom he undertook the raid on Aqaba. Such an identification fits in much better with everything that the mythical S.A. suggests. Besides, it would explain, at least in part, the care which Lawrence took to hide the real name of his friend. At the time when he was writing the *Seven Pillars* the Franco-Syrian crisis had reached a bitter stage, and by revealing the name of one of his partisans in Damascus he would have risked exposing his relations or confederates to reprisals from the French.

This is of course purely hypothetical; equally hypothetical is another suggestion. To be sure, by putting the *Seven Pillars* beneath S.A.'s invocation, Lawrence almost certainly wished to recall the memory of a lost loved one, but he was also pursuing a literary aim and was obeying his taste for obscure mysteries.

This mystery which he created intensified the interest of his work by exciting the curiosity of present and future readers. It gave him pleasure to think that there would be an S.A. riddle, like the W.H. riddle in Shakespeare's Sonnets.

We know that these poems were dedicated to a certain W.H. the Begetter, but despite all the research that has gone into it, we do not know who it was. This point has been endlessly studied, but with no definite results. It will doubtless never be known whether the Begetter was Henry Wriothesley, William Hews, the Earl of Pembroke, or somebody else. It is in any case a man, the Master-Mistress of the twentieth sonnet, and the love which the author ardently declares is not very orthodox.

Lawrence had a particular devotion to Shakespeare, and he once said of him in a letter: "There was a man who hid behind his works, with great pains and consistency. Ergo he had something to hide, some privy reason for hiding. He being a most admirable fellow, I hope he hides successfully."

By imagining S.A., Lawrence if the hypothesis is correct

achieved several objects: he was dedicating the *Seven Pillars* to a loved one for whose loss he wept, creating out of nothing a literary enigma which added spice to the interest of his book, and finally linking his work mysteriously to Shakespeare's, and to the *Sonnets* whose lyricism he admired and whose troubled environment and equivocal tendernesses he loved.

The Man who has Lost his Shadow

LAWRENCE, a little skimpy silhouette, wandered through the streets of London. He was one of the most famous men in England; he knew all the great men of the hour; flattering or lucrative careers were open to him and he had just finished a magnificent book, and yet he was sinking into the most profound disorder. Since leaving the Colonial Office in 1922, his friends had watched with anxiety the progress of his neurasthenia. To some he had confided with his twisted smile and his sarcastic air: "You know that I am going mad." To others he spoke of unexpected expenses that had reduced him to beggary: he was wretched, he said, and was nearly dying of hunger; which was ridiculous as he still had the All Souls Fellowship and was being offered positions in the administration, the Army or the world of letters on all sides. He confided to his intimates his profound distaste for vain human activities. All authority, he said, was noxious, since its ends were unjust and sordid, and from now on he no longer wished to command, he no longer wished even to act. The final putting into shape and printing of his book in Oxford had cost him an effort that had exhausted him. This work completed, he felt himself emptied and finished. And the book itself was the most cruel disappointment for him: the cherished work, which had gestated for years, seemed to him to be mediocre and uninspired, whereas he had dreamt of writing something exceptional, a *Don Quixote* or a *Divine Comedy*.

He also said that his sojourn in Arabia had taught him to look on Europe with the eyes of an Oriental, the result being that he no longer believed in anything, neither in the East nor in the West. The revolutionary had become a nihilist.

It is not easy to distinguish the real reasons for so profound a crisis. The years of war had put the nerves of a man who treated himself intellectually and physically with inhuman toughness to a very severe test; he had been wounded several times, he had been half killed in an aeroplane accident, and the tortures he suffered in Deraa had probably left an indelible trace on his extreme sensitivity. However, at Paris he had fought like a demon and his colleagues had admired his dynamism and tenacious pugnacity; in Cairo and in Amman with Abdullah, he had been seen to be equal to himself; something new must have intervened in his life to explain so great a collapse.

Who can sound a man's most inner feelings? Who will know whether he was upset by political disappointments or whether some intimate sorrow gnawed at his heart?

With the results of his last stay in the Near East he had no reason to be satisfied. He had announced for all to hear that everything had been settled; that Churchill, following his suggestions, had given the Arabs more than they could have hoped for; that England had kept all the promises made by him, Lawrence, and that a young Arab nation set up in Mesopotamia was entering on an era of peace and happiness.

He knew perfectly well that this was not all entirely true. Since the end of 1921 Iraq had been in a state of chronic rebellion. Sir Percy Cox, the English representative, had been booed in the streets of Baghdad, and he had had to declare martial law and exile the ringleaders. The English had bombed villages, and instead of sending the troops back to England Cox had asked for more. The situation was alarming and nobody knew how things would turn out. Thus it looked as though the reassuring words spoken after the Cairo Conference were in danger, in the event, of contradiction, and as if the political and military system advocated by Lawrence would prove inoperative and eventually disastrous.[1]

But there was more. Lawrence had come back from Trans-Jordania with some bitter memories. The Arabs had greatly changed since Aqaba and victory did not reveal them in a very good light. Liberated by English blood and English

---

[1] In fact, everything was put straight in 1922 thanks to the tactful diplomacy of Sir Percy Cox and to some fairly important concessions on the part of England. See Sir Percy Cox's contribution in the *Letters of Gertrude Bell*.

gold, they showed not the slightest gratitude, and sharply and harshly clamoured for more. Lawrence no longer recognised the men who in other times had treated him like a prophet and a saviour. Feisal, who had become King of Iraq with the help of the English, was distant and patronising to the man who had made his entire fortune. It appeared that he had never liked this adviser to whom he owed so much and whose name alone pronounced in front of him recalled the humiliating subjection of a prince of Mecca to an infidel without rank or title.[1] In Amman the slippery Abdullah had put up with him without pleasure and the old companions of the Revolt had cried that the settlement agreed upon in Cairo had trampled underfoot the Arabs' liberties, of which Lawrence had spoken so much during the campaign. Why all these vacillations, why did not Lawrence and the English Army come and help them to kick the French out of Damascus?

Put out by an attitude to which he was so little accustomed, Lawrence, who had been the inspiration of the war, had to defend himself, plead, and apologise for the peace. "Like a tedious pensioner he showed them his wounds as proof he had worked sincerely on their side." But he came away embittered from these struggles. It is hard for an idol to fall from so high. His wounded pride burnt his heart; having read everything he could meditate on the saying of Gobineau: "The East is a delicious meat, but it poisons those who eat it."[2]

In fact, in studying this troubled period of Lawrence's life, one is led to formulate an hypothesis which could in part explain the crisis through which T.E. was passing on his return from the Levant: that of a conflict with the Intelli-

[1] Ronald Storrs says in his memoirs: "There were moments he (King Hussein) and his sons suspected him (Lawrence) of working against them, and more than once let fall hints to confidants that he should not be allowed to mingle too much with the Arab tribesmen. Feisal spoke of him to me with a good-humoured tolerance which I would have resented more if I had ever imagined that Kings could like Kingmakers."

[2] George Antonius in *The Arab Awakening*, p. 230, conveys the feelings of Abdullah's entourage towards Lawrence at this time; in his pro-Hashemite ardour he is not far from considering Lawrence as a traitor to the Arab cause.

gence service. It is likely, as I have said before, that
before the war he belonged to that vast organisation, a network at once political, military and economic, and that
during the hostilities and later on during the Cairo Conference and whilst in Trans-Jordania that he received certain
instructions from it[1]; had he had a disagreement around
1921 or 1922 with the bosses of the organisation? Although
unsupported by any documents it is tempting to believe this
supposition. In 1921, in fact, British policy in the Hejaz
underwent radical changes: after having staked all on the
Grand Sherif Hussein and his sons, England was led to believe that she had made a mistake and began to support the
Emir of the Nejd, Ibn Saud, the sworn enemy of the Hashemites. This was to conform to the ideas of St. John Philby
who, throughout the war, had been violently opposed to the
pro-Hussein policy of Sir Reginald Wingate, Clayton and
Lawrence. Did Lawrence rebel against this *volte-face* and
did he therefore incur the disgrace of the Intelligence
Service which does not like its agents to show too much
independence? To cease to be *persona grata* with so powerful
an organisation and thus to lose all hope of influencing Near
Eastern policy in the future would have severely harmed
Lawrence. All this is hypothetical and one has only the
suspicion of a conflict of this kind. Later, Lawrence spoke
of the Intelligence Service in tones of great bitterness and
in one of his customary moods of rancour.[2]

With a proud and hypersensitive man, worn out by the
war, such cruel disappointments could cause a collapse of
nerves and health. Was there nothing else, more profound,
more intimate? In the tormented life of this complex man,
one is always tempted to imagine something obscure in the
background. His reticence, his half confessions, the mystery
in which he wraps himself compel one fatally towards it.

It is certain that his sentimental life, strange and ill-
balanced, and of which we must speak, had a great influence
on his destiny.

[1] Periodically English newspapers in articles on Lawrence ask to
what degree he was a super-spy. The Intelligence Service not being in
the habit of opening its archives to the public, it is probable that the
question will remain unanswered for some time.
[2] See Forster's contribution to *Lawrence by his Friends*.

THE MAN WHO HAS LOST HIS SHADOW

The almost persistent tradition would have it that
Lawrence was inverted and that this vice weighed heavily
on his behaviour and on the whole of his life. There is
certainly some truth in this accusation, but to define it thus
is to express a complex subject in a very elementary way.
Woolley, Vyvyan Richards, Lowell Thomas, Graves, Liddell
Hart, Colonel Newcombe, and several others have asserted
that he was not a homosexual and that his life was pure. One
is tempted to believe them or at least to believe them in part.
Everything that one has seen of Lawrence's character, his
severe self-control, his horror of the sensual world, of physical
contacts, his fear of any interference with his liberty, allow
us to suppose that on reaching manhood he never allowed
himself to go very far in these "strange and sad" mistakes. It
is difficult to imagine him pursuing Proustian intrigues or
soliciting the services of the corydons of the cross-roads.

None the less there hovers around him all his life the unpleasant phantom of inversion. The fact that the men whom
I have just cited, naturally little inclined to broach a subject
of this kind, should have been under an obligation to defend
him shows that the problem arose. The intimacy with
Dahum, the too pretty ephebe, had from all accounts an
equivocal basis; during the war unkind rumours were continually circulating, since Brémond, if discreetly, made
allusion to it.[1] After the war, passages from his letters, and
such remarks by his friends show that this suspicion continued to float around him. In all this there could have been
no more than youthful errors, imprudences or tittle-tattle
born of his juvenile appearance and of his propensity for
shocking his contemporaries, but it was Lawrence himself by
his writings who gave birth to the most definite suspicions.

In the *Seven Pillars*, he feels a need which he cannot contain, from the second page of the book, to make a sort of
explanatory declaration excusing the homosexual habits of
the men who fought in the desert. He talks of "our men,"
and one feels that he has nearly said "us"; he speaks with
embarrassing fervour of the joys "of friends quivering to-

---

[1] Brémond, in his foreword: "he was always strictly shaven in a
country where the lack of a beard gave rise to suspicions which he was
not spared."

314 T. E. LAWRENCE

gether in the yielding sand". It is pointless and has nothing
to do with the stories of the war in Arabia. In the life of an
army there are a host of other unpleasant things of which
one does not speak. He tells of the heterodox love of Daud
and Farraj with evident pleasure. These things haunted him.

His attitude towards women is not that of a normal man.
He has never hidden his distance towards if not all women,
at least to femininity. He seldom had a relationship with
members of the opposite sex unless they were very virile (like
Lady Astor) or maternal (like Mrs. Bernard Shaw): with the
others, if they were intelligent and good, he sometimes had
fairly cordial relations, but they were very guarded. One
senses that beauty, charm, the aptitude for love, all in fact
that constitutes the essence of a woman, frightened and
disgusted him.

One of his friends, who had for him a great admiration,
told me with vehemence: "the head perhaps, the heart perhaps, but further down, certainly not!" One would like to
believe it, but the head and the heart is much with a creature
who was all intelligence and sensitivity.

Whether or not he gave way to his leanings is not in the
final analysis very important: in his intimate nature he was
certainly a homosexual, and this fission in the depths of his
personality created a lack of stability. He recognised in
himself this dissonance which separated him from normal
humanity, he hated it but he took pleasure in it. He had a
double character. Within him there lay a being of strength,
of an indomitable will, of an intransigent conscience, a
leader, a fanatic and a puritan. But there was also an
hysterical woman, perfidious, lying, unstable, with a taste
for travesty and treason, and a love of causing quarrels.

One is thus led to believe that this anomaly in the subsoil
of his nature played a part in the access of neurasthenia
which overturned his life during 1922. Was he despairing
for an unhappy and inadmissible love? Perhaps this puritan,
haunted by the idea of original sin, by his contempt for the
flesh, felt stirring within him monsters that horrified him?
He has spoken in his book of his companions of Arabia, of
whom "several, thirsting to punish appetites they could not
wholly prevent, took a savage pride in degrading the body

and offered themselves fiercely in any habit which promised physical pain or filth", and at the time of his nervous depression at the beginning of 1918, he admitted to Hogarth and to Clayton his fear that he also was drifting towards dangerous shoals. "I feared to be alone lest the winds of circumstance, or power, or lust, blow my empty soul away." It is not unreasonable to suppose that a crisis of this order was threatening him at the beginning of 1922.

We shall probably never know the paths down which this despairing soul wandered and whether there was a body and a face involved in this struggle. What is certain is that he was completely crippled. His physical condition reveals this internal collapse. He had moments of nervous disorder which without his ferocious will-power would have led him to the brink of epilepsy. His friends saw him, his forehead bathed in sweat, clenching his fists, gritting his teeth, his body shaken with trembling, his eyes full of anguish, making desperate efforts to gain control of himself. He felt that forces were dragging him to what he knew not: madness, vice or suicide. He sought for something to cling on to. That to which he did cling seems extraordinary, and his friends, like ourselves, remain amazed at his choice: he decided to join the professional English army and to become a private soldier in a flying unit.

*   *   *

Ne suis-je pas un faux accord
Dans la Divine comédie

....

Je suis les membres et la roue
Et la victime et le bourreau.

BAUDELAIRE

When a young, happy and beautiful girl becomes a nun, when a man marries an impossible woman, becomes a Trappist or joins the Legion, it is rare that their friends manage to understand such decisions. And meanwhile the convents and monasteries are full of nuns and monks, bad marriages take place every day, and Danish princes, the sons of millionaires and orthodox bishops continue to join the service of the white kepi.

No one has really understood nor will ever understand Lawrence's persistence in losing himself in the ranks of an army whose spirit and discipline he hated and in submitting his free and complex soul to a mean yoke intended for the common herd. To each of his intimates he gave vain and contradictory explanations which throw no light on anything, and yet his decision, monstrous in its absurdity, must correspond to something very deep within him, for he stuck to it for thirteen years, although nothing obliged him to remain in the service.

Everything that he said or wrote at the time to his friends contains parcels of truth and elements of dissimulation. One sees above all a distracted soul which cannot even understand itself, and which in its doubt takes the most painful solution, judging it to be the most noble.

"Seven years of this will make me impossible for anyone to suggest for a responsible position, and that self-degradation is my aim", he said to a friend, and to Graves: "I am going into the army to eat dirt." But to others, he let it be understood that, overcome with weariness, he wished to find peace of mind in a regulated life and manual labour.

Some days before joining up, he went to see Young and spent part of the night in discussion with him. With this comrade of the war and of the Colonial Office, Lawrence had the relaxed relationship of affectionate enmity which the great actors of life have with those who know them too well and with whom they can neither put on airs nor tell lies. Young pleaded for hours, begging Lawrence not to commit this folly, or at least to join up as an officer. Lawrence said that he did not think much of the officers of the Royal Air Force. "Then why not help raise the standard?" Young retorted. But nothing made any impression, he was up against a brick wall.

"The night before I did (join the army) a very wonderful night by the way: I felt like a criminal waiting for daylight", he said later. Lawrence walked up and down his room and wrote on a piece of paper his reasons for enlisting. He found none, save that "it was a necessary step, forced on me by an inclination towards ground-level". An aspiration towards sorrow, an obscure masochism, should he rather have said.

The morbid need to be his own executioner is certainly the most profound failing in this character, so difficult to analyse.

He had asked Trenchard, the Air Marshal with whom he had made friends in Cairo, for the authority to join up as an ordinary airman under an assumed name. "The conquest of the last element, the air, seems to me the only major task of our generation", he said to that officer, and he wished to take part in it, even were it in an obscure rôle; further, he wanted to get to know the life of a private soldier, and to write a book about it. Trenchard, with much repugnance, agreed to help him, and arranged things for him. "It is understood", he said, "that this is a contract which the R.A.F. and yourself can break at any time."

On the morning of the 30th of August, 1922, Lawrence reported to the recruiting office in Henrietta Street and attempted to join up under the name of John Hume Ross. The papers which he presented to justify this assumed identity were clumsily forged and attracted the attention of the officers in charge of enlistment. They noticed that T.E. carried the scars of a whip across his shoulders, which could make it supposed that he was an ex-convict who had suffered the punishment of the 'cat o' nine-tails' in an English prison. Because of these suspect details, they refused to enrol him.

Lawrence sought the intervention of the Minister for Air, who, despite the opposition of the doctors who considered that the recruit was not fit for service, obliged the control commission to accept him; the next day he was at the recruit training depôt at Uxbridge not far from London. He was to remain thirteen years in the army as an ordinary soldier.

His first experience of the depôt was terrible. In the restriction of the barracks he was like a wild animal caught in a trap. He had dreamt of finding stability once more in the relaxation of manual labour, amongst simple friendly beings co-operating joyously in the performance of a noble task. He loved handling anything mechanical or to do with motors, and he had a weakness for the proletarians, of whom he had formed a generous and inaccurate idea. He found himself surrounded by coarseness, rowdiness, drunkenness, the screaming and shouting of N.C.O.s and a harsh and petty discipline, which was intended to break the recruits. They had to sweep the square, wash the plates, carry the refuse bins and feed the camp pigs; the arms drill was stupefying; the ex-Colonel Lawrence was put in the guard-room because he had left his overalls on his bed. His comrades, when drunk, were sick in their sheets and worse.

He gritted his teeth and wagered himself that he would stick it out to the end. The absurd and shabby side of the situation excited him. There are souls who can only live in a tragic climate: when circumstances do not provide them, they create them. Uxbridge, the barrack room, the discipline, the fatigues, all this sublimated by his imagination, became a Golgotha.

Having given up all, he did not give up literature, and from the first day in barracks he started to write, blackening with his experiences as an ordinary soldier pages full of a keen melancholy and a vengeful wrath. To his friends, he wrote letters in which he described his voluntary punishment and complained at length.

The training of recruits at the depôt lasted two months. Early in November he was sent to the camp at Farnborough, where the young pilots and photographic observers were instructed. He watched other young men learning to fly, whilst he was given inferior tasks to do. But he had found at last the calm for which he had sought, he took care of the motors, busied himself around the aeroplanes, and spent a part of his time in the photographic dark-room. Without obligations and without needs, he achieved that apathy and that complete calm of the soul of which he had dreamt after the years of struggle. His nerves regained their equilibrium. Had he reached harbour?

Meanwhile, his indiscretions and his strange and mysterious ways had soon revealed his identity at Farnborough and the officers of the camp knew that the 2nd Class airman (non-specialist) Ross was the famous Colonel Lawrence. No one could understand why a man of his quality should take the King's shilling and restrict himself to material tasks instead of serving more usefully and more honourably as an officer in the R.A.F. An ex-officer who no longer wishes to be an officer has something of the quality of a defrocked priest. Lawrence did not hide his aversion for the men who commanded the Air Force; he certainly had some unfortunate ways of expressing himself, and many of his officers did not consider that his presence was good for discipline. In any case they did not think that the army was a refuge for psychopathic intellectuals: they regarded with suspicion this submissive, correct and jeering airman; some of them wondered whether he was not a spy of the Minister for Air.

All this created a hostile environment around him. Early in January 1923 the papers were tipped-off and started to speak of the ex-uncrowned king of Arabia who was serving as an ordinary soldier; photographers besieged the gates of the camp; the press in general was not favourable to Lawrence, who had often been rude to journalists, and spoke of him without warmth. The R.A.F. were worried by the stir caused by their singular recruit. Trenchard obliged Lawrence to choose between becoming an officer or leaving the service. T.E. refused the former and returned to civilian life on the 23rd of January, 1923.

Lawrence was desperate. He stayed in the neighbourhood of Farnborough as if he could not take himself away from the airfield, asked help of his friends, and he even went to the extent of soliciting a post as a light-house keeper so as to be able to continue his life of calm and anonymity. The connections which he had with the War Office helped him to contract a new engagement, this time in the army, in the Tank Corps, and under the name of Shaw he joined up again early in March 1923 at Bovington Camp, where his unit was stationed.

He bitterly regretted the flying, the engines, the smell of hot oil in the hangars, the noise of aeroplanes in the air, and meanwhile he persisted in his strange determination, his desire to live in a barracks, among troops.

He had to go through all the recruit's training again and he made a tragedy of it. Never was a courageous soul less resigned: T.E.L. to Edward Garnett: "The army is unspeakable, more solidly animal than I believed Englishmen could be. I hate them, and the life here; and am sure that it is a good medicine for me."

T.E.L. to Lionel Curtiss: "To record the acts of Hut 12 would produce a moral-medical case book, not a work of art.

but a document ... I lie in bed night after night with this cat-calling carnality seething up and down the hut ... and my mind aches with the rawness of it. ..."

The army, however, did not treat him so severely. They gave him an easy job in a clothes store, and the Oxford graduate, the author of the *Seven Pillars*, the hero of the Arabian war, occupied himself with putting regimental numbers on pants and tunics. He had some leisure, and could devote himself to the revision of his book. To make some money he translated some French novels.[1] He bought a large motor-cycle and spent hours riding around the countryside.

[1] In particular Adrien le Corbeau's *Le Gigantesque*, published by Jonathan Cape, and Pierre Custot's *Sturly*.

Cloud's Hill

BOVINGTON, hewn from the wastes of Dorset, is some way from the sea and far from the great cities. The Tank Corps barracks, the wretched little soldiers' shops, and the guard-room, lost in this solitude, are found along a scarce fre-quented road; as far as the eye can see, the barren land is ploughed up with tank tracks and pitted with trenches.

The camp and the countryside exude boredom, and Lawrence, despite his anchorite's vocation, sought some escape from it. He discovered, a mile and a half from the camp, a small ruined house and started work on turning it into a refuge for himself. It was a cube of whitewashed bricks, seventeen feet by twenty, with an attic reached by a ladder, and a tiled roof that was falling in. This tiny tumble-down cottage was buried beneath banks of rhododendrons which hid it from the road, but which also deprived it both of daylight and of its view in a country whose only beauty lay in its vast horizons.

Lawrence undertook to put it back in good order. To raise the necessary money he sold the golden dagger that he had brought back from Mecca to his friend Lionel Curtiss.[1] Then with the help of one of his friends in the camp, Sergeant Knowles, who being married had a cottage of his own quite close, he turned himself into a mason, a plumber and a thatcher, and in a few months had made himself a home where he could put his books and his gramophone and live at ease during his hours of leisure.

T.E. and a few of his friends in the Tank Corps made the house at Cloud's Hill their refuge. Around Lawrence gathered a small court of young men attracted by the prestige of his intelligence and his magnetic personality. Once again he was the undisputed oracle, the leader of these hasty youths, and it was a delicious balm to his vanity; moreover,

[1] This dagger is now in All Souls College, Oxford.

it was something for which he had always sought; among the
navvies at Carchemish and with the camel-men of his guard
or the drivers of the armoured cars in Arabia, he had made
a sort of retreat far from his equals, whose company and
whose critical minds in particular irritated him. He let it be
understood that he was thus obeying his taste for equality
and that he felt that he was intended for a worker-priest
mission among simple people; was it not rather the reaction
of an imperious soul needing to surround itself with elementary beings whom it could the more easily dominate?

This bevy of troopers watched him with veneration. With
them he was like a prince, and he could make them do as he
pleased. On the rare occasions when his famous friends were
invited to this Thebaid, his young vassals busied themselves
around the house, polished the tile floor, shone up the
brasses, made the tea, and while the visit lasted, remained
deferent and silent around the painter or celebrated poet
who had come to see their idol.

But if one of these strangers to their little world arrived
without having been asked and surprised Lawrence amongst
his comrades, T.E. would scarcely conceal his anger and the
intruder feeling that he had fallen among a hostile clique,
could but go away again.[1]

Consequently men of the class of Thomas Hardy, Bernard
Shaw, or Forster were flattered to be asked to Cloud's Hill
to drink tea (alcohol was forbidden in the cottage) and eat
buttered toast between Sergeant Knowles, his son Pat, and
some obscure recruits.

[1] On the strange atmosphere which reigned at Cloud's Hill see Eric
Kennington's contribution to *Lawrence by his Friends,* in particular
page 277, and the curious incident of the soldier with the girlish face.

Friends

APART from the camp routine and from his limited life as an ordinary soldier, literature was the only thing which really interested Lawrence. To write was for him a necessity: he studied at length the works of the great masters, hoping to discover the secret of literary perfection. But here also the criterion for which his avid soul was searching, escaped him: "That's one infuriation of letters, of all artistic efforts... their lack of an absolute", he said to a friend. He sought for contact with writers. He frequently saw Graves, the poet and novelist whom he had met at Oxford. Graves would have liked to patronise and advise him since he regarded him as an apprentice, but T.E. was evasive and the relationship of these two hypersensitive characters was often stormy. Lawrence solicited Graves' advice, but did not follow it; he annoyed his friend by not showing him the *Oxford Edition*. One day he submitted to him the poem to S.A., "I loved you, etc.", asking him with feigned humility whether this was prose or verse. Graves took his rôle as a professor of style seriously, criticised the piece and suggested a final stanza of his own in which he spoke of white chargers and black chargers and other poetic appurtenances. Lawrence thanked him effusively, said that the stanza was admirable, much too good to be mixed with his own wretched attempt and altered nothing in the poem.

He had a close friendship with Eric Kennington and his wife Celandine. He liked the man as much as the artist. Coarse and upright, he was uniquely illuminated by his art. His terse straightforwardness did not prevent him from understanding the most complex problems. Lawrence, fundamentally incapable of thinking simply, admired and envied his stability. Kennington did a bust and some excellent portraits of him and a sketch in black and white which T.E. called the Cheshire Cat, and which is the only one of his many portraits which seems to throw any light on the secrets of his soul. To the painter we owe a striking written portrait of Lawrence at the time of Cloud's Hill: "The wide mouth smiled often ... sometimes extending to an unusual curve, warning of danger. . . . These crystal eyes were almost animal, though, when he would ignore the presence of others retiring into himself, they would diverge slightly. Then he was alone and as inscrutable as a lion or a snake."

In his anxious search for the secrets of the art of writing, Lawrence went to an acknowledged master, Thomas Hardy, the author of *The Dynasts* and of *Jude the Obscure*. Hardy, one of the celebrities of English literature in the eighties, was very old, but in his broken-down body, in the mind dimmed with age, could still be distinguished the nobility and elevation of a man who had devoted his life to art and thought. On Graves' recommendation Lawrence went to see the old writer in his house at Max Gate, within reach of Bovington by motor-cycle. Thomas Hardy and his wife received him with kindness, and he came to this haunt of artists several times a month to steep himself in pure intellectuality.

But Lawrence's greatest moral and intellectual support came from George Bernard Shaw and his wife Charlotte. It was a close friendship which had a major influence on T.E.'s life, but which equally left traces in the ideas and work of G.B.S.

It was Sydney Cockerell, the curator of the Fitzwilliam Museum, who brought Shaw the soldier and Shaw the great humorist together. The two men liked each other, a rough friendship grew up, and T.E. was frequently asked to their home. Charlotte Shaw was an intelligent and humane woman; life with her old *enfant terrible* of a husband had taught her how to handle the unstable animals that are artists and celebrities with amused tact and indulgence. As to the cynical writer, he had a heart of gold. In this childless household their treasures of unused affection were lavished upon this distressed man. The Shaws were for T.E. both a family and a sure guide in the profession of letters. When Shaw had read the *Seven Pillars*, he was full of admiration, but he also saw the weaknesses of the work, its *longueurs* and its clumsy passages; he compelled Lawrence to recast his text, to cut it, and to condense his style. Lawrence rebelled, became angry but submitted. "G.B.S. read the proof, and left not a paragraph without improvement . . . but some nearly died in the operation. Not a trace of anaesthetic!" he was to say later.

When Lawrence was exiled to India with his regiment, Mrs. Shaw wrote to him by every post. It was an intimate and maternal correspondence, in which Charlotte opened herself more than she could with her egocentric and humoursome husband, who was absorbed in his work. When after his wife's and Lawrence's death he saw the letters which they had exchanged, he was rather ill-tempered: "She told Lawrence things which she never spoke of to me!" he complained.

Shaw with his hatred for war and for the conformity of the Army had never known any soldiers well. This revolutionary hero captivated him, and he gleaned in their conversations certain ideas which are to be found here and there in his work. In his play *Too True to be Good*, which is unfortunately not one of his best, he brings in a character that is entirely inspired by Lawrence. The actor, Walter Hudd, who physically resembled T.E., took the part. Lawrence went to see the play and was enchanted. He had always loved looking at his own portraits. It seems probable that when he wrote the preface to *Saint Joan*, Shaw was thinking of his friend when he said of the Maid: "She lectured, talked down and overruled statesmen and prelates. She pooh-poohed the plans of the generals, leading her troops to victory on plans of her own. She had an unbounded and quite unconcealed contempt for official opinion, judgement and authority, and for War Office tactics and strategy. . . . There were only two opinions about her. One was that she was miraculous: the other that she was unbearable."

It would be impossible to mention by name the innumerable friends whom Lawrence saw from time to time or with whom he kept up a close correspondence, politicians, intellectuals, generals, high officials, or his very modest comrades in the army. His epistolary relations with the critic Edward Garnett do, however, deserve special mention.

22

Garnett, an independent and original mind, enjoyed a wide authority in the world of letters. Endowed with an immense culture and with an exclusive love for things literary, he had an exceptional flair for discovering unknown talent. It was claimed that so bent was he on this pursuit, that he ceased to be interested in writers once they had succeeded. Having appreciated all the qualities of Lawrence's book, he was one of those who encouraged him most to publish the *Seven Pillars*, of which, as we have said, he even produced an abridged version. In his long missives Lawrence confided to him his anguish and his doubts on the subject of his work. Later he was to dedicate to him *The Mint*, his memoirs of the R.A.F. The two men wrote to each other about books and their considerable correspondence deserves to be published by itself, for it makes Lawrence appear in his least known aspect as a literary critic.[1]

Thus Lawrence remained in touch with an infinite number of men. His retreat was only relative and this intense need for intellectual contacts clashed strangely with his set purpose of obscurity and renouncement.

[1] A part of Lawrence's correspondence was published after his death by David Garnett, the novelist, and son of Edward Garnett. The notes that accompany these letters constitute a veritable biography of Lawrence, probably the best that has been written.

Return to the R.A.F.

ONCE we admit that Lawrence wanted at all cost to serve in the ranks, the camp at Bovington must have assured him of an acceptable life. But for some obscure reason he detested the Army and only dreamt of returning to the R.A.F. This became a gnawing *idée fixe* and he besieged the Minister with requests for a change which were all turned down; Bernard Shaw wrote to Baldwin, but without result; Trenchard, the head of the Air Force, was in favour of allowing him back, since he admired and pitied him, but certain politicians were keenly opposed to his return.

The clamorous modesty of the ex-Colonel created for him as many enemies as admirers—both equally extreme. Lowell Thomas's work *With Lawrence in Arabia* had just appeared and had caused a stir. It was a mixture of child's adventure story, Western and journalism. Grossly exaggerated stories were mingled with accurate facts. This log-rolling did nothing to help Lawrence, who had already been reproached by the R.A.F. for being too conspicuous. He complained loudly that the book was disgusting, omitting to say that he had furnished much of it himself. Whatever the case, in the delicate situation in which he found himself it was an unfortunate publication.

Trenchard meanwhile had Lawrence informed that they would allow him into the R.A.F. again if he would agree to devote himself to writing the History of English Aviation during the war. It was an enormous task which had already discouraged several writers, of which Hogarth was one. Lawrence refused and remained in the Tank Corps.

At the end of 1924, his hatred of the Army and his desire to wear the blue Air Force uniform again became an obsession: "The army is muck, stink, and a desolate abomination", he wrote to Kennington. He was quite well aware that his *idée fixe* had become pathological and he wrote to one of his friends: "Sometimes I wonder how far mad I am, and if a madhouse would not be the next (and merciful) stage. Merciful compared to the place which hurts me body and soul. It's terrible to hold myself voluntarily here. . . ." And to Buxton these desperate lines: "I might go off: a burst front tyre, or weariness, or the other fate I'm always fearing. You know, Robin, I am hardly sane at times."

On the 14th of June, 1925, he sent to Edward Garnett a short note which finished with these words: "I'm no bloody good on earth. So I'm going to quit. But in my usual comic fashion I'm going to finish the reprint and square up with Cape[1] before I hop it! There is nothing like deliberation, order and regularity in these things."

Edward Garnett, in a panic, wrote to Bernard Shaw, who in turn went to Hogarth for help. There was an exchange of correspondence between these men who were sincerely fond of T.E., but who were disarmed by his sudden moods. Bernard Shaw to Hogarth: "Lawrence is not normal in many ways and it is extraordinarily difficult to do anything for him! In some measure the life of letters is best suited to him. He will not work in any sort of harness unless this is padlocked on to him. He enlisted in order to have the padlocks riveted on to him!"

Shaw had also written direct to Baldwin, who was then Prime Minister, remarking to him that Lawrence's suicide would give rise to a frightful scandal. He had some credit with politicians and in the end he got his way; at the beginning of July 1925 Lawrence was put back into the R.A.F. and posted to the air base at Cranwell, in Lincolnshire. Arriving at Cranwell, he made known his identity to his officers and comrades and was accepted without too much trouble by the first as by the second. He was employed in the squadron office; once more he had his own little corner and sufficient leisure, but it is difficult to understand why he should have threatened to commit suicide in order to obtain this quill-driving job, which was not very different from the one which he had had at Bovington.

[1] Jonathan Cape, his publisher.

* * *

The typesetting and the engravings for the *Seven Pillars* went on slowly. Amidst the crises of his military life, Lawrence occupied himself with his book, paying scrupulous attention to the smallest details of typography, format and the correcting of the proofs; he spent hours with Kennington, taking pulls off the coloured blocks. *The Seven Pillars* appeared in October 1925. Lawrence had scarcely time to hear what were the reactions of the subscribers and of his friends to whom he sent the work before he was sent by the R.A.F. to India at the end of December 1925, to serve on an aerodrome close to Karachi, at Drigh Road.

Karachi

THE airfield of Drigh Road is six miles from Karachi. It is a piece of desert scorched by the sun and eroded by the wind. "We eat dust and breathe dust and think dust..." wrote Lawrence. Meanwhile for some incomprehensible reason, probably out of a taste for self-mortification, he decided never to leave the camp.

He worked in the office of the mechanics workshop, typing circulars and administrative letters; his officers were kindly and tried to make life easy for him; he had leisure and could turn his ear to the sounds that were reaching him from Europe and which the appearance of his book had provoked.

The Seven Pillars came out at the end of 1925, *Revolt in the Desert* in 1927. The sale of the first work was limited by the small number of copies printed, whilst the second, published in a popular edition, reached a vast public in England, America, and before long in other countries. Lawrence followed the reviews avidly: "So you know I'm absolutely hungry to know what people think of it—not when they are telling me, but what they tell to one another." That is, alas, the wish, never gratified, of every author.

To see his child dissected in the press tore at his heart. The critics, almost all favourable, did not agree in their praise: some admired the science and the music of his style, others his "simple and direct" approach. Wells said that the *Seven Pillars* was an admirable human document, made more moving by the absence of all artistic pretention. Thomas Edward was wild: "But I have enormous pretensions to art", he cried indignantly.

We do not know the reaction of most of his companions of the Arabian War to whom he sent copies of the *Seven Pillars*. In the story Lawrence retained the limelight and their part was not painted in glowing colours; even his best friends were not spared some of his harsh cracks. Young alone rebelled. In his account of the night of Sheik Saad when Young had in vain opposed his project of cutting the Turks' line of retreat, considering that his colleague's attitude had been an inglorious one, Lawrence avoided mentioning him by name, and referred to him under the false name of Sabin.

"You know very well that it did not happen like that", Young said when he saw the passage. "One day I will write an accurate account of the operations around Deraa. In any case, I have no regrets for what I did and said, and I demand that you do not change my name in this episode." But Lawrence laughed and altered nothing.[1]

Lawrence was pretty irritated by Andrew Macphail's book, *Three Persons*, in which a long chapter was devoted to him. Macphail, greatly praising the *Seven Pillars* from the literary point of view, was rather harsh on Lawrence as an historian and as an officer, and handled him severely. Angered, T.E. wrote: "*Three Persons* wasn't as good as it seemed at first ... upon me he was irritating. He patronised me, I thought, damn him. What does he know about prose that he dares praise mine?"

The Indian Army had never forgiven Lawrence for his biting criticisms at the time of the siege of Kut el Amara. An officer of this army called Bray, who had been with Lawrence for some months and had taken part in the attack on Wedj in 1917, published in 1934 a work of memoirs called *Shifting Sands*, in which he violently criticised Lawrence's policy in Arabia. At the end of the book he tells the heroic story of the life and death of an officer in the civil service in Mesopotamia called Leachman. Leachman was the opposite to Lawrence: his policy had been purely European and English, he hated publicity, and never allowed himself to be photographed; he had been assassinated by the nomads whilst he was attempting to pacify Iraq—for England; in brief, he should have had Lawrence's glory, but his modesty had kept him in obscurity.

At the time of its appearance Lawrence did not take this

[1] Young's book, *The Independent Arab*, appeared in 1937. He describes in detail the march on Damascus, in very different colours to those of the *Seven Pillars*.

diatribe badly and did not protest against the obvious errors which the book contained, nor against its biased approach:[1] "Bray is quite an honest, muddle-headed sort of chap, who believes everything he wrote," was all he said. But the defence of Leachman must have been very disagreeable for him. He detested Leachman, of whom he had spoken very coolly in his letters, saying that he was "a fourth rater", a fool who had got himself killed because of his brutality and clumsiness.

Neither Pisani nor Brémond received a copy of the first edition of the *Seven Pillars*. In the case of the colonial captain it was an inelegant omission, since he had accompanied Lawrence on some of his most hazardous operations. Pisani, it is true, did not perhaps understand English. Brémond only saw *Revolt in the Desert*, of which the translation appeared in France in 1929 and whose manner of telling the story angered him. He wrote a book called *Le Hedjaz dans la Guerre mondiale* which is anti-Lawrence and constitutes a very interesting restatement of the question. Brémond was a very cultivated man; he had encyclopedic opinions on history and he had an admirable knowledge of the Islamic countries in which he had lived for twenty years, but unfortunately his work is confused and difficult to read. If he had produced a better book, the Colonel, who had seen beneath the surface in Arabia, might have done great harm to some of the Lawrencian legend. In fact, his work was only read by a very few people in France, and in England it was ignored.

* * *

It was while he was at Drigh Road that Lawrence was sent the proofs of the book which Robert Graves had written on him, *Lawrence and the Arabs*. It was puerile hagiography, containing exaggerations, grossly romanticised anecdotes, and some obvious inaccuracies. In his introduction the author formally declared that he had not submitted his manuscript to Lawrence; in fact, as he had to admit on the death of the latter, this assertion was deceitful, for T.E. not only corrected every line of the book but he added entire paragraphs of his

[1] Field-Marshal Allenby, on the contrary, defended Lawrence in an interview with the press. See the *Letters*, p. 829.

own. It is distressing that a man of his quality, driven by a
morbid vanity, should have contributed to the spread of such
indifferent fables about his own life.[1]

* * *

All this happened five thousand miles from the Indian
aerodrome where Lawrence was filling in forms and sorting
files. He had asked his officers that he should never have to
go out of camp—the Hindus, he said, disgusted him. He
strove to carry out a moral mission amongst his comrades:
professional armies are full of strange flotsam, *déclassés* of
every kind with unhappy pasts; he tried to help them, introduced them to classical music, lent them books, but he never
achieved a real intimacy with any of them. He complained
of it bitterly. Here also, the absolute escaped him.

[1] The hatred of France is diffused throughout the entire work.
Graves, for example, wrote that when a French publishing house asked
to publish a translation of *Revolt in the Desert*, Lawrence declared
that he could not authorise them to do so unless the French edition
said on its cover that the profits of its sale would be reserved "for the
victims of French cruelty in Syria": as the publishers refused, there
could be no French translation of the *Revolt* so long as Lawrence was
in control of the book. This story was in fact doubly inaccurate, not to
mention the gratuitous insult to an old ally. The *Revolt* appeared in
France in 1929 with, of course, the author's agreement and the
Librairie Payot, which published it, has stated in writing that they
never received the demand to put this offensive statement on the cover
of the book.

"The Mint"

LAWRENCE had a succession of passions, first for archaeology, then for war, and finally for Oriental politics; but from now on he had but one thing at heart: to write. Sincerely or not, he declared that the *Seven Pillars* had been a fiasco. He wished in fact to produce a great work.

At the depôt at Uxbridge, whilst he was experiencing the most painful side of the soldier's profession, he had taken some notes of a melancholic mood, pouring out his spleen in vitriolic comments on the harsh training to which he had submitted. At Karachi, he put the finishing touches to what he considered to be the book of his life and sent the manuscript to Edward Garnett with this dedication: "You dreamed I came one night with this book crying, "Here is a masterpiece. Burn it. Well as you please." Needless to say, Garnett did not burn it.

The book was entitled *The Mint*, a word which conveys the idea of violently stamping an indelible mark on coarse material. The Army, which moulded the soldier's body and soul into a uniform pattern, was the Mint.

It is legitimate for a conscientious objector to rebel against military discipline, but it is the less so for a man who has freely chosen the career of a soldier, and the violence of the diatribe written by Lawrence is astonishing. There were, however, some legitimate reasons for his project: he was in revolt against the clumsy methods with which it was intended to train the recruits for a technical army whose task was either flying or delicate mechanical work, and against the application of the very harsh, almost Prussian methods of the old English mercenary army.

His starting point is therefore just and many of Lawrence's criticisms went far, but the artist and the fanatic betray the logician, and the violence of the satire weakens the scope of the work. The adventure was too petty for the misfortunes of the hero to be moving, the persecution mania is obvious and it is difficult to feel sorry for the *declassés* (whom the author besides describes in pretty unattractive colours) subjected to the abuse of the sergeant-major and the classical punishments of the barracks. The righteous wrath of the author falls flat. The inspiration of *Le train de 8 h. 47* or *Les Gaiétés de l'Escadron*[1] are not worthy of the whip of a Juvenal.

Certainly there are some pages in this book in which one recognises the fist of a great writer, his vigorous prose, the choice of words, the imagery, and the magical power of evocation: *The Mint* is composed of short chapters of two or three pages, of which some are excellent, such as those which describe the Church Parade, the sermon on the sin of the absurd padré, barrack-room life, drill, and such passages as depict the mentality of the English people, and their finicky and complicated formalities. But apart from these pages of quality, there are unfortunately others of either an odious cruelty or in very bad taste, and others which leave the impression of childishness and, even worse, are deadly boring. The almost physical hatred which the author nourished for the officers is insupportably dragged out, and he describes with a sadistic pleasure the camp commander, a war-cripple, falling into the mud and unable to get up, being dragged along the ground by his dogs. What he says of the N.C.O.s makes one think that they are worse than the worst re-enlisted men charged with drilling the habitual inmates of Biribi,[2] which is not very likely. Here again the excess of realism detracts from its credibility and one is regrettably aware of a certain baseness in this literary vengeance on his old officers.

Lawrence wanted to write the whole book in the language of the English soldier which (like that of all soldiers) is candidly and constantly obscene and filthy. The effect is disagreeable, because if for the soldiers who use them the foul words have lost some of their evocative power, it is different for the reader who has forgotten his barrack life, and the marching songs he used to sing. It is painful to see in black

---

[1] Humorous studies of military life by Courteline, in the style of P. G. Woodhouse.

[2] A town in Southern Algeria where French convicts do their military service.

and white the song, once so funny, which the soldier sang. Some of the expressions ought never to be printed. One detects the influence of *Feu*,[1] which Lawrence had read, but Barbusse, despite his brutality, used the argot of the soldiers with much greater discretion and the subject of his book— the trench war—allows of licences which the infinitely less tragic theme of the tribulations of recruits in a barracks, does not.

Meanwhile, despite the poverty of the story and the incongruity of the vocabulary, *The Mint* attains in places a tragic intensity which is astonishing for such a subject, but one realises that it is moving because it reveals the anguish of an unbalanced mind.

It exposes Lawrence's persecution mania, his morbid need to suffer, and above all his unhealthy desire to humiliate himself morally and physically. The author rolls himself deliciously in his own filth, and the enjoyment with which he describes himself eating the remains in the kitchens or splashing through pig dung is distinctly pathological. If *The Mint* is not the artistic peak which Lawrence hoped it would be, it remains a curious human document which is indispensable to the understanding of the latter part of his strange life.

Lawrence attributed to *The Mint* a considerable importance. It would be, he thought, his major work and it is curious to see him under-estimate the *Seven Pillars* in favour of this work of excessive naturalism, which is nearer to Zola than to Swift. He was tormented by the desire to publish it, but he could not do so without Trenchard's agreement. The Air Marshal, when consulted, was a little staggered by this description of the life which his flock led and withheld the desired authorisation. Lawrence's friends were secretly relieved, for they wondered what the reaction of the English public would be to so crude a nourishment. *The Mint* has not yet been published.[2]

[1] By Barbusse.
[2] Written in 1954. *The Mint* was published in 1955.

Miransha

LITTLE by little, Lawrence recovered his moral health. His correspondence reveals the stages of his convalescence. The demon of adventure he claimed, was returning to excite him. "This travel, or rather this residence in the East, is one perpetual temptation to me to cut loose again on some further project of my own," he said in a letter; in another he announced to one of his friends that he had just missed being appointed as secretary to the English Legation at Kabul, and only his lack of training on a typewriter had prevented him from going. He regretted it. "From '14 to '18 I served a decent apprenticeship in semi secret-service work, and Russia interests me greatly. The clash is bound to come."[1]

But it is doubtful whether he really wished to start again. Everything that we know of his life at this time shows his indifference to this Orient in which he was engulfed. Far from thinking of "some project of his own" he was writing to his friends in London to get himself repatriated. In fact he was living the life of a bureaucrat and he occupied his leisure hours in literary activities. At the instigation of an American writer, Bruce Rogers, he had undertaken for a United States publishing house the translation of the *Odyssey*. He devoted himself with meticulous care to this work which was to bring him in the fairly large sum of eight hundred pounds sterling. "After all, I have hunted wild beasts, I know how to bend a bow and I have killed plenty of men; I am therefore qualified to talk about Ulysses", he said.

At the end of 1927 Hogarth died. Lawrence was deeply affected by this loss, as he had a real veneration for his master.

[1] Later he said that he had frequently flown across the North-West frontier of India, which he knew backwards, but since on the other hand he complains in his letters of this period of never being able to fly, there is every reason for believing that he was romanticising this period of his career, something that he had rather too great a tendency to do towards the end of his life.

"He was more than a father and mother to me", he had said. He was equally affected by Thomas Hardy's death a few months later. He wrote some bitter letters on the brevity of life: his hair was turning grey, his hearing was going and his eyesight was starting to fail. These deaths caused him to look to his own destiny. He drew up his will.

In the middle of the summer of 1928, he was moved to the aerodrome of Miransha, a frontier post close to Afghanistan. It was a small fort in a plain bordered with "peaks . . . sharp like bottle-glass", a savage and desolate country. Twenty-five Englishmen and a few hundred Hindu irregulars lived in the brick buildings surrounded by barbed wire, and defended by machine-guns and searchlights. At night it was not safe to leave the perimeter for fear of being shot by the Afghan partisans.

In such an environment Lawrence immersed himself in the austere and contemplative life of a Tibetan llama. His commanding officer was indulgent and friendly, and he achieved the relative happiness of perhaps a monk, who though not entirely convinced of the necessity for religion, is sufficiently resigned to his life and is friendly with his abbott.

But he was not made for calm waters and the squalls came to seek him out in his distant refuge.

In July 1928 an American journalist short of copy, who had got wind of Lawrence's presence on the confines of Afghanistan and who wished to profit from the stir caused by the recent publication of *Revolt in the Desert*, wrote an article on how the "uncrowned King of Arabia" was touring the Orient organising obscure political intrigues on England's account. The article was sent in to the *New York World*, who refused to publish it, but the British press agencies in the United States heard of it and pricked up their ears.

A few months after that, in December 1928, the King of Afghanistan, Amamillah, who was trying to modernise his country, was overthrown by the Afghan conservative party, indignant at the Western novelties which their sovereign was imposing upon them. The affair caused some excitement in England where people of advanced opinions, who approved of Amamillah's reforms, were convinced that the Indian government, by definition retrograde, had encouraged this reactionary and pietist revolution in Afghanistan. There were rumours about Lawrence's mysterious activities in the Orient caused either by the unpublished article of the American journalist, or more probably by imprudent passages in the letters which Lawrence wrote to his friends in England and the United States and in which his vanity forced him to say that he was playing a secret rôle in Indian politics, whilst as far as one can tell he was typing out circulars in an office.[1]

The liberal papers were set ablaze. The *Daily Herald* followed by the *Daily News*, published sensational articles on the activities in the Middle East of the ex-Colonel, of the super-spy (6th January and 4th February, 1929). There were meetings in the big Labour centres; during one of these, in a suburb of London, Lawrence was burnt in effigy; in India, the nationalists seized the opportunity to demonstrate against the English domination and an unfortunate Hindu, mistaken for Lawrence disguised as a native, was almost torn to pieces by the mob; in the British Parliament, a left-wing member, Ernest Thurtle, accused the government of sending agitators into a friendly country; he was astonished that someone had been able to join the English army under a false name and demanded that the Lawrence farce end as soon as possible.

The government of India, alarmed at a scandal of which they understood nothing, decided, from the beginning of January 1929, to rid themselves hastily of the undesirable. Without being given the time to pack his bags and leaving his books and his records at Miransha, Lawrence was packed, dazed and furious, into an aeroplane, sent from Miransha to Lahore and from there to Karachi. On the 12th of January, he boarded the steamer *Rajputana* bound for England; at Port-Said the quay was guarded to prevent him landing or receiving visitors; at Plymouth, an officer came to fetch him in a launch in order to avoid the reporters and took him

[1] It must be observed, however, that we are here concerned with Secret Service affairs, and that probably no one will ever know the truth.

ashore by a round-about route so as not to alert the curious.
Brought to London, he was ordered into civilian clothes, and
told to go into hiding until he received further orders.

Indignant and humiliated, Lawrence had to go to ground
in Barton Street with his friend Baker, without having much
idea of what they would decide to do with him. There was
nothing for which they could reproach him, apart from a
few unwise boasts in his personal letters, but as a soldier he
was an encumbrance, who was indefatigably pursued by
publicity, and they did not know how to deal with him.

He then had an idea which was typical of his character.
He would go and see Ernest Thurtle, the M.P. who had
spoken of him in Parliament, and quite simply put his case
to him: did a man not have a right to serve his country in a
humble employment without being thus persecuted? Thurtle
was captivated by his strange personality, declared that he
was convinced, and promised to halt his campaign.

Lawrence stayed several more weeks in London. He spent
some of his time in the Bumpus library in Oxford Street, of
which the manager, J. G. Wilson was a friend of his, and
whilst browsing in the vast honeycombs of this city of books
he could hear the newsvendors announcing his arrest in
Kabul or Teheran. At the end of February, the Air Minister
decided to keep him on in the R.A.F. and he was posted to
the seaplane base at Cattewater, close to Plymouth.

Plymouth

THE exile, suddenly brought home to the cold of an English winter, suffered from a climate to which he was not accustomed, but there were friendly influences at work: Colonel Sydney Smith, who had met him on board the *Rajputana*, had become interested in this strange lost child. He had a command at the Cattewater base; he treated Lawrence with sympathy and took him on as his secretary. The officer was engaged at the time with the preparation of the seaplane that was to compete for the Schneider trophy. The year before England had won the cup from the Italians and she wanted to keep it. Lawrence was employed on this work, and threw himself into it with ardour, happy to occupy his mind with a task that was according to his taste. He liked mechanical things more and more, and loved tuning up complex and delicate engines, fiddling with magnetos and regulating valves. "I am a mechanic", he said, showing his rough and corny workman's hands. His Oxford friends hardly recognised the old intellectual in this rather dense soldier, with his heavy figure, whose smile was spoilt by a row of gold teeth and who spoke a garage English instead of the slightly affected language of the University which he had used formerly.

Lawrence was allowed plenty of liberty. Piloted by Captain A. A. Nathan, he often flew in a Moth seaplane. The machine had dual controls, and he was sometimes allowed to take over, an exquisite sensation for a man who adored flying and who lived among aeroplanes but was seldom allowed to go up in them.

Mr. and Mrs. Shaw had offered him a powerful Brough motorcycle on which he went for long trips, intoxicating himself with speed and reaching 80 m.p.h. Speed, which he had always loved, became his greatest pleasure; it was his drug; a virtuoso on a motorcycle, he took terrifying risks that horrified his friends.

He maintained that he was happy.

1930—1935

THE last years of Lawrence's military life passed without too many untoward incidents, usefully occupied, but with little glory in a manual labour that he found pleasant. It is an epoch of relative equilibrium in his tormented life. His relations with the higher authorities were not always amicable. He retained the protection of Trenchard and of his assistant Salmond, but the Air Minister, Lord Thompson, was not fond of him and did not like the idea of keeping him in the Royal Air Force. "A self-advertising mountebank", he said and never lost an opportunity to show his hostility.

At the time of the Schneider Cup in 1930, Lawrence once more just avoided getting his ticket. During the trials, he was on the ground, and from friendship or curiosity a crowd of people gathered round him. He went from group to group, shook hands with important people, and some of the officers were annoyed that an ordinary soldier should steal the limelight.

Balbo was at the head of the Italian team and the English were antipathetic to the representative of a rival country and close collaborator of Mussolini. Lawrence, on the other hand, laid himself out to please the Italians, intervened to have their tar-mac cleaned up, and pushed himself a little too far forward.

All this caused a bit of a scandal in the R.A.F. and Trenchard threatened T.E. with expulsion. He could not be at one and the same time the ex-Colonel Lawrence and Airman Shaw, they would be very pleased to retain him as a simple soldier, but he would have to keep in his place, no longer make a show of talking to important people, journalists or politicians, abstain from flying, and lead the normal life of a mechanic for as long as he wished to remain one.

Trenchard named the people whom Lawrence was to avoid: Winston Churchill, Austen Chamberlain, Lord

Birkenhead, Siegfried Sassoon, Lady Astor. "Am I one of
them?" asked Bernard Shaw. He was not, and did not
conceal his annoyance at this omission.

The Shaws showed an ever-increasing affection towards
T.E., and the old couple acted as a family for this isolated
man, none of whose close relatives remained in England, for
Mrs. Lawrence was in China, working in a remote mission.
Some people thought that Lawrence, who had taken the
name of Shaw by deed poll, was the natural son of the writer.
"Shaw should have repeated the effort", said a mutual friend.

Lawrence would not accept promotion, but he could never
give up playing a part wherever he was. This was the absurd
part of his position and it disposed many of his superior
officers against him. He was preoccupied with bettering the
lot of the English airman, and thanks to his friendships in
high places, he did obtain a few reforms. He wished to see
this technical arm freed from the stereotyped discipline of
the Army, but little by little the work which he was given,
and to which he gave himself with passion, put a distance
between him and the other ranks.

His job at Cattewater was the maintenance of the launches
which refuelled and rescued the seaplanes, and he suggested
to his officers the adoption of a craft lighter and swifter than
those which were in use. The R.A.F., perhaps as the result
of his suggestion, decided to order some speed-boats and
Lawrence was put in charge of one of the crews whose job
was the tuning up of these machines. It was work which he
liked and he enjoyed handling these small, powerful and
responsive vessels, with their roaring motors. He tested the
speed-boats and delivered them to the different naval flying
bases in England; in this way he cruised round all the
English coasts. He wore civilian dress and no longer lived in
barracks.

In this relatively free life he was able to see his friends,
and despite the admonitions of the Air Minister he remained
in contact with the most influential among them. When he
went to London, he made the rounds in a few hours of all
the high-up people that he knew in political and military
circles, and his intimate friends made ironical comments on

this weakness in a man who so loudly proclaimed his desire
to remain in obscurity.

Did he have any intimate friends? He knew numbers of
people, keeping up on all sides a very active correspondence,
but there were very few people with whom he had close
bonds of confidence. In human relationships he oscillated
between domination and antipathy. He would only try to
captivate or to shock, and from this sprang his extremely
different approach to different people. It led him to keep his
friendships in watertight compartments. Later, his friends
when they compared their opinions of him discovered that
they had only known one facet of his multiple, agile and
fugitive character. Some were annoyed by this, others upset,
and others thought that they alone had in fact known the
real Lawrence.

There was meanwhile a small privileged group with whom
he was relaxed and charming and with whom he did not
experience the need to put on airs. But even with them his
morbid vanity was always alert and would suddenly wreck
the relationship. His sharp criticism did not spare those
whom he loved the most, and when his correspondence was
published many were wounded by things which he had said
and accused him of perfidy. But did not the treachery consist
in making personal letters public after the author's death?

His celebrity continued from time to time to cause him
trouble. One day he learnt that a certain man was going
round England passing himself off as the famous Colonel
Lawrence, and had succeeded in borrowing money from
various people. He was arrested and T.E. was confronted
with him at the police station.

Lawrence was not very flattered that so poor a specimen
of humanity could have been confused with him. "An
obviously feeble character with the wrinkling face of a
chimpanzee", he said; and added, "We persuaded him that
he was not me. To my relief he agreed at once. Had he stuck
to his statement I should have begun to question myself."

His enormous vanity increased with age and drove him off
and on to a sort of mythomania. He exaggerated the rôle
which he had played at different times in his life; in his
mind, or at any rate in what he said, he became the *deus ex*

machina of everything that had happened in the Near East during the war. At the Cairo Conference he had done everything. In some of his letters he spoke as if he was a big influence in English aviation ("I do not want the R.A.F. expenditure increased", he wrote in March 1934) although he was finding it difficult not to be expelled from the R.A.F. In his conversations with his biographers he often strove to mislead them, creating in advance his legend instead of establishing the real stages of a life which was anyway sufficiently glorious. His ego was abnormally developed, and at the same time he had a taste for mystery and a morbid love of complexity and pointless secrets.

Despite these irritating failings, his rich and multiple character still had some extremely attractive sides to it. In fact, his detractors were mostly people who only knew him by hearsay. All those who came close to him were won over by his intelligence as by his profound idealism, his intransigent disinterestedness, and the obvious good faith that emerged from behind his pirouettes, his childishness and his lies. Living poor, doing arduous work, refusing the lucrative positions that were offered to him and not touching a penny of the enormous sums which his book had earned him, he compelled admiration.

His method of pursuing the absolute to which he aspired could have been absurd, but he was paying the price. The thirteen years which he devoted to the life of an ordinary soldier suffice to guarantee his good faith. No impostor has ever made such sacrifice to make his imposture credible.

Some who had known him or thought that they had known him for a long time believed that as he had grown older he had lost his power of thought and that an overstrained will-power had obscured his intelligence. His mind still sparkled, but no longer burnt with the powerful fire that had enabled him to carry on the Arab war and write the *Seven Pillars*. No doubt some interior breakdown occurred around 1923 or 1924 and sapped his power of action and his faculty of artistic creation, but his mind retained its singular quality. His enormous correspondence is full of interest, and we can find in it the sparkle, the subtlety, the art of evocation, the inexhaustible vocabulary of his book on the war. It is a firework display of original, amusing, poetic and often contradictory but always striking ideas. It must be said, all the same, that there is more wit in them than real gaiety and that Lawrence's anxiety to be always brilliant does give to some of the letters a taut and irritating quality that often spoils them.

Those who came near to him were still struck by the almost hypnotic power that emanated from him. He seemed to possess like an apostle or a healer, a quasi-physical fluid which enveloped some of his friends to such an extent that twenty years after his death they still dimly feel the effects of this secret power. Others have said that he was above all else an extraordinary actor, which comes to the same thing, for only those who exercise an exceptional physical ascendancy over their fellow men can be actors.

And meanwhile although in many ways so patrician, he was invincible attracted not towards vulgarity, but to the most ordinary of beings. Living voluntarily among the proletarians, whose company seems to have been indispensable to him, he became more and more like them. The photographs that we have of him at the end of his life are those of a typical English workman. He was happy to be among people of a humble social class and of a rough-and-ready turn of mind. For his holidays in 1934 he set off with two friends, a Scottish horse-dealer and an old soldier of the Tank Corps, and camped on a beach in the North of England, cooking his meals with his two friends in a fisherman's house.

People came across him with strange companions, with unpleasant expressions on their faces and one whole side of his life seems to have remained secret. He was just as furtive and mysterious when he was meeting a cabinet minister as when he was seated at table with a mechanic.

A life without woman or home had morally dried him up. Marriage and paternity imply a certain sacrifice for the sake of their benefits: one has to keep oneself within the limits of normal humanity, accustom oneself to criticism from someone else, and overcome one's vanity when tempted by pride. Lawrence lacked this stabiliser and a part of him appeared to harden. "At moments he seemed like a horny old maid," said one of his friends, which does not besides fit in with other aspects of his character, with the roughness of the mechanic which he acquired, nor yet with that incorrigible childishness of a half-grown boy which he retained all his life.

He detested physical contact with animals as with men; he never stroked a dog or cat, and went in for every sort of slightly ridiculous trick in order to avoid shaking or even touching the hands of the friends of whom he was most fond. One of them, a thickset, tough, sporting character, took hold of him by the shoulders and shook him during an animated discussion. He saw in Lawrence's eyes a look of fear and horror which he never forgot.

Without apparent reason, if not perhaps as the result of Bernard Shaw's influence, he had reverted to his Irish origins, and stated that he was Irish. "If I start writing again, it would be to write a biography of Sir Roger Casement," he said one day.

He no longer believed in anything very much. "Of the creed of my youth, I have kept the four first words", he used to say. Little by little he slid towards a complete agnosticism and seemed to feel neither regret nor anguish. From a pious childhood he retained not his faith, but his taste for asceticism and sacrifice. He did not smoke, and but rarely drank anything alcoholic, and only allowed himself the minimum of comfort and material satisfaction. To deny himself, to constrain himself, to despise his body had become second nature to him.

His head seemed always to be far away in the clouds.

Was he thinking of the Levant, of that country where his personality had asserted itself, where his glory had been born and which had been his second fatherland? He had drawn a veil across that part of his life. He avoided talking about it; for him the Orient was dead. In India he never left the airfield at Drigh Road nor that at Miransha; every time that one of his friends offered him a position in a distant country, he refused it; it seems that all curiosity for these things had been extinguished and that the man of the Desert had become as stay-at-home as the proletarians with whom he lived, and who usually hate leaving their cabbage-patch or their suburb.

Did he know that everything which he had known belonged to a past that was gone for good? The Syria of his

youth was as out-of-date as Chateaubriand's America,
Lafcadio Hearn's Japan or Claudel's China. Was he aware
that, above all, the projects which he had elaborated no
longer had a place in an Orient that was carried along by
new political and economic currents?

In a moment of lucidity he had written these lines on the
Syrians and Mesopotamians:

"They were weak in material resources, and even after
success would be, since their world was agricultural and
pastoral, without minerals, and could never be strong in
modern armaments. Were it otherwise we should have had
to pause before evoking in the strategic centre of the Middle
East new national movements of such abounding vigour."

All these words tell, and are prophetic, but in them he
condemns himself; he had foreseen everything except the oil
by which his most pessimistic views were realised. He had
been the apprentice sorcerer.

Did he know it?

His biographer, Liddell Hart, whilst preparing his book
on the Arabian War, compelled him by his questions to return to an already distant past. For once he seems to have
done it with pleasure, accentuating still further the light
thrown on the Arab campaign that is to be found in the
Seven Pillars. But it is surprising to find how little his ideas
had evolved. He does not appear to wish to see the profound
transformation that had taken place in the Islamic world. In
1934 he still had the same passions, the same hatreds as in
1921, and had not in the light of recent events either
learnt or forgotten anything. But Syria, the garden of the
Enchantress, was no longer full of flowers and youthful
gaiety. It was an enclosure filled with thorns and venomous
plants.

The End of the Road

IN April 1935 Lawrence's engagement in the R.A.F. came to an end. He felt a little sadness at leaving the blue uniform which he had worn for more than ten years, but he declared, however, that he was happy to be able at last to have some rest. The translation of the Odyssey had brought him in a little money, Buxton had made some good investments for him, and it seems that his father's family had promised to make him an annuity. He thus had the few necessary shillings for a very modest life.

He had decided to set himself up in a definite way in his cottage in Cloud's Hill. A strange decision: it was a sinister place—the house had no view and was as ugly as any house in a mining town, but he was close to his friend Pat Knowles, who lived on the other side of the road, and a mile from Bovington camp. He was unable to draw himself away from the proximity of barracks and soldiers.

Demobilised at Plymouth, he loaded his baggage on to a motorcycle and set off for Cloud's Hill. He found the garden full of reporters, who wished to photograph him and write an article on the return of the celebrated soldier colonel to civilian life; they crowded on his drive, perched on his wall and machine-gunned him with their cameras.

In a rage Lawrence shut the door in their face and the angered journalists threw stones on to his roof and broke some of the tiles. It was a ridiculous and irritating way to return. Several days later, he was attacked in the same way and ended by punching in the eye a reporter whom he had found in his garden. He went back into the house thunderstruck, and looking at his fist, he said to Eric Kennington, who was standing by him: "I have just struck a man. It is twenty years since I last struck a man."

The same evening, he left for London, where he lay low. He did not go back to Cloud's Hill until the excitement had died down, and tried to divide his life between his books, his gramophone, and his motorcycle. He loved more than ever the long trips on his powerful machine, and he rode it faster and faster.

On the 13th of May, 1935, he received a letter from one of his friends, Henry Williamson. He was a rather visionary writer who dreamed of universal peace and thought that Europe would experience a golden age if England and Nazi Germany could contrive to become Allies. "You alone are capable of negotiating with Hitler," he wrote to T.E. "I must speak to you about this immediately."

Lawrence took his motorcycle, reached the post office in the camp at Bovington and sent a telegram to Williamson: "Lunch Tuesday wet fine cottage one mile north Bovington Camp."

Returning to Cloud's Hill, he tried to avoid two children; his motorcycle skidded and threw him on to the road, where he fractured his skull. He lingered for six days, in the depths of a coma, and died on the 19th of May, 1935. He was forty-seven years old.

He was buried two days later a few miles from Cloud's Hill, in the cemetery at Moreton. Storrs, Newcombe, Kennington, Pat Knowles, a Tank Corps soldier and an Air Force mechanic helped to carry the coffin, while Winston Churchill walked behind it.

On his gravestone can be read that name of Lawrence which he pretended to hate and which he had renounced, together with a pious quotation.

* * *

England, in recognition of one of the most brilliant of her sons, has placed his bust in the crypt of Saint Paul's in London.

The place, in its chilly greyness, breathes of sadness and desertion, but the names which can be read are flamboyant: Nelson, Wellington, Van Dyck, Constable, Blake, the heroes of war, the lights of the arts and of the intellect, all have their inscription or their statue there. At the foot of one of the vaults are buried the bones of the oldest sovereigns of England, from Sebba to Ethelred. It is a moving way to honour the hero and the artist that was Thomas Edward Lawrence.

What are the thoughts of a Frenchman as he stands before his effigy? He admires the soldier, like the writer, but he cannot help thinking that a little less passion and a little more balance would have made of the dead man someone more useful to England and to Europe. Lawrence cannot alone carry the responsibility for a particular policy in the Levant, but it must be realised that he was its most ardent apostle and that he laid down its two fundamental principles: the exaltation of Arab nationalism and open rivalry with France.

Particularism in human communities is the equivalent of individualism in men: a fine and respectable thing but dangerous in times of strife. If Europe had continued to exercise her domination over the countries of the Near East and if she had succeeded in entirely absorbing them by an intelligent but firm colonial policy, she would have increased her powers of resistance to outside attack, formed a more powerful ethnic and economic bloc, and perhaps avoided her later enfeeblement. It is not certain that it could have been possible, but it was worth trying even if a few local patriotisms had to suffer for it. But France and England, instead of supporting each other and reaching an understanding on the administration of their colonial patrimony in the Levant, never ceased to intrigue against each other to the great detriment of their respective positions; today the whole of the east of the Mediterranean has escaped the English, the French and above all Europe, and we are witnessing there, as elsewhere in the world outside the Soviet bloc, the break-up of political groups, a centrifugal movement in face of a firmly centralised communist world.

Besides, Anglo-French rivalry in the Near East contributed to the moral separation of two countries who had just withstood side by side a terrible war, and whose obvious interest lay in remaining closely united. A solid alliance of England and France—an alliance of the mind, of the heart and of fact, would probably have avoided the creation of the Nazi power. Divided, the two countries delivered themselves enfeebled and ill prepared to Hitler's attack.

Everything that has come between England and France during the last half century has been harmful to the civilisation and to the Peace of Europe.

January 1950–June 1954.

Paris
Labbeville
Alhamar.

Bibliography

WORKS BY T. E. LAWRENCE

Seven Pillars of Wisdom. Oxford Edition, 1922.

Seven Pillars of Wisdom. (Subscribers' Edition). London, 1926.

Seven Pillars of Wisdom. London, 1935.

Revolt in the Desert. London, 1927.

The Letters of T. E. Lawrence. Edited by David GARNETT, London, 1938. With a remarkable commentary by David GARNETT that is equal to a biography.

Letters to Bruce Rogers. London, 1933.

The Home Letters of T. E. Lawrence and his Brothers. Oxford, 1954.

Carchemish. Report on the Excavations at Djerabis on behalf of the British Museum conducted by C. Leonard WOOLLEY, M.A., and T. E. LAWRENCE, B.A. With an introduction by D. G. HOGARTH, M.A., F.B.A. London, 1914.

The Wilderness of Zin. By Leonard WOOLLEY and T. E. LAWRENCE, London, 1936.

Oriental Assembly. By T. E. LAWRENCE (Posthumous collection). London, 1939.

The Mint. Private Edition.

Crusader Castles. By T. E. LAWRENCE, London, 1936.

"The Evolution of a Revolt." In the *Army Quarterly.* Vol. I, no. I, October–January, 1921.

The Odyssey of Homer. Newly translated in English Prose. By T. E. SHAW, 1932.

Secret Despatches from Arabia. By T. E. LAWRENCE London (no date).

T. E. Lawrence to his biographer Robert Graves. Information about himself in the form of letters, notes and answers to questions, edited with a critical commentary. London, 1938.

T. E. Lawrence to his biographer Liddell Hart. Information about himself in the form of letters, notes, answers to questions and conversations, London, 1938.

The Forest Giant. By Adrien LE CORBEAU. Translated from the French by J. H. Ross, London, 1924.

356 T. E. LAWRENCE

PRINCIPAL WORKS CONSULTED

T. E. Lawrence by his Friends. Edited by A. W. LAWRENCE, London, 1937. A collection of eighty articles written by Lawrence's friends two years after his death. The diversity of the opinions expressed is enough to discourage any attempt at biography, if biographers are capable of being discouraged.

Orientations. By Sir Ronald STORRS, London, 1937.

The Independent Arab. By Major Sir Hubert YOUNG, C.M.G., D.S.O., London, 1933.

Dead Towns and Living Men. By C. Leonard WOOLLEY, Oxford, 1920.

Shifting Sands. By Major N. N. E. BRAY, Oxford, 1934.

Steel Chariots in the Desert. The story of an armoured car driver with the Duke of Westminster in Libya and in Arabia with T. E. LAWRENCE. By S. C. ROLLS, London, 1937.

Rapport du Capitaine Pisani. (Les armées françaises dans la Grande Guerre. Tome IX, volume d'annexes, page 881).

Le Hedjaz dans la guerre mondiale. Général Edouard BRÉMOND, Paris, Payot, 1931.

Safety Last. By Lieutenant Colonel W. F. STIRLING, London, 1953.

Portrait of T. E. Lawrence. The Lawrence of the Seven Pillars of Wisdom. By Vyvyan RICHARDS, London, 1936.

World Crisis. Volumes I and IV. WINSTON CHURCHILL.

Les Armées françaises dans la Grande Guerre. Tome IX.

The Palestine Campaigns. By Colonel A. P. WAVELL, C.M.G., M.C., London, 1928.

Great Contemporaries. By the Rt. Hon. WINSTON S. CHURCHILL, London, 1937.

Memory hold the Door. By John BUCHAN, London, 1940.

Two Cheers for Democracy. By E. M. FORSTER, London, 1951.

With Lawrence in Arabia. By Lowell THOMAS, New York, 1924.

Lawrence and the Arabs. By Robert GRAVES, London, 1927.

T. E. Lawrence, in Arabia and After, by Liddell HART, London, 1934.

Three Persons. By Sir Andrew MACPHAIL, London, 1929.

338171 T.E. (Lawrence d'Arabie). By Victoria OCAMPO, Paris, Gallimard, 1947.

Le secret du colonel Lawrence. By Leon BOUSSARD. Editions A.M., Paris, 1946.

Portrait de l'aventurier: T. E. Lawrence, Malraux, von Salomon. By Roger STEPHANE, Paris, Le Sagittaire, 1950.

Lawrence of Arabia. By R. H. KIERNAN, London, 1935.

T. E. Lawrence. A Bibliography. By Elizabeth W. Duval, New York, 1938.

Journal of the Royal United Service Institution. Vol. LXVII, no. 467, August 1922.

Cinq ans de Turquie. By Liman von Sanders, général de cavalerie. Translation by commandant Mabille, Paris, Payot, 1923.

What Really Happened at Paris: The Story of the Peace Conference, 1918, 1919. By E. M. House and Charles Seymour. New York, Scribner, 1921.

The Truth about the Dardanelles. By E. Ashmead-Bartlett, special representative of the English press in the Dardanelles (1915).

Les Origines orientales de la guerre mondiale. By Jean Pichon, Paris, Lavauzelle, 1937.

Le partage du Proche-Orient. By Jean Pichon, Paris, Lavauzelle, 1938.

Sur la route des Indes un siècle après Bonaparte. By Jean Pichon, Paris, Societe d'Editions Géographiques, Maritimes et Coloniales, 1932.

The Arab Awakening. By George Antonius, London, 1938.

Franco-British Rivalry in the Post-war Near-East. The decline of French Influence. By Henry H. Cumming. Oxford, 1938.

Traditions et politique de la France au Levant. By André Bruneau, Paris, Alcan, 1932.

Angora Constantinople Londres. By Berthe Georges Gaulis, Paris, Armand Colin, 1922.

La Tactique au Levant. By Colonel Clement Grandcourt, Paris, Lavauzelle, 1926.

The Letters of Gertrude Bell. London, 1927.

Travels in Arabia Deserta. By Charles M. Doughty, with an introduction by T. E. Lawrence, London, 1936 (the book was first published in 1888).

A Pilgrim in Arabia. By H. St. J. B. Philby, London, 1946.

Cedar. By Bernard Vernier. Carnets d'un Mehariste Syrien, Paris, Plon, 1938.

La Révolte druze et l'insurrection de Damas. By General Andrea, Paris, Payot, 1937.

Mœurs et coutumes des Musulmans. By E. F. Gauthier, Paris, Payot, 1929.

Berbères et Arabes. By General Brémond, Paris, Payot, 1942.

Nomad. By Robin Maugham, London, 1947.

Too True to be Good. By Bernard Shaw, London, 1934.

Thirty Years with G.B.S. By Blanche PATCH. (Mr. Shaw's private
    secretary for the last 30 years of his life), London, 1951.
The Life of Charles M. Doughty. By D. G. HOGARTH, London,
    1928.
L'equipage de l'Ayesha. Aventures des rescapes de l'Emden. By
    Lieutenant de Vaisseau von MUCKE, Paris, Payot, 1929.
Good-bye to All That. An Autobiography. By Robert GRAVES.
    London, 1929.

While the present book was being published, I had no
knowledge of the important work by Richard Aldington. It is
an extremely severe critical study of Lawrence, of his character,
of his rôle during and after the war, and finally of his veracity
as a writer of memoirs.